FINDING LOST

SEASON 4

NIKKI STAFFORD

ECW Press

Published by ECW PRESS
2120 Queen Street East, Suite 200, Toronto, Ontario, Canada M4E 1E2
416-694-3348   info@ecwpress.com

LIBRARY AND ARCHIVES CANADA CATALOGUING IN PUBLICATION

Stafford, Nikki, 1973–
Finding Lost, season four : the unoffical guide / Nikki Stafford.

ISBN 978-1-55022-878-6

1. Lost (Television program). I. Title.

PN1992.77.L67S734 2009   791.45'72   C2008-907562-5

Developing editor: Jennifer Hale
Cover and text design: Tania Craan
Typesetting: Gail Nina
Front cover photos: iStock;
pocket watch © Andrew Parfenov; desert © Alexander Hafemann
Printed by Printcrafters

The publication of *Finding Lost, Season Four* has been generously supported by the OMDC Book Fund, an initiative of the Ontario Media Development Corporation, and by the Government of Canada through the Book Publishing Industry Development Program (BPIDP).

Canadä

PRINTED AND BOUND IN CANADA

ECW PRESS
ecwpress.com

Table of Contents

Acknowledgments

A big thank you to ECW Press for continuing to believe in these books. Thanks to Crissy, my awesome editor, for being the perfect sounding board for my ideas and finding a lot of the photos and being my cheerleader. Thank you to Gail Nina for laying out the book, and to my wonderful publicists, Simon Ware and Sarah Dunn.

Thank you once again to the brilliant (and award-winning!) Gil Adamson, who took her pen and smoothed out my rough edges once again.

As usual, I cannot thank Oahu resident Ryan Ozawa enough for the amazing behind-the-scenes photos he contributed to the book. He promises for season 5 he'll go spelunking for me. I'm holding him to that.

To my dear friend and *Lost* nut Fionna Boyle, thank you for reading through the episode guide and pointing out anything that was out of place.

A big, big thank you to the *Lost* fans out there who bought my first two books and emailed me letters of praise and encouragement. The biggest thanks are reserved for those *Lost* fans who joined me on my blog, Nik at Nite (nikkistafford.blogspot.com) this year every Friday morning to chat about *Lost*, offer their theories, and argue about the mechanics of what we'd just seen. You all have brilliant ideas, and you posted comments throughout the season that made me think, laugh, or write more: Roland, cartographer, Brian Douglas, dansmot, fiveagainst, redeem147, chapatikid, fb, Brandon, Matthew D, Pete, Emilia, Crackedout, Jason, Jazzygirl, Steve Gee, atruebluehusker, Barry, Leor, christemple, Don, tanyam, dk, ekrs, LoyallyLost, Cindy, Martin, Jeff Heimbuch, Kris Eton, The Question Mark, Eric, Danielle, Ann, Amy, Michele, Matt, michelle woolley, Karolyn, poggy, scrvet, not that jj, thisguypossessed, humanebean, teebore, don edwards, Kristin, Frank, David, mags, sdbrian, myselfixion, batcabbage, Daniel Larsh, Elizabeth, KeepingAwake, Wawa, Jeremy Barker, DanM, Mark, Karole, Joshua, Mighty YT, Josh, Fletcher, James, Tim, MW, memphish, Jonni Bravo, Ludi, Shane, alxmnslv, Saza, Sarah in MI, Marvin T, Yussi, David in TN, Power, and the many anonymous posters.

Thank you to my family and friends, especially Sue, who all felt like they needed a prescription for Losticil just to understand what I was rambling about for months.

To my husband, Robert, who put our daughter to bed every night so I could get more writing done, and supported me throughout the process, thank you. Big hugs and kisses to my wonderful daughter Sydney, who kept my mind sharp with reciting the alphabet behind me while I was typing, and to my amazing son Liam, born right before the season began and deciding to be the perfect sleeper right from the beginning. And finally, my biggest thanks, as always, to Jennifer Hale. You'll always be my constant.

How Not to Get Lost

Season 1 of *Lost* was immensely popular. But by season 2 the ratings had begun to decline. This was either thanks to the inefficient scheduling of episodes (a couple of weeks of new episodes followed by a month of reruns, then three weeks back on and three more weeks of reruns) or thanks to the exposition of the story lines and the deepening of the mysteries (with no answers) that had fans scratching their heads. By season 3, when the network aired six episodes that were heavy on the Others, Kate, Jack, and Sawyer, and very light on everyone else, and when they ran the rest of the season a full three months later, those fans who were already frustrated by the show jumped ship, which left only the hardcore fans behind.

Thank goodness we stayed. We've loved *Lost* unbendingly from the beginning, but season 4 was mind-blowing.

In fact, the fourth season won back many viewers. Reduced to a mere 13 episodes due to the WGA Writers' Strike, this season was short, but packed with intrigue, drama, mysteries, and answers. During an interview I did while the Writers' Strike was on, a journalist asked me why I thought season 4 was getting great ratings and was so critically acclaimed. Was it because of the strike?, he asked. I said the answer was manifold. Yes, the Writers' Strike (which lasted from November 2007 to February 2008) created a dearth of new programming in January and February, precisely the time *Lost* began rolling out brand new episodes. Or it could have been the timing of the DVDs. In previous seasons, new fans of the show would buy the DVDs when they came out — usually around September 7 or 8 — and try to make it through the episodes in two weeks before the new season started. But unless you're a die-hard television viewer, such a schedule could be tough. When some viewers couldn't finish the season, they wouldn't dare begin the new one. So, they'd wait for the *next* season's DVDs to come out a year later. These fans wouldn't be counted in the ratings for that season. For season 4, however, the previous season's DVDs were released on December 11, and the new season didn't begin until January 31, giving new fans plenty of time to watch not only season 3, but the first two seasons as well.

But in my opinion, the main reason the new season was so good is because showrunners Damon Lindelof and Carlton Cuse have an end date. ABC has done the unthinkable and given them an end date of 2010, with three seasons of 16 episodes each. Knowing there are 48 more hours in which to tell the story, "Darlton" (as fans like to call the two men) have mapped out a plan. They know how to answer certain huge questions, when to drop the clues in there, and when they should start on the big reveal. This plan has allowed the storytelling to be smooth, it's given us so many answers, and the new questions seem to be leading into more obvious territories than in previous seasons.

In other words, it's starting to unveil itself like a beautifully told fairy tale, one where the writer already knows how it's going to end and how many pages he has left in which to tell it.

If season 1 was about trying to be rescued, season 2 was about learning to live with each other on the island, and season 3 was about dealing with the native people on the island, then season 4 is about the invasion by the outside world into the microcosm of the island, and what that does to the people on it. Do the freighter people come in peace? Do they want to rescue the Losties? Or, as Ben famously says in "Through the Looking Glass," is making contact with that ship "the beginning of the end"?

As I've written in the introduction to my previous books, *Finding Lost* and *Finding Lost — Season 3*, this book is intended to be read alongside the episodes. You could watch the entire season and then read through the book, or you could watch an episode and read the corresponding guide to it. I strive for these guides to be more than simple plot summaries (if you're looking for plot summaries so you don't actually have to watch the series, this isn't the book for you). Instead you'll find analytical, detailed, in-depth readings of each episode that will help you sort out the clues, work through the mysteries, and figure out all that physics that happened to be a big part of season 4.

Aside from writing these books, I keep a blog called Nik at Nite (nikkistafford.blogspot.com) where, during the season, I analyze each episode the night of the show and my readers and I discuss the episodes at length for the next week. In season 4 there was a *lot* to discuss, and many of the blog entries had close to 100 comments or more. I owe a great deal to the regular commentators on that blog who show up day after day to discuss their favorite TV shows.

As with my other books, this book will be primarily an episode guide, analyzing the development of characters and plotlines, asking questions along the way, and acting as a companion for viewers. I want you to read the episode guides as if you were discussing the shows with a friend.

Finding Lost is *not*, however, a substitute for watching the show. I will not provide plot summaries or transcripts or anything that would allow a reader to read my book instead of actually watching the show. You must watch the DVDs or the aired episodes. This book will provide a deeper understanding of the characters, the events, and the mysteries, but it will not be a replacement for *Lost* itself. No book could ever hope to do that.

The text is formatted episode by episode. Almost every guide is broken up by some tidbit of information, like a small sidebar of interest, or a larger chapter on the historical significance of something. These are "intermission" sections. Just as the plot of life on the island is interrupted by flashbacks of the characters, so too will this episode guide be broken up by these sections. You can skip over them at first and just focus on the guide in the beginning, or you can read through them to get a better understanding of the references or the actors playing the characters.

The sidebars are usually compilations of small themes or motifs in the episodes. The book summaries provide a more in-depth study of the books referenced on the show. In each book summary, I will give a brief rundown of the plot, and point out the deeper meaning in each book (warning: the book chapters contain spoilers for important plot details), and then offer some suggestions about the importance the book has on the show, and why it may have been chosen by the writers. For example, in "The Constant," Kurt Vonnegut's landmark novel *Slaughterhouse-Five* is referenced when a character quotes a line from the book (he never actually says the title); I believe reading that book would give people a better idea of what is going on in the show when it comes to the aspects of time travel. There are chapters on other books mentioned this season, as well as new philosophers, and show timelines.

Some of the intermission chapters will touch on historical explanations of various allusions on the show, such as a philosopher who is name-dropped in the season 4 finale. Others will take a facet of the episode and explore it more closely than you might have seen on *Lost*. Still others will look outside the show to things like the *Find815* alternate reality game (ARG) or the mobisodes, the latter of which preceded the season, giving fans some "missing pieces" from previous seasons.

The guides to the individual episodes will contain some spoilers for that particular episode, so I urge you to watch the episode before reading its guide. I've been careful not to spoil any episodes beyond what you're reading, so if you watch an episode, and then read the corresponding guide to it, you will be pretty safe from being ruined for future surprises. The episode guide will feature a brief summary of the episode, and then an analysis. Following each analysis, you'll find special notes of interest. These sections require some explanation:

Highlight: A moment in the show that was either really funny or left an impression on me after it ended.

Timeline: Lostpedia is an online wikipedia for *Lost* fans, put together by *Lost* fans. By paying close attention to the time that has passed in each episode and using key moments where a character mentions the actual calendar date, fans have put together a suggested timeline for what the date is in each episode. Since the estimation of dates has already changed from what I'd written in my previous book, take these dates as general suggestions only.

Did You Notice?: A list of small moments in the episode that you might have missed, but they are either important clues to later mysteries, or were just really cool.

Interesting Facts: These are little tidbits of information that are outside the show's canon, explaining allusions, references, or offering behind-the-scenes material.

Find815: In the *Find815* alternate reality game (see page 31), there were season 4 clues in each chapter. This section recounts in which episode each of the clue words was actually used.

Nitpicks: Little things in the episode that bugged me. I've put these things in nitpicks because I couldn't come up with a rational explanation myself, but maybe you have explanations, and if so, I'd love to hear them. What makes the Nitpicks section difficult is that, particularly with *Lost*, what appears to be an inconsistency now could be a deliberate plot point by the writers that will take on massive significance later. So I'm prepared for several of these to be debunked by the show. Please read these knowing that I nitpick only to point things out, not to suggest the writers aren't on their game. These are meant to be fun.

Oops: These are mistakes that I don't think could be explained away by anything.

4 8 15 16 23 42: In the late season 1 episode "Numbers," Hurley reveals a set of numbers that have had an impact on his life, and it turns out those numbers have popped up everywhere, on the island and in various other Losties' lives before the crash. This section will try to catalog them.

It's Just a Flesh Wound: This is a list of all of the wounds suffered by the characters on the show. I've decided to leave off the emotional injuries, as those would take pages to list.

Lost in Translation: Whenever a character speaks in another language that is not translated for us or we see something written that's not immediately decipherable, this section will provide a translation, wherever I could find it. Thanks to all of the fans who have provided these to the English speakers like me.

Any Questions?: These are questions and ideas that I think viewers should be thinking about. A question in an episode from early in the season might be answered later, but because these guides are meant to be read as one goes through the season episode-by-episode, these questions are the ones you *should* be asking yourself at the end of each hour.

Ashes to Ashes: If a character on the show dies, this section will provide a brief obituary.

Music/Bands: This is a list of the popular music we hear on the show. In most cases I've provided in italics the name of the CD where you could find the song, but if I haven't, it's because it's a song that is featured on several compilations. I owe most of these findings to LostHatch.com. The analyses of the lyrics are my own.

And there you have it, a guide to the guide. I hope you enjoy the book, and I welcome any corrections, nitpicks, praise (please? just a little?), and discussion at my email address, nikki_stafford@yahoo.com, or come on over to my blog. I cannot stress this strongly enough, however: the opinions in the following pages are completely my own, and if anyone out there has contrary opinions, I respect those. I don't expect everyone to have the same views as I do. What makes *Lost* so much fun to watch and discuss is how many possibilities this show presents to us. Ten fans can come away with ten different interpretations of what they just saw, and that's what makes the show great, in my opinion.

Nikki Stafford
nikki_stafford@yahoo.com
nikkistafford.blogspot.com
October 2008

"The Beginning of the End": Season 4

Of all the endings of all the seasons of all the shows we've seen, few have offered such a shocking twist as the one that ended *Lost's* third season. With the stunning revelation that the flashback we'd just seen was actually a flash*forward*, fans suddenly realized the twist would send the show in a new direction for season 4 and onward. But it wasn't the only twist that got fans excited about what was to come.

In an unprecedented decision, ABC and Touchstone reached a joint decision with Carlton Cuse and Damon Lindelof in May 2007 to set an end date for *Lost* of May 2010. Fans and critics (and Darlton) had been calling for an end date for some time. After all, if the show's complex mythology meant the writers would have to reveal the ending bit by bit until the final mysteries would be solved, wouldn't it be easier if they knew exactly how many episodes they had left? The plan, released to the public on May 6, 2007, would be to have three more seasons of *Lost*, each comprised of 16 episodes, running from January/February until May of 2008, 2009, and 2010. (This strategy followed that of the hit show *24*, which was lauded by fans and industry people alike.) The writers would be able to map out the 48 chapters that were left and plot out exactly how much information they could reveal in each installment to build up to the best possible ending. With a show as rich and depthless as *Lost*, that could be tough. When asked what would happen should they come up with some exciting ideas that they can't fit into the truncated schedule, Lindelof joked, "We'll do it as a radio play."

Fans and critics applauded the decision. It met with kudos all around; only the network itself saw the negative side — after all, if *Lost* remained in the top 15 shows, which is where it was when the announcement was made, they'd cut loose a show that could easily continue to make them money. But clearly some executives at ABC looked at the bigger picture. They realized the money they could make in DVD sales for a show that could go down in history as one of the best, rather than having a potential disaster on their hands that simply dragged on with no end in sight.

The only other downside: now fans had to wait *eight months* to see a new episode of *Lost*. It was going to be a long fall.

Season 3 was all about the Others. First, the survivors were split up, with Jack, Kate, and Sawyer held captive in the Others' barracks. We met Juliet, a fertility doctor who works for the Others and who came to the island to try to save the lives of the pregnant women. We discovered Ben's backstory, and saw that he had come to the island as a child, had killed most of the Dharma Initiative, and was now the leader of the Others with some serious daddy (*and* mommy) issues. The survivors were eventually reunited, but Juliet joined them too, amid much suspicion. After the hatch explosion in "Live Together, Die Alone," Desmond began seeing the future, which was punctuated by images of Charlie dying. He tried to keep him alive, but both men eventually realized that destiny would have to take over. When a woman, Naomi, dropped to the island from a helicopter and said she was there to rescue them, the survivors nursed her back to health and began a trek across the island. In the final episode, Charlie and Desmond went to an underground station to stop a radio frequency that was jamming their communication signal; Sayid, Bernard, and Jin were stationed on the beach to ambush a group of Others who were coming to steal the pregnant women; Locke was lying in a pit of decomposed corpses where Ben had left him to die with a bullet in his gut; and the rest of the gang had headed across the island to the radio tower to try to send a message to Naomi's ship. The finale ended with Charlie dying; a miraculously recovered Locke throwing a knife into Naomi's back; Sawyer, Juliet, and Hurley heading back to the beach and saving the day; and Jack making contact with a boat that was presumably going to send rescuers.

Or, maybe not.

Even more interesting in that episode was the series' game-changer, the flashforward, that showed viewers what the future held for at least two of the characters. Jack gets off the island, slowly goes mad thanks to his various addictions, and becomes obsessed with returning to the island. He reads an obituary of someone clearly connected with the island, goes to the funeral home, and is surprised to see no one else there. He meets up with Kate and tells her that he's been taking flights over the Pacific in the hopes the plane will crash and he might actually find the island again. He insists they need to go back. She replies that nothing will get her back to that island. If we know Jack and Kate get off the island, it means that the rescue call might actually be legitimate. Or that it wasn't, but another rescue attempt was coming soon. But what happened to the other survivors?

More importantly, fans knew the writers would give us more flashforwards. Did anyone else get off the island? Would we see their futures, too? What about those who are left behind or killed? The possibilities were endless.

In July 2007, it was announced that a cast member who had previously left

Flashforward: Carlton Cuse and Damon Lindelof tease fans at Comic-Con 2008 about what season 5 will have in store. (DONABEL AND EWEN @ FLICKR)

the show would be returning (I won't say who, simply because if you don't actually know, then knowing will only ruin the surprise of that person's return; it was definitely ruined for the rest of us who knew). On July 26, 2007, Darlton appeared before a standing-room-only crowd at the San Diego Comic-Con to answer questions from people bursting with excitement. This time, they sat with little bells they placed on the table in front of them, and if either man thought the other was about to say too much, he would ring his bell, and the other would instantly stop talking. During the panel, they said they'd be doing a Libby flashback, and hinted she might have ties to Dharma. They also said (again) that Rousseau would get a flashback, probably not in season 4, but definitely in season 5 or 6. Damon also said Jack and Claire would probably find out in season 4 something viewers already knew: they're half-siblings.

At the end of the panel, they showed the audience a new Dharma orientation video. This time the doctor said his name was Edgar Halliwax, but the footage appeared to be a series of outtakes taken while filming the actual video. (If you want to watch it, go to www.lostpedia.com/wiki/Orchid_Orientation.) Halliwax complains about putting on makeup and saying he's a scientist, not an . . . one presumes he was going to say "actor" before he is cut off. He is rude and diva-like to the people on the set, but eventually readies himself and holds a large white rabbit in his hands with the number 15 written on its side. Halliwax introduces himself, and says this is the video for station six, the Orchid. He says the viewer has probably realized this is not a botanical station, and apologizes for making them deceive their family and friends. He says the unique properties of the island have created a Casimir effect, and he says the work that will be done in that station is potentially dangerous. Something white drops from the ceiling behind him, and he stops mid-sentence and says, "What the hell?" and turns around. Sitting on a shelf behind him is the exact same rabbit he's holding, with a number 15 on its side. People in the room begin screaming, and a female assistant runs in to grab the other rabbit as Halliwax shouts, "Don't let them near each other!" She says she'd set the switch at negative 20, and there are still nine minutes left. Halliwax screams at the cameraperson to turn the camera off. There's a break, and we cut back to the beginning, with Halliwax calmly holding the rabbit and introducing himself, again repeating the words, "As you've no doubt surmised, station six — or, the Orchid — is not a botanical research unit." The video is grainy, with a lot of scratches on the frames. There are also hidden frames inserted throughout — an image of Gerald DeGroot teaching a class of students; a skyscraper; the words "God loves you as He loved Jacob"; and an upside-down video of someone riding a bike through New Otherton.

So what does it mean? By the looks of the video, it would appear the rabbit was involved in a time travel experiment and accidentally ended up existing twice in the same time frame. Halliwax is insistent the two rabbits don't come near each other, and he's probably worried about some rip in the cosmos that might happen should an entity physically contact another version of itself in a time where it wasn't meant to be. Did this mean time travel would play a part in season 4?

In August, new cast members were announced — Lance Reddick (known to fans of excellent television as Lieutenant Cedric Daniels on *The Wire*), Ken Leung (best known as Carter Chong, the guy who hooks up with Uncle Junior to scam people in card games on *The Sopranos*), Rebecca Mader (familiar to some fans from FOX's *Justice*), Jeff Fahey (from *The Lawnmower Man* and *Grindhouse*), and Jeremy Davies (from several movies, including *Saving Private Ryan* and *Rescue Dawn*). Rumor had it that the characters would include Charlotte, a woman in her twenties who is "a successful academic"; Arthur Stevens, a "ruthless corporate recruiter"; and Russell, "a brilliant mathematician in his late thirties who is 'capable of great insights and has a tremendous knowledge across various scientific fields.'" Darlton explained in an interview that of those three names, only one was correct, and some of the information in the character descriptions isn't accurate, simply to throw off anyone looking for spoilers of the fourth season.

In September, *Lost* was nominated for several Emmy Awards. "Through the Looking Glass" was nominated for Best Writing (Darlton) and Best Directing (Jack Bender) and there were nominations for Sound Editing and Single Camera Picture Editing. In the Supporting Actor in a Drama Series category, both Terry O'Quinn and Michael Emerson were nominated, and to everyone's delight, O'Quinn took the award. Accepting the award, O'Quinn gave a very short and funny speech: "Sometimes when we're rolling around in the jungle in the mud, and we're hitting each other and stabbing each other and shooting each other, and they're pouring on the blood and turning on the sprinklers, I wonder what it would be like to bake up a sheet of cookies on Wisteria Lane. And get one of their checks," he joked, as the camera panned over to the *Desperate Housewives* actresses and the audience laughed loudly. "Then I think about my castmates and my crewmates, represented here by the great and glorious Michael Emerson, and I realize why I have the best job in the world."

October 2007 brought some bad news. First, the Writers' Strike caused all production on the show to cease as of November 6 (see page 103). Then, on October 25, Daniel Dae Kim was charged with driving under the influence. Fans first wondered aloud if there are no taxis in Hawaii. Then they worried for his character's safety: Cynthia Watros, Michelle Rodriguez, and Adewale Akinnuoye-Agbaje were each slapped with serious traffic violations in Hawaii and their characters were subsequently killed off the show. In fact, Watros and Rodriguez, who were arrested together for DUI, saw their characters fatally shot in the same episode. Kim released a statement to TMZ, in which he expressed his deepest apologies and shame. "It saddens me to know that I jeopardized the welfare of the kind people of Hawaii, a community that I love and call my home. It is my intention to cooperate fully with the police and I am grateful to them for their sensitivity throughout this matter." In September 2008, Kim pleaded no contest to the charge and was ordered to complete community service and lost his license for six months.

With the strike ongoing in January, ABC made a decision, after much thought, to air the eight episodes of *Lost* that had already been filmed, and hope that the strike would end in time for Damon Lindelof and Carlton Cuse to add some more episodes to the year. By the time *Lost* premiered, it was one of the only dramatic shows on television airing new episodes, and it was a welcome arrival for a lot of television viewers.

"The Beginning of the End" premiered on January 31, 2008, to over 16 million viewers, which was *Lost's* best ratings in over a year, and this put it in the top 10 shows for the week. The reception was generally a positive one. Robert Bianco of *USA Today* raved that the show was a "heart-stopping, perfectly pitched episode that fulfills all the promise of last season's stunner of a finale." In the midst of the Writers' Strike, he added, "Let *Lost* remind you of how spectacular scripted network programming can be . . . We need shows like *Lost*, and we only get them when great writers combine with big-network budgets and exposure." Matthew Gilbert of the *Boston Globe* asked, "How great is it that 'Lost' can still make the pulse race and the brain tingle?"

And it would continue to do so, right up to its heart-stopping fourth season finale.

SEASON 4 – January–May 2008

Cast: Matthew Fox (Jack Shephard), Evangeline Lilly (Kate Austen), Terry O'Quinn (John Locke), Josh Holloway (James "Sawyer" Ford), Jorge Garcia (Hugo "Hurley" Reyes), Naveen Andrews (Sayid Jarrah), Yunjin Kim (Sun Kwon), Daniel Dae Kim (Jin Kwon), Henry Ian Cusick (Desmond Hume), Michael Emerson (Benjamin Linus), Elizabeth Mitchell (Juliet Burke), Emilie de Ravin (Claire Littleton), Jeremy Davies (Daniel Faraday), Ken Leung (Miles Straume), Rebecca Mader (Charlotte Lewis)

Recurring characters: Sam Anderson (Bernard), L. Scott Caldwell (Rose), Alan Dale (Charles Widmore), Jeff Fahey (Frank Lapidus), Blake Bashoff (Karl), Mira Furlan (Rousseau), Tania Raymonde (Alex), Lance Reddick (Matthew Abaddon), Fisher Stevens (George Minkowski), John Terry (Christian Shephard), Marsha Thomason (Naomi Dorrit), Zoë Bell (Regina), Kevin Durand (Keamy), Grant Bowler (Captain Gault), Marc Vann (Dr. Ray), Anthony Azizi (Omar)

4.1   The Beginning of the End

Original air date: January 31, 2008
Written by: Damon Lindelof, Carlton Cuse
Directed by: Jack Bender
Guest cast: Michael Cudlitz (Mike Walton), Billy Ray Gallion (Randy Nations), Steven Neumeier (Lewis), Grisel Toledo (Nurse)

Flash: Hurley

When Desmond returns to the beach with Charlie's final message, the survivors must decide if they believe the rescuers are hostile, or if they're really going to rescue them. Hurley's flashforward reveals that he will be one of the rescued, but on the island, he leads some of the survivors away from Jack's camp and over to Locke's.

It had been eight long months since the season 3 finale. Fans spent the summer and fall speculating on who was in the coffin, why Jack wanted to go back to the island, who might have been left behind, and whether the survivors were about to be rescued. But nothing could have prepared us for the words that were uttered by Hurley at the beginning of *Lost's* season 4 premiere: "I'm one of the Oceanic 6!"

Whoa, dude. I didn't see that coming.

"Through the Looking Glass," the season 3 finale, gave the show many potential directions to go. Jack and Kate clearly get off the island, and Jack is feeling guilty about what happened before they left. Fans wondered if a few survivors were sacrificed, or if all the survivors but Jack and Kate were left behind. With Hurley's proclamation that he's one of six survivors, the entire game changed. Have the so-called Oceanic 6 lied about what happened? At the end of season 3, I asked in my episode guide (see *Finding Lost — Season 3*, page 192) how the survivors were going to explain the deaths of so many people on the island, or why they left the others behind. But when Hurley tells Ana Lucia's partner in this episode that he'd never met her, one wonders if they're just going to pretend the people who didn't come back had died in the crash.

The opening of "The Beginning of the End" echoes the openings of other *Lost* season premieres. There's a new location we haven't seen, and jarring events that disorient the viewer, making us wonder if we'd tuned in to the right show. Season 2 opened with a man we hadn't yet met working out in a 1970s-style bachelor pad, which turned out to be inside "the hatch," while the sounds of Mama Cass played in the background. He looks in a mirror to shave, and we see in his face the uncertainty of who he is and what he's doing. Season 3 opened with an unknown woman having a very bad day, and gradually we realize she is one of the Others, also living on the island. She looks in a mirror while listening to Petula Clark, and we see her trying to keep it together, but she falls apart and begins to cry. So by season 4, we were prepared to see another new character we didn't know, with some 1960s tune playing in the background, glancing into a Lewis Carroll–type mirror that is about to take the series in a new direction. Instead, the episode opened with a stack of mangoes on the sand, which for one brief moment makes us think we're on the beach and this *won't* be a discombobulating opening. But this shot is followed by a KTLA-style car chase through Los Angeles. When the car door opens, and our beloved Hurley steps out and says what he says, we know we're seeing another flash-forward, which is the new direction of season 4.

Why open the season with Hurley? The first three seasons gave us Jack-centric flashbacks, and while it was probable the season wouldn't open with him, simply because season 3 *ended* with him, giving the flash to Hurley was an interesting choice. Hurley flashbacks have always seemed at first like standalone episodes, but later they take on greater significance. Season 1's "Numbers" was a comic episode that revealed that Hurley was a millionaire who had played some throwaway numbers that he later believed were cursed. When those exact numbers became an integral part of the show, all fan eyes turned to Hurley, wondering if he was more important than we'd originally thought. Season 2's "Everybody Hates Hugo" showed us the fallout of Hurley winning a lottery, and while again it seemed like the sequel to "Numbers," it also revealed Hurley to be something more than the funny guy with the one-liners. Instead he was a broken man with real fears, and those fears had followed him to a mysterious island. Now Hurley worried the friends here would regard him as a fake and turn on him the way his friend Johnny had. In "Dave" we saw the extent of Hurley's depression and psychosis when the writers explored what his life had been like in the institution — and we meet his imaginary friend "Dave," whom he believed had followed him to the island. That episode addressed one of the big fan theories — that the island and all the other characters are a figment of Hurley's imagination — and pretty much laid it to rest. The season 3 episode "Tricia Tanaka Is Dead" again seemed to have no significance beyond Hurley's character, and was more of a look at how Hurley had been abandoned by his father and how Hurley was trying to put an end to his curse. But that episode

"I said, shut UP." Rousseau (Mira Furlan) clocks Ben (Michael Emerson) for talking about "his" daughter. Fans cheer wildly. (MARIO PEREZ/© ABC/COURTESY: EVERETT COLLECTION)

took on greater meaning when the vw van he discovered on the island became a key feature in the events of the season 3 finale.

All of those episodes now seem to have been leading up to this one. Again, we see Hurley's paranoia, his return to a mental institution, his conversations with someone who couldn't possibly be there (or could he?). When we see what Hurley's future holds, it's sad, because Hurley is the Everyman on the island, the regular guy like the rest of us, the innocent person who's been used as a pawn. A lottery win once ruined his life, and now that he's been rescued, fate has once again bitten his hand. Hurley is the perfect character with which to begin this season, because, other than Claire, he's not only the closest person to Charlie and the one who will be most affected by his death, he's also the guy who didn't go with Jack. The question now is, how will the two be reunited?

For three seasons we've watched Jack and Locke bicker, fight, argue over science versus faith, and want to kill each other. But their feud escalates to all-out war in this episode, when Jack confronts Locke for killing Naomi in "Through the Looking Glass." When we last left Locke, he'd just been shot and left for dead by Ben, only to have a vision of Walt, who told him to get up because the rescuers were not who they said they were. Without asking any further questions, Locke threw a knife into Naomi's back, and held a gun to Jack as Jack dialed the satellite phone. Unable and unwilling to pull the trigger, Locke slinked back into the jungle, warning the others they were making a mistake. Now he stands before the survivors, insisting that everything he's done that seems crazy to them — accidentally killing Boone; blowing up the Flame station along with all of the books that explained what exactly Dharma was; blowing up the submarine that would have been Jack's ticket off the island; killing Naomi — has been done in their best interests. Despite the fact that Rose wants to stay on the island, she refuses to go with Locke because she thinks he's crazy. After all, he'd just killed someone in cold blood right in front of her.

But facing off against Locke, in this corner, weighing 175 pounds of pure self-righteousness, is Jack, the "sane person's choice." Jack is a doctor who has been their leader from the beginning. He's led them into traps, and he's led them to safety. He was initially reluctant to accept the mantle of leader, but now that he's taken on the job, he wants others to accept his leadership without question. He refused to believe that pushing the button was anything other than a pointless Sisyphean task, and he was wrong. When Kate insisted there was a second blood trail they needed to follow, he brushed her off. And once again, he was wrong. He bartered with the Others — the people who had killed or kidnapped many of their number — to get himself a one-way ticket off the island and he called the freighter without listening to any of the warnings of the naysayers around him.

Locke might very well be the bad choice in this situation, but when Jack, the white knight, holds a gun to Locke's head and pulls the trigger, everything changes. Jack, the doctor who has taken up the Hippocratic oath to "do no harm," intends to do the ultimate harm. (Things between these two have come a long way from two guys arguing about a button in the hatch.) Rose refuses to go with the cold-blooded killer, Locke, but the only reason Jack *isn't* one too is because Locke had only one bullet in the gun, which he fired into the ground in the previous episode, showing us he really never intended to kill Jack. What makes the standoff between these two men so fascinating is that we know where Jack's story is going — we've seen his flashforward and the miserable state he'll be in in only a few short years. Despite all the times Jack's been wrong, people continue to follow him because they think he has their best interests at heart. The reason is that in the midst of the craziness on the island, Jack is the only person who seems to make sense. When he tells Kate in this episode that there's no way Naomi would be worrying about making a dummy trail if she was bleeding to death, it makes perfect sense. And yet, Locke will probably continue to be proven right — his insistence that the rescuers aren't really rescuers might actually be true if Charlie's final message to Desmond was correct, and his suggestion that the island is a living thing that won't let them leave also will prove true, since we see Jack become obsessed with returning to the island. Knowing Jack's future adds dramatic irony to how fans see his present, and this makes his decisions even more foreboding. And yet, when we see Hurley and Jack meeting in the future (clearly prior to Jack's nervous breakdown), Hurley apologizes for having gone with Locke, as if Locke really was the wrong choice. The fact that Jack appears to be silently threatening Hurley in this scene adds to the suspicion that Jack isn't the white hat everyone thinks he is.

Our beloved Hurley, played by Jorge Garcia. If I was stuck on a desert island with only one character from *Lost*, it would be Hurley. (TONY DIMAO/SHOOTING STAR)

This episode was all about division: Jack's group versus Locke's; whether the people on the phone are rescuers or invaders; if the rescue we see in the future is a good one or a bad one; whether making that call was the happiest moment of their lives or the worst. "The Beginning of the End" was a fantastic way to come back to the series after such a long wait, but the real standout of the episode was Jorge Garcia's performance. Never before has he shown such range, from happiness at discovering they're about to be rescued, to despair when he has to tell Claire what's happened to Charlie.

The key moment in this episode is when Hurley tells Bernard that he's always wanted to cannonball into the water, but never has. He's been afraid to. After all, he played the lottery and won, and it led to his downfall. He allowed himself to fall in love with Libby, and she was dead before anything could happen between them. Hurley lives in a constant state of paranoia, sure that if he allows himself any happiness, something terrible will happen to balance things out. His paranoia certainly isn't unfounded. All his life he's been held captive by his circumstances, his weight, his cursed money, a mysterious island, or the Others.

But in that one moment, he realizes he'd just been a hero: he came charging out of the jungle in a vw van (as one does on a desert island) to save the day; he's watched the "good guys" triumph over the bad; he's just gotten word that Charlie made it to the station and fulfilled his task (he was worried Charlie might die) and that they're all about to be rescued. As he stands with Bernard, he thinks nothing can go wrong. His money is gone, the Others have been defeated, his friends are safe, and he's about to go home. As he says to Bernard, "I'm gonna be free." So . . . he cannonballs. The look on Hurley's face as he floats under the water is one of pure, unadulterated joy, and one that we've yet to see on him or anyone on this show. It's a look of complete happiness, something it seemed none of the survivors were capable of.

And then, the moment his head comes back out of the water, everything falls apart around him. Charlie is dead, the bad guys have been replaced by new bad guys, they're not going to be rescued, and everything terrible is about to start over again. Garcia handles the whole scene beautifully. If you watch the scene from his point of view, it's possibly the most deflating moment of the series thus far, and makes Hurley's about-face at the end of the episode more understandable.

In the season 3 finale, Ben looked at Jack and said, "If you make that phone call, it will be the beginning of the end." The title of this episode suggests that Ben was right, and if so, we're all in for a rollercoaster ride this season.

Highlight: Ben's snarky remark when Kate announces Naomi is really dead: "Better call the boat, tell them she's getting a really big bundle of firewood."
Timeline: The events immediately follow the ones in "Through the Looking Glass," and the episode takes place on December 21, 2004.
Did You Notice?:
- Going into season 4, we know that the series will end after season 6, so technically, this is the first episode of the last half of the series (i.e., the beginning of the end).

OMGWTFPOLARBEAR!!

In "The Beginning of the End," fans noticed several hidden references to the North Pole. They're not the first ones we've had. What could the references mean? Is it pointing to where the island is located? Could the island be trapped in a bubble bobbing along in arctic waters and it only appears to be tropical? Or is it an indication of something that could happen in the future?

Polar bear — This one is the obvious one, the moment in the second episode of the series that made some fans say, "Awesome!" and others say, "Uh . . . I'm changing the channel." We've seen a few polar bears on the island, and they seem to have been brought to the island by the Dharma Initiative to be involved in experiments to see how a polar bear would adapt to a tropical climate. Answer: they become *really* angry.

"What did one snowman say to the other snowman?" — When Locke first encounters Desmond, this is the question Desmond asks him. It's a coded question to help him determine if Locke is his replacement. We later find out the correct answer was, "Smells like carrots."

"We're stuck in a bloody snow globe!" — When Desmond leaves at the beginning of season 2 and sails away, only to find himself right back where he started, he becomes convinced that the island is inside a snow globe and there's no way away from it.

Two Portuguese men in the blizzard — At the end of "Live Together, Die Alone," we see two men in a blizzard, possibly at the North Pole, receiving a message on a computer. It seems that when Desmond turned the key, it rendered the island momentarily visible to the outside world.

Ho Ho Ho — It's what Santa says, but in "The Beginning of the End," it's so much more. Hurley freaks out in a convenience store when he sees Charlie standing next to the Ho Hos. When he plays basketball with Jack, they play H-O-R-S-E, but Jack quits after Hurley wins H-O. Ho is also the chemical symbol for Holmium, which is the most magnetic of metallic elements. It has been used to create artificial magnetic fields.

Eskimo — When Charlie first shows himself to Hurley at Santa Rosa, Hurley is drawing a picture of an Eskimo standing outside an igloo.

- The Camaro that Hurley crashes at the beginning is the car his father had been working on when he was a kid.
- As the police officers are trying to subdue Hurley in the parking lot, you can see a man standing in front of the store where the car crashes, video-

taping what is going on. That man is Randy, Hurley's awful boss from the Chicken Shack, and Locke's boss at the box company.

- The cop who interrogates Hurley is Mike from "Collision," who kept yelling at Ana to holster her weapon when they were responding to a domestic call.
- When Hurley hallucinates that Charlie is swimming up to the one-way glass, if you pause the scene just before the glass smashes, you can see "They Need You" printed on Charlie's hand in marker.
- At one point you can see Juliet digging graves on the beach for the Others who were just killed. She might be working with the survivors to get off the island, but the Others were once her friends, and this moment is the only one where we see how difficult it must have been for her to watch them mowed down, one by one.
- When Abaddon visits Hurley in the mental institution, you can see several interesting things in the background. There's a chalkboard behind Hurley at one point, upon which is drawn a shark, a palm tree, a raft with a makeshift sail, waves, and a sun. Behind Abaddon you can see the word "Victory" written on the wall. Considering the significance of Abaddon's name (see page 153) this word is worrying.
- When Abaddon leaves and the camera moves to the door closing, there appears to be a dark shadow (or, perhaps, black smoke?) on the door. Some fans speculated Abaddon was a manifestation of the smoke monster.
- When Locke went to Jacob's cabin, the camera pauses on a painting of a dog sitting in the corner. The painting is there again, but when we first see it, it's on the wall to Hurley's right, and when the camera pans back to it, it's on the wall facing Hurley, as if the painting is as ephemeral as the cabin itself.
- The man rocking in the chair in Jacob's cabin is none other than Jack's father, Christian Shephard. (Jorge Garcia later revealed in an interview that they filmed the scene in the chair with everyone else off the set, so Christian's presence would come as a surprise to the rest of the cast.)
- Hurley's eye is framed by the broken glass in the window. In season 1, we always had a close-up of the eye of the person whose flashback we were seeing. This is a clever way to show Hurley's.
- Locke tells Hurley that Charlie had written "Not Penny's Boat" on his hand, but Locke wasn't around to hear Desmond tell anyone that. Hurley must have just mentioned it to him off-screen.

- Rose refers to Bernard as "Rambo" when they are reunited. In "Through the Looking Glass," she made Bernard repeat over and over, "I am a dentist. I am not Rambo."
- Sayid seems to be particularly hostile to Locke, and that's because the last time he saw Locke was in New Otherton, right after Locke had blown up the Flame station and had thrown Mikhail through the sonar fence. Sayid would have learned about Locke blowing up the sub shortly afterward.
- Charlie hits Hurley in the face when Hurley says he doesn't believe in him, which is what Dave did in "Dave."
- When Hurley makes his big speech to the group about how Charlie was trying to tell them something, he says he doesn't know what made Charlie change his mind, and Desmond doesn't tell him about seeing Penny transmitting a message. While Desmond couldn't have known what Penny was saying, he could easily surmise that Charlie had gotten his information from Penny herself.
- Desmond doesn't go with Locke, even though he delivered the very message that convinced the others to follow him.
- At the end of the episode, Hurley tells Jack, "Never say never, dude." In the *Lost* mobisode, "King of the Castle" (see page 133), Ben tells Jack, "I've learned never to say never."

Interesting Facts: The name "Abaddon" is Hebrew for "The Destroyer." For a longer explanation of the significance of this name, see page 153 (be warned: the explanation contains spoilers up to "Cabin Fever").

The dog painting in Jacob's cabin was painted by Thomas Hannsz, who is a former roommate of Sophie Bender, director Jack Bender's daughter. Sophie had rescued a dog from the Humane Society, whom she named Lulu (short for Honolulu), and the dog is always on the *Lost* set. Hannsz's wife is Bender's production assistant, so Hannsz is also on set a lot, and he has become a caretaker of the dog. He painted Lulu in a pose that was meant to parody da Vinci's *Mona Lisa*, and presented the painting to Bender, who promptly put it in Jacob's cabin. Hannsz has also appeared as a background Other (though he was killed off in the season 3 finale).

Find815: "Matthew," "Abaddon," and "Santa Rosa pill bottle" were clues in the game.

Nitpicks: Hurley is in a variety store, takes his food up to the counter to pay, sees something, tries to run away, and falls over a display. The cashier doubtless tells him to stop and clean up his mess, but Hurley keeps running. And that's enough to get 10 cruisers to chase him down the freeway? I think part of the story must be missing. Unless he held up the store before crashing into something and then drove over a person on his way out of the parking lot, it seems strange they'd waste all that manpower on someone who was spooked and knocked over a display of peanuts. Was it because of his celebrity status?

4 8 15 16 23 42: Jack is watching Hurley's car chase on Action**8** News. Hurley plays Connect **4** at the mental institution. When Hurley closes his eyes to get rid of the cabin, he repeats, "There's nothing here" **4** times. When Hurley and Jack are playing H-O-R-S-E on the basketball court, Hurley says, "That's H-O." H is the **8**th letter of the alphabet, and O is the **15**th.

It's Just a Flesh Wound: Rousseau gives Ben another elbow in the face when he refers to Alex as his daughter. Jack tries to beat the faith out of Locke when they're reunited in the jungle.

Lost in Translation: There is a lot of controversy about the whispers that Hurley hears when he sees the cabin. Some people think they hear the whispers saying that Jack's dad is hiding, or that Jack and his dad are hiding. Some have heard discussions about Desmond or Nikki (horrors). However, probably the most reliable translation of the whispers was done by two fans, Sara and Chelsy, who posted their transcription on Lostpedia. They used special equipment to isolate the whispers into different tracks, and slowed the audio right down to pick it up (note the name Sarah, which is Jack's ex-wife's name):

> Man: "Come to me, I need you. You're an alchemist and uh . . ."
> Woman: "I need—"
> Man (*sounds like Christian Shephard*): "Sarah, is somebody coming?"
> Woman: "They must be coming, you—"
> Man: "Hush! One of these—"
> (Shushing: "Shhh, shht!")
> Woman: "Richard!"
> Man: "Come with us."
> Woman: "Here's the recipe."
> Man: "Oh thank you, I thought I'd lost—"
> Hurley: "Uh-oh."

Any Questions?:

- Who are the other three people in the Oceanic 6? When did they all get together to make this pact that they would stay hush-hush about the island?
- Ben takes a serious interest in Jack and Kate discussing the two blood trails.

Is he interested in their relationship? Or Jack's dismissal of Kate's theory?

- Who is Abaddon? Why is he interested in Hurley?

- Who does Abaddon mean when he asks Hurley if "they" are still alive? Does he know what really happened during the crash? Is he referring to the rest of the people on the plane? Just the people who survived the crash but were not part of the Oceanic 6? The Others? The people sent to rescue them?

- Did Naomi send out a secret message to the people on the boat?

- When Locke comes to Jacob's cabin, it takes a while before he sees the man in the rocking chair, and even then, it's only a fleeting glimpse. Hurley sees the man right away, and for a longer period. Could it be because Locke sought out the cabin, and the cabin came to Hurley? Why did it come to Hurley?

- Whose eye is in the window? There has been speculation that it was Locke, Jack, Mikhail, or Jacob himself.

Charlie (Dominic Monaghan) makes a ghostly appearance to Hurley in the season 4 opener. (CHRISTINA RADISH)

- What did Charlie mean when he said, "I *am* dead. But I'm also here"? Is it a spiritual reference, that even though he's dead, his spirit remains in the air or in Hurley's heart? Or could it be less abstract, and he's suggesting that he exists on more than one temporal plane? Could it be a reference to time travel? Does death mean something different when you've been on the island?

- Is Charlie really there? When Charlie first appears to Hurley at Santa Rosa, another patient points him out. This would suggest that Charlie really is there, since he's not just a figment of Hurley's imagination. But could the other patient also be a figment of Hurley's imagination? In the previous scene where they're playing Connect Four, the nurse addresses the other patient and gives him his meds, but then again, the other nurses and doctors used to address "Dave," too, for Hurley's benefit.

- Who does Charlie mean when he says, "*They* need you"? Are "they" the people who were left behind?
- What terrible thing did the Oceanic 6 do??

Ashes to Ashes: Naomi Dorrit was . . . oh wait, she's not dead yet. Just a second . . . okay, *now* she's dead. Naomi Dorrit was from Manchester, England, but could speak several languages, including Italian, Spanish, Chinese, and Portuguese. She is sent on a mission to an island by someone with ties to Penelope Widmore, and while she survives being impaled by a tree branch, she doesn't survive being stabbed in the back by John Locke. She wants her sister to know she loved her.

4.2   Confirmed Dead

Original air date: February 7, 2008
Written by: Drew Goddard, Brian K. Vaughan
Directed by: Stephen Williams
Guest cast: Kanayo Chiemelu (African Man), Jill Kuramoto (Female Anchor), Azure McCall (Ms. Gardner), Necar Zadegan (Translator)

Flash: freighter folk

Through flashbacks, we're introduced to the four new characters who have been sent to "rescue" the survivors. On the island, Charlotte is held hostage by Locke's group, while the other three are with Kate and Jack. The survivors discover the real reason the freighter folk have come to the island.

Imagine watching a television news report saying the wreckage of a plane that was lost has been found. You see graphic footage of dead, bloated bodies floating in the water, strapped to the seats. You see the fuselage of the plane with the airline's logo emblazoned on the side. Would you accept the report as true? After all, you're staring at the evidence, and "seeing is believing," so they say. Would you ask any questions?

"Confirmed Dead" introduces us to the four people who have been sent to "rescue" the survivors. It's an episode about points of view, truth versus lies, and asking questions. The four people sent to the island — Daniel Faraday, Miles Straume, Charlotte Lewis, and Frank Lapidus — all share a common belief that the Oceanic recovery mission was a hoax. Frank and Charlotte are more vocal in their questioning, whereas Daniel seems to have an innate sense that it's not true (he cries when he hears the report, but doesn't know why) and Miles, in his very Miles way, just stares at his radio as if to say, "What a load of crap." By the end of the episode we know they're not coming to rescue the survivors (score another one in the Locke column), but they are not a unified force. Charlotte and Miles seem very comfortable with spinning a wild lie to the survivors, but Daniel and Frank are more sincere, either saying nothing, or, in Daniel's case, saying too much.

Miles Straume (Ken Leung) shows us the real reason the freighter folk are here. (MARIO PEREZ/© ABC/COURTESY: EVERETT COLLECTION)

Why did Abaddon choose these four people for the mission? What advantage did he have with a band of non-believers? Despite what Abaddon says to Naomi — that there "*were no survivors*" — many of the passengers of Flight 815 are alive and well and being chased all over an island. When the foursome lands on the island, Charlotte is the only one who is surprised to see them, but we discover later she's just a really good liar. There is clearly a hierarchy among them comprised of those who are in the know and those who aren't. Daniel doesn't seem to have a clue about much of what's going on. Miles knows that Naomi's final words were the tip-off that the survivors were hostile. Frank keeps referring to multiple trips to the island, which suggests he really believes they're going to rescue them in batches, or he could be lying to them. Frank and Miles both know they've really come for Ben, because Frank tips off Miles that Juliet is a native and would therefore know Ben. Charlotte seems to have knowledge of the island — the way she looks at the Dharma collar she finds on the skeleton of the polar bear made it seem like she knew the significance of it, and her happiness when she lands in the water seems to be more than just the joy of someone who's survived jumping out of a chopper.

What's interesting about the freighter folk is that they are no different from the people on the island. The relationships between the survivors have been changed and informed by withholding information from each other, conning each other, not asking important questions, and looking out for themselves while putting up a front that they are working together. At the beginning of this episode, we see Locke and his band of followers walking through the jungle, and Sawyer is peppering Locke with questions, asking him where they're going and why. When Locke finally tells the truth — that he's following instructions given to him by Walt — it's not the answer anyone was expecting. Sawyer's response, "What, you didn't ask any follow-up questions?" gets to the heart of the episode: has *anyone* been asking any follow-up questions? Nobody on the island knows what Kate really did, or that Hurley's a millionaire, or that Rose had cancer, or just about any detail of the lives of anyone else. Only a couple of people know that Locke was paralyzed or that Jack was married. Rousseau knows more about Sayid than anyone else on the beach does, but that's because she interrogated him. After three months, the follow-up questions between passengers have been few and far between.

From a writing and directorial perspective, this is also an episode about point of view. It opens with Daniel being thrown out of the helicopter, and the camera shows us his perspective as the helicopter gets further away above him, as the trees below him get closer, and as his breathing becomes panicked and shallow. It's a beautifully shot scene that is both frightening and exciting. Later we see what the island looks like upside-down, as we see through Charlotte's eyes what she sees while suspended from a tree branch by her parachute. As we follow Frank up the hillside, we are face to face with a cow, and momentarily share his bafflement. Miles is the only character whose perspective isn't shown, but perhaps it's because he's so abrasive the only way we'll ever look at him is from the outside.

These few moments put us right in the heads of the new people, yet we will naturally see them as outsiders. We've been onside with the survivors for three seasons, so their point of view is also ours, and we regard these new people with suspicion and caution. However, try watching the episode from the perspective of the freighter folk, and a very different world unravels. You're dropped on a mysterious island where you've told the survivors you will rescue them. Daniel lands, and he's met by two people who don't hug him, don't jump for joy, they just stare at him like they're trying to figure him out. Miles finds out they killed Naomi, when he meets the Losties for the first time he assumes they are hostile, and he sees Kate try to steal a gun from Daniel. Just when Miles thinks he has the upper hand, two more people come from the bushes holding guns to his head, and suddenly he and Daniel are hostages. Charlotte also knows Naomi has been killed by them (hence the bullet-proof vest) but she expects gratitude from the people she's going to rescue, and instead they barrage her with questions, stare at her like she's a different species, and hold her hostage while refusing to help her reunite with her team. Kate explains to Miles and Daniel that they didn't kill Naomi, that Naomi was killed by John Locke. So imagine how they must feel when Jack sees Charlotte's transponder around Vincent's neck and says, "Locke's got her." It would be a similar feeling the rest of the group would have had in seasons 2 or 3 if someone had said, "The Others have her."

"What the hell have I gotten myself into?" Frank Lapidus (Jeff Fahey) gets more than he bargained for when he lands on the island. (MARIO PEREZ/© ABC/COURTESY: EVERETT COLLECTION)

The difference between the freighter folk and the Others is that we, as viewers, have been given a glimpse of the world from their perspective, through the flashbacks and the point-of-view shots in the episode. They are clearly carrying secrets of their own, yet they are each fascinating in their own way and make us want to know more about them.

The surprise at the end of the episode, however, is that while they are new to the survivors and to us, they are not anonymous to Ben, who knows all about them. The game has shifted again.

Highlight: The looks on everyone's faces when Locke says he's getting his orders from Walt. They each look like they're thinking, "*Crap* . . . I should have gone with Jack."

Timeline: The episode begins on December 21 around midnight, and moves on to December 22.

Did You Notice?:

- Dan looks at Kate and Jack and says, "I'm here to rescue you," which is an echo of *Star Wars*, when Luke Skywalker says the same thing to Princess Leia. In this case, however, the line has about as much machismo as when Marshall Flinkman said it to Sydney Bristow on *Alias*.

- Locke stands in the rain with his face to the sky, eyes closed, a throwback to "Pilot, Part 1," when he sits on the beach in the same pose while the other survivors on the beach race for cover. He also predicts the rain in "All the Best Cowboys Have Daddy Issues" when he tells Boone to turn back, and Boone doesn't believe him (just like Hurley doesn't believe Locke here) until the downpour happens moments later. Again, in that scene, Locke's face is skyward, and he is smiling. In season 1, Locke had complete faith in the island, and his faith has been restored once again.

- Vincent, a.k.a. the dog of death, is with Locke's group. That can't be good for them.

- Locke looks at Hurley with shock when he mentions the cabin, which means it wasn't his eye in the previous episode looking out or else he'd have known Hurley was there.

- Sawyer calls Locke "Colonel Kurtz," which is probably the most apt nickname he's ever given someone. Not only is Locke bald like Kurtz in *Apocalypse Now!*, but everyone believes he is deranged, and he is now leading others down his dark path with him. Charlie had also called Locke Kurtz in "Numbers" (see analysis of *Heart of Darkness* in *Finding Lost*, pages 99–101).

- Locke shows everyone his bullet wound and says if he still had a kidney, he would be dead. The insinuation is that Locke has been correct all along when he's been saying he's following a destiny and his fate has been laid out for him. In this case, he was meant to be conned by his father, because it saved his life.

- Miles appears to have landed on the flats where Inman died.

- The name Miles Straume sounds like "maelstrom."

- In the young man's bedroom, there's a poster on the wall for the fictional band Dirt Spigot. In "Fire + Water," the director of the diaper commercial that Drive Shaft is filming complains about the band, saying he had wanted to hire Dirt Spigot instead.

- When Locke insists that Sawyer not kill Ben, Sawyer looks at Hurley, who quietly shakes his head, and only then does Sawyer walk away. This is an interesting moment, because in the first two seasons Sawyer and Hurley were constantly at each other's throats, and last season they seem to merely tolerate each other. Now it seems that Sawyer not only tolerates Hurley, but respects him.
- When we first see Frank's flashback, he's dropping a toy plane into an aquarium and it lands upside-down. It looks like he's been doing this for a while, always with the same result, as if he knows the plane found on the ocean floor — right-side up — is a fake.
- Frank's toy plane looks a lot like Kate's plane, which we see in "Whatever the Case May Be" and "Born to Run."
- Note the way Abaddon says to Naomi, "There were no survivors of Oceanic 815," as if to say, "You will make sure there were no survivors of Oceanic 815." Perhaps their mission is to make that statement a reality.
- Naomi refers to the foursome as "a head case, a ghostbuster, an anthropologist, and a drunk." Charlotte is the only one of the group she doesn't belittle in this statement.
- Charlotte is from Essex, England, and Daniel is from Essex, Massachusetts.

Interesting Facts: Jeremy Davies' character is named Daniel Faraday. One of the names used by the villain in Stephen King's *The Stand* is "Russell Faraday." In the original casting call for the character, he was named Russell, but by the time they started filming they changed it to Daniel. More importantly, Dan is named after Michael Faraday (1791–1867), a British chemist and physicist who conducted several experiments into electromagnetism. In particular, he discovered through experiments with light and electromagnetism that by applying a magnetic field, he could rotate a light beam's plane of polarization. The result of the experiment was called the Faraday Effect. It is referenced briefly in this episode when Dan is staring at the way the sunlight falls through the trees, and says the light doesn't scatter quite right.

Miles does an exorcism for a woman named Mrs. Gardner. In 1941, a skeleton was found on Gardner Island, and many believe it to have been the remains of Amelia Earhart. Some fans have theorized that the Adam and Eve skeletons of season 1 are based on Amelia Earhart and her male companion.

Frank is from Eleuthera in The Bahamas; eleuthera is derived from the Greek word for "free."

Charlotte Staples Lewis is clearly named after Clive Staples Lewis, a.k.a. C.S. Lewis, author of the Narnia series. That series of books is about stepping from one world into the next, as if the universe is a series of parallel realities. One of the favorite fan theories is that all of the action in the flashbacks, flashforwards, and island is happening at the same time, in parallel universes.

Find815: "*Christiane I*," "Sunda Trench," "Frank Lapidus," "Miles Straume," "Charlotte Lewis," "Daniel Faraday," and "Tunisian newspaper" were all clues in the game.

Nitpicks: Why does Charlotte require a translator when she's in Tunisia? Surely an anthropologist would know how to speak French. Also, if the freighter folk are here for Ben, why wasn't Charlotte more interested in him when she first saw him? Didn't it raise a red flag for Locke and Co. when Charlotte didn't bother to ask, "So who's the guy with the pulpy face and bound wrists?"

Oops: In Miles's flashback, the camera zooms in on the photos of the young man whose ghost is haunting his grandmother's house. The main picture is a close-up of the man, in a wooden frame. There is another photo above it in a white frame. When Miles comes back down the stairs after communicating with the spirit, the main photo is suddenly much larger, and in a brass frame. There are several other photos around it, also in brass frames. It's possible, of course, that the photos somehow changed to indicate the man had left, but it's probably, like a lot of very strange occurrences on the show, a production error. Also, when the gang first encounters Frank and he sits up, he has two pieces of grass stuck to the cut on his forehead. The camera cuts away for a second and when it cuts back, the grass is gone.

4 8 15 16 23 42: When you see the two ROVs (remotely operated underwater vehicles) underwater, the second one has a fuel reading of 64 (**8** x **8**). There are **4** team members in the helicopter. When Miles enters the grandson's room, there's a **15** on a football poster on the wall and when he puts his ghostbuster device on the table, there's a coupon stuck to the board on the wall saying something is $**15**. If you add up the numbers in the Oceanic hotline, the sum is **48**. The helicopter has the number N**842**M on the side of it. Charlotte was born on July 2, 1979, **42** years to the day after Amelia Earhart was pronounced missing.

It's Just a Flesh Wound: Sawyer beats up Ben . . . again. Frank suffers a gash on his forehead and appears to have hurt his leg when he was putting the chopper down. Ben shoots Charlotte, and even though she's wearing a bulletproof vest, her chest would be very sore.

Any Questions?:

- In the script, the woman talking to Dan in his flashback is his "caretaker." Why does Dan require a caretaker?
- So why *was* Dan so upset when he watched the news?
- Did the magnetic anomaly bring the helicopter down?
- Why did they have gas masks on board? Are they planning on wiping out everyone on the island through chemical warfare?
- Did Miles's dustbuster machine actually help him talk to ghosts, or is it all for show?
- Why does Ben goad Sawyer? It's like he wants Sawyer to lose it and beat him up. Is he a masochist?
- How did the polar bear end up in the desert with a Dharma collar on it? Did Charlotte recognize the Dharma symbol?
- Why wasn't Frank flying Oceanic 815 if he was supposed to have been the pilot that day?
- Was that one of Mikhail's cows that Frank comes face to face with?
- Who was Naomi? When Abaddon is recruiting her, he acts like she's a superhero. She says there's only so much she can do, and he tells her she's being modest. Why was she carrying a photo of Desmond and Penelope, when the mission clearly had something to do with the survivors of Oceanic Flight 815?
- Why were these four people chosen? Is Dan there because of the electromagnetism? Is Miles there to talk to the numerous dead people on the island? Or are they hoping to kill these people because they are living proof the Oceanic recovery was phony?
- Abaddon tells Naomi that everything relies on her getting them in and out unharmed. Since she's dead and can't fulfill her task, does that mean the mission cannot succeed?
- When Dan tried to contact the freighter's communications officer, George Minkowski, why was George unable to come to the phone?
- Why have the people on the helicopter all been given different information? Charlotte is wearing a bulletproof vest and Miles knows about Naomi's phone call, as if they were both told that Naomi was dead. Frank and Dan don't know about Naomi's death. Were each of the freighter folk given different information according to their specialty?
- Why is Miles so angry when talking about Ben?

- Why go to all the trouble just to get Ben Linus?
- Why does the photo of Ben look like it was taken in the 1970s, by the looks of the clothes he is wearing in it?
- Is Ben telling the truth when he says he doesn't know what the smoke monster is?
- Why wasn't Naomi more excited when Ben first joined the group in "Through the Looking Glass"? Was she not aware of the greater mission? When she pounces on Kate in "The Beginning of the End," she sounds like she truly believed she was getting them rescued.
- This is the place where I'd usually ask if Ben's telling the truth about having a spy on the freighter, but if he was looking to make believers out of us, recounting Charlotte's biography pretty much did it for me.
- Who is Ben's man on the boat?

The Freighter Folk

Lance Reddick (Matthew Abaddon)

Known for his intense dramatic roles, Lance Reddick was most recognized for his role as a beaten-down lieutenant in one of the best shows on television before he appeared to mainstream audiences as the enigmatic and mysterious Matthew Abaddon on *Lost*.

Born in Baltimore, Maryland, Reddick had aspirations of becoming a musician. He attended the University of Rochester as a physics major (hmm . . . a clue to his character, perhaps?). The school was affiliated with the prestigious Eastman School of Music, and by the time Reddick was entering his second year of university, he realized he'd made a mistake, transferred to Eastman, and focused on music composition. Upon graduation he moved to Boston in the hopes of becoming a pop singer, but he injured himself while working a delivery job, and had to give up the part-time work that would have supported such a career. Realizing he might have to make yet another career shift, he entered Yale's graduate school of drama and focused on acting.

His first major role was as the understudy in Tony Kushner's critically acclaimed play, *Angels in America*. He appeared in other theater roles, including *Henry V* in Central Park, before landing supporting roles on television shows such as *The Nanny* and *The West Wing*. But it was the role of Detective John Basil on HBO's *Oz* (with fellow *Lost* cast members Adewale Akinnuoye-Agbaje and Harold Perrineau) that gave Reddick the breakthrough he needed. He appeared in other HBO shows, like *The Corner*, produced by David Simon and Edward Burns, and when they were casting for their new series, *The Wire*, he came in to read for the role of Detective Bunk, followed by the drug addict Bubbles. He was turned down for both roles, but in season 2 he landed the role of Lieutenant Cedric Daniels. *The Wire* went on to become one of the most critically acclaimed television series of all time, and suddenly Reddick was in demand.

The dashing Lance Reddick has appeared in *The Wire* and, most recently, *Fringe*. (AP PHOTO/PETER KRAMER)

Damon Lindelof and Carlton Cuse were both fans of *The Wire*, and they originally wanted Reddick for the part of Mr. Eko, but Reddick was unavailable. When filming on *The Wire*'s final season had wrapped, Darlton leapt in to snatch him up for the role of Matthew Abaddon, a "corporate recruiter," as his casting call read. J.J. Abrams was clearly impressed, and Reddick now does double-time between *Lost* and Abrams' *Fringe*, where he plays Agent Phillip Broyles.

Almost all of Reddick's roles have been unsmiling, powerful men who get the job done no matter what gets in their way. And while Reddick always plays them pitch-perfect, sometimes he wishes people would see the other side of him. "I'm really goofy," he says. "I've had a hard time getting an opportunity to do any comedy since I started doing a lot of television because what I've become known for is intense dramatic character acting." Maybe in an upcoming season we'll get a goofy showdown between Abaddon and Sawyer. We can only hope.

Jeff Fahey (Frank Lapidus)

As the grizzly Frank Lapidus, Jeff Fahey has created a character we may sympathize with the most of the freighter folk. When looking for someone to play Lapidus, Damon Lindelof said they specifically wanted someone who wasn't immediately recognizable to the fans. And while he's starred in a cult hit that many genre fans have watched repeatedly, the man with the long blond hair in *The Lawnmower Man* looks nothing like the character Fahey now plays on *Lost*.

Born in New York on November 29, 1952, Jeff Fahey is one of 13 children. In his teens he traveled around the world to places like Afghanistan, India, and Israel. He took up dancing in his early twenties, and secured a scholarship to the Joffrey Ballet school in New York at the age of 25, an age when many dancers would be close to retirement. After an injury, Fahey landed a role on *One Life to Live*, where he starred for three years. Roles in shows like *Silverado*, *Miami Vice*, and *The Demon Within* followed, and he became a cult figure when he starred in *The Lawnmower Man*, a sci-fi film very loosely based on Stephen King's short story of the same name (so loosely based, in fact, that King successfully sued the studio to have his name removed from the film).

Fahey is not only an amazing actor, he's a humanitarian. When Darlton contacted Fahey for the role of Frank, he was in Venezuela, setting up an orphanage that would be based on a model of another orphanage he'd already been running in Kabul, Afghanistan. As the alcoholic helicopter pilot on *Lost*, Fahey has won over the fans . . . and the showrunners. "[H]e has the most intense eyes of any guy out there," says Carlton Cuse. "And I say that as a non-gay man."

Jeremy Davies (Daniel Faraday)

He has worked with some of the greatest directors in the indie film world — Wim Wenders, Werner Herzog, David O. Russell, Steven Soderbergh, Lars von Trier — and has starred in films directed by Steven Spielberg and Jan de Bont. In a matter of two episodes on *Lost*, Jeremy Davies managed to make himself one of the most beloved characters on the series, despite being the new guy. He brings to the role one of the most impressive resumés of anyone on the show.

Born October 28, 1969, Davies was born Jeremy Boring, and is one of four children of

Mel Boring, who is a children's author (Davies is Jeremy's mother's maiden name). His first acting stint was in a Subaru car commercial, where he was discovered and immediately offered movie roles. Davies starred in David O. Russell's first film, *Spanking the Monkey* (2004), with Alberta Watson (*La Femme Nikita*), which dealt with an incestuous relationship between a mother and son. Davies' jittery moves and wavering voice became his trademark, and he soon was offered more roles, including his breakthrough part in *Saving Private Ryan* as Upham, a cartographer and interpreter who is pushed into the horrors of war, despite his lack of combat training. Viewers of that movie will remember his complete breakdown in a stairwell during the movie's final battle scene.

After *Saving Private Ryan*, Davies returned to his first love — indie films — and starred in several movies, many of them by Miramax, including *CQ*, *Teknolust*, *Secretary*, *Solaris*, and *Dogville*. His turn as Charles Manson in the 2004 film *Helter Skelter* garnered Davies some rave reviews, and in 2007 he offered a groundbreaking turn in *Rescue Dawn* opposite Christian Bale. Playing a POW who has been imprisoned in a camp for two years, Davies lost 35 pounds off his already incredibly slim frame, bringing his weight down around 100 pounds. In one scene in the movie where his character, Gene, removes his shirt, audible gasps were heard in the movie theater at the show's premiere.

While Davies has been building up an impressive resumé, what he really wants to do is write and direct. "I never expected that a misfit like me could get very far in this business," he says. "You know how competitive it is. It's almost like winning the interplanetary lottery to get anywhere within [it]. But, above all, I've always had a real strong desire from way back to become a filmmaker, so I've actively been taking these acting experiences over the years with the active desire to hijack them and turn them into film school." One of the advantages of working with such unique directors is that Davies has been able to pay close attention to their filmmaking styles and learn from them. In fact, he wasn't even looking for an acting role when he won the part in *Dogville*, but instead wanted to sit on the set and watch von Trier work. "I wrote Lars a letter and said, 'I think you're one of the greatest filmmakers in the world, and I'd love the privilege of coming to watch you,'" he explains. "And he invited me out and made me take a small role in his film *Dogville*, which I didn't even want. He's one of my best friends now."

Because Davies didn't do television, Darlton were thrilled when he showed an interest in the part of Daniel. "He's usually the smartest guy in the room in any part he plays," says Lindelof. "[T]hat transformative quality, plus the tremendous intelligence that seems to emanate from him, sort of seemed perfect for this particular character." One can expect Davies is paying as much attention to the directors and writers of the series as he is the other actors. Perhaps we'll see him behind the *Lost* camera one of these days.

Rebecca Mader (Charlotte Lewis)

Rebecca Mader arrived at her *Lost* audition to try to obtain the part of a woman in her mid-twenties who was "precocious, loquacious and funny . . . a very successful academic who also knows how to handle herself in the real world." The part called for an American, and she read the lines as such. When the producer checked over her resumé and saw she had done a lot of British television, he asked her if she was British. She said yes, and reread the part as a Brit. Suddenly, Charlotte Lewis became English.

Mader was a relative unknown when she was cast in her role on *Lost*. Carlton Cuse described her as a "young Nicole Kidman," and he's right. Born in 1979 in Cambridge, England, Mader had small roles in several television shows (including a week-long stint on *All My Children*) before appearing in *The Devil Wears Prada*, which brought her talents to a larger audience. Her big break came when she was cast in a starring role in FOX's show *Justice*, also starring Victor Garber, Kerr Smith, and Eamonn Walker. But FOX moved the show from Wednesdays to Mondays to Fridays, all within its first few episodes, and then they canceled it. (Big shock there.)

While Charlotte has a tendency to be a little cold in the beginning, Mader played the character carefully, making sure to keep the audience guessing at Charlotte's background. By the end of the fourth season, she became one of the show's most intriguing characters.

Ken Leung (Miles Straume)

His special brand of snark is what makes Miles Straume such a fun character to watch, but it's not a coincidence that he's so similar to the previous television character Leung played.

Ken Leung was born on January 21, 1970, in New York City. He studied acting at NYU and began taking small roles in movies such as *Rush Hour*, *Keeping the Faith*, and *Vanilla Sky*. Not limited to movies, Leung also appeared in shows like *Law & Order* and *Oz*. His roles in the movies *X-Men: The Last Stand* (as Kid Omega) and in *Shanghai Kiss* with Hayden Panetierre made Leung's face a little more familiar. But it was his stint as Carter Chong, the irritating guy with serious anger management issues who befriends Uncle Junior in *The Sopranos*, that caught the eye of Carlton Cuse and Damon Lindelof. Lindelof saw the episode first, and told Cuse to watch it, asking him to tell him the next day if there was one particular actor who stood out for him. After Cuse had watched the episode, he simply said to Damon, "You mean Ken Leung?" Anxious to see if he was available, the duo contacted Leung's management, and discovered he was now considered a hot property, but he wanted to do *Lost*. So, they created a role for him. "The part he's playing — it's a character we wrote very specifically for Ken. Nobody else read for it. It had to be him," says Lindelof.

Considering that the only part they knew Ken Leung from was the one on *The Sopranos*, it's not surprising that Miles is also annoying and has his own anger issues. Despite his rudeness, however, Miles is beloved by fans, who take delight in his sarcasm, and I, for one, look forward to seeing where he plans to take this character in the future.

Find815: The 2008 *Lost* ARG

After the extraordinary success of the online alternate reality game (ARG), *The Lost Experience*, which gamers played between seasons 2 and 3, the writers of *Lost* decided to try it again, and the result was *Find815*. Told mostly through videos, this one was a little less intense than *The Lost Experience* but still told a compelling story about one man trying to find answers. It was divided into five chapters, starting on December 31, 2007, and running until a couple of hours before the season 4 premiere on January 31, 2008. The following is a summary of the story. Throughout the game, the videos would stop and players would be asked to complete a task to continue the story (they had to decode messages, find clues in screen captures, and complete certain tasks for protagonist Sam Thomas). If they failed, they would see a video of Sam screwing up and paying the price. But if they succeeded, the story moved on. I'll put in boldface the clues that pertained directly to season 4 (see the individual episode guides for the references).

Sam Thomas is an IT guy at Oceanic Airlines, and his girlfriend Sonya was a flight attendant on Oceanic Flight 815. They had been dating for almost eight years and he was going to propose to her when the flight went missing. Upset at Oceanic's lack of interest in an investigation following the plane's disappearance, Sam has become a very vocal critic of his employer in the media. He receives an email from an anonymous person saying they're an old friend of Sonya's and they send an attached photo. Embedded in the photo are the messages **Christiane I**;

Sunda Trench; **Black Rock**; and Tell No One — Grave Consequences. Hidden in the notification message is a website: the-maxwell-group.com. Sam walks over to a giant world map that adorns most of one wall of his house, covered in Post-its and tacks (he's clearly been doing his own investigation) and circles the Sunda Trench. Sam emails his friend Tracey R to ask her about the *Christiane I*, and she says it's a boat that is leaving from Jakarta on a confidential mission. He then emails his friend David and asks for a plane ticket to Jakarta, Indonesia, which David gets for him. (Considering how quickly Sam responds to this email, let's hope an "ambassador from Nigeria" doesn't write to him asking if he could lend him $10,000.)

Sam goes to sleep, but awakens in the night to the sound of his shutters opening and closing in the wind. He closes them, but sees an image of Sonya in the window saying, "Love you madly." The next part of the game asked players to find clues from each season hidden in a screen capture of Sam's bedroom. The season 4 clue on the ABC.com site was "**Matthew**," and in Australia it was "**Abaddon**." In the meantime, Sam's mother calls his cell phone to tell him she's worried about him and about what he's been saying. Sam receives an email from his manager at Oceanic saying he's being fired for being so outspoken against the company. Sam writes a message to Austral Air inquiring about job openings. He leaves a video diary, which is much like one of the Dharma orientation films, full of glitches and jumps and missing dialogue. At one point, a man's face appears for half a second, and at the end of the message, there's a brief screen capture from J.J. Abrams' *Cloverfield*. Sam leaves for Jakarta, and asks Tracey to find out anything she can on "black rock."

Chapter 2 opens with Sam trying to board the *Christiane I*. The captain, Mr. Ockham, refuses him passage, saying they're not going to give him a free ride. But when the ship's chart plotter short-circuits, Sam says he will fix it in return for a spot on the ship. Oscar Talbot, who is Ockham's superior (and the man whose face was in the frame of Sam's video diary), is standing there when it happens, mentioning his "employer" is in a hurry. He asks Sam why he's so interested in the Sunda Trench, and asks if he's running away from something. Later, in Sam's quarters, Sam looks at some websites about the Sunda Trench that detail the many planes and ships that have gone missing there, usually citing electrical failures. He turns on an old radio he finds and hears a radio broadcast saying Amelia Earhart's plane has disappeared and people are looking for her. Tracey R emails him to say she's not finding anything on the Black Rock, but she looked up Oscar

Talbot and suggests Sam stay away from him. Season 4 clues to the game that follow this section are "**423 Cheyne Walk**" and "**Daniel Faraday.**" A bonus clue was **020 7946 0893**. Sam emails the Broadcasting Authority, asking them why he was hearing a 1937 broadcast, and they suggest possible ham radio enthusiasts playing historical recordings. He then pulls up a website talking about the Black Rock, and discovers it was a slave ship that sailed in the 1880s and was lost at sea. He leaves a video diary saying he's having second thoughts about the whole thing and wonders if that email from the Maxwell Group was a hoax.

At the beginning of chapter 3, Sam asks Ockham to let him off at Christmas Island, but Ockham says they missed Christmas Island by 150 miles. He says he's got a job to do and that Talbot gave him a grid in which to search for the *Black Rock* and he's going to stick to it, because he wants to get paid. As Sam leaves, he sees Talbot, clearly seasick, leaving his quarters, and Sam enters. He finds a briefcase and when he opens it, sees a file with a document entitled, "Proposed Salvage of 'The Black Rock' Shipwreck." At the top of the page it says "The Maxwell Group," and adds that it's a **division of Widmore Industries**. Talbot catches him leaving the room, and Sam tries to say he was simply closing the door, but Talbot is suspicious, and tells Sam that while others think he's an asset to the expedition, Talbot himself is not one of them. (By the way, we've only ever seen Sam, Ockham, and Talbot, so it appears to be a pretty sparse expedition.) Sam receives a strange email that contains a string of letters, and then a second email from Sonya's parents asking him to come stay at their place. He politely declines.

Later, on the deck, Sam hears strange high-frequency noises coming from below. He finds the source of the feedback and pushes a button on a panel, which makes it stop. Players then had to search the bridge for clues from each season, and the season 4 clues were **36-15-28**, **Frank Lapidus**, and **Charlotte Lewis**. The bonus clue was **Tunisian newspaper**. Back in Sam's quarters, he does an Internet search for "Maxwell" and finds James Clerk Maxwell, a "pioneer of **electromagnetism**." He sends an email to Tracey about the strange frequencies, and she replies that they could have been caused by a burst of electromagnetism. More clues in the game reveal **Morse code** as a clue. Sam leaves a video diary saying that in the strange emails he found geographic coordinates and he will be checking them out. He adds that Sonya would hate what he's doing, but at least it's been keeping his mind off things.

In chapter 4, Sam is steering the ship when Ockham leaves for a moment. Sam quickly pulls a wire out of the chart plotter, turning it off. Ockham returns, baffled that his computer screen is dark, and asks Sam to look at it while he goes to get Talbot. Sam rushes over, hacks into the plotter, and pulls up the coordinates, which are inside the grid they're looking at. He brings the computer back online and returns to steering the ship. When Ockham and Talbot return, everything's working perfectly. Soon after this, Talbot corners Sam and says he knows he's lying about the plotter, and that he'd found Sam's piece of paper with the coordinates. After first denying it, Sam admits the numbers came from the Maxwell Group. Talbot smiles and tells him not to get caught up with them. Sam returns to his quarters and gets a phone message from a friend saying he's made some money due to an investment — a box company he invested in on his friend Randy's advice has burned down and the investors are somehow collecting the insurance money. (Randy is probably Randy Nations, Hurley's boss from the Chicken Shack, who went on to be Locke's boss at the box company which Hurley owned. Maybe Randy burned it down. . . .) Tracey R emails to say Sam's mother is upset, but Tracey has assured her that Sam is okay. Sam receives an anonymous email with a coded message that, once deciphered, says, "Love you madly."

Sam goes out to walk along the ship's deck at night and sees some glowing lights in the distance. He grabs some binoculars from inside the ship, but by the time he returns, the lights are gone. Players were then asked to play another clue hunt. The season 4 clues were **Frank Lapidus** (the last Frank clue was for Australian players; this one was for Americans) and **Miles Straume**. The bonus clue was **Santa Rosa pill bottle**, and when the serial number on the bottle was decoded, the clue was **campmillar bonusclue**. Sam emails Tracey to ask about the lights and she says they could be aurora borealis, caused by magnetism and generally spotted around polar regions, but she says they shouldn't have disappeared so quickly. In Sam's video diary he appears agitated and angry, and he says he's upset about the coded message, which was a phrase he and Sonya would use with each other all the time. He says it's not a comfort to him to see that, it seemed instead like something meant to goad him. He says he's going to continue to search for the coordinates.

Sam tells Ockham the truth about his coordinates and convinces him to change course to help him find the *Black Rock*. As they do so, Talbot catches on and tells them to turn the ship around and return it to its original course, but Sam sees something intriguing on the radar, and they decide to head for it. Back in his quarters, Sam receives a phone message from Tracey expressing her worry. He gets an email from the airline service he'd emailed earlier saying they might have a job opening. He receives yet another anonymous email with the hidden message, "All is lost." Sam goes up on deck and hears whispers that sound like Sonya saying, "Sam, love you madly," but as Sam begins shouting her name, Ockham approaches and tells him it's the wind. Players then had to find the season 4 clues, which were **Southfields** and **Red Sox**, and a bonus clue, **Queen's College**.

In Sam's video diary, he says they've found the *Black Rock* and will be investigating. He says the weather is too rough to explore, and it reminds him of the storm that caused his chance first meeting with Tracey eight years earlier. When the weather clears, they lower the rov and Sam pilots it through the water. Just as Ockham's about to give up, Sam sees something. But it's not the *Black Rock* . . . it's Oceanic Flight 815. Sam breaks down in tears.

A few days later, we see Sam back in his apartment as he watches the news broadcast announcing they'd found the remains of Oceanic 815. Talbot gives a statement, and mentions Sam being on the ship, saying that he was trying to get away from things, but an "extraordinary twist of fate" put him on the ship and helped him discover the plane. Sam stares at the screen in stunned silence.

This was technically the end of the game, but in March the Find815.com site was updated to show a page in Sam's diary (and at the time of writing, the page is still there), in which he says he's losing sleep, and that, while the rest of the world has moved on, he hasn't. He still wants answers.

4.3   The Economist

Original air date: February 14, 2008
Written by: Edward Kitsis, Adam Horowitz
Directed by: Jack Bender
Guest cast: Armando Pucci (Mr. Avellino), Thekla Reuten (Elsa)

Flash: Sayid

Sayid, Kate, and Miles travel to Locke's camp to retrieve Charlotte, while Daniel conducts an experiment near the helicopter. Sayid's flashforward shows us that his future career will be similar to the one in his past, but with a different motivation.

Four down, two to go. With this episode we discover the fourth member of the Oceanic 6 is Sayid. Sayid is one of the few characters on this show who has

Despite just arriving, Daniel (Jeremy Davies) looks like the one who has been stuck on a desert island for several months, while Charlotte (Rebecca Mader) and Juliet (Elizabeth Mitchell) look like travelers waiting at an airport. (MARIO PEREZ/© ABC/COURTESY: EVERETT COLLECTION)

come to an epiphany about himself and not died. One of the factors fans use to support the theory that everyone on the island is in purgatory (despite the creators saying they are *not*) is that, often, when a character realizes something about themselves that allows them to put the past behind them and focus on a new future, they soon after die. Charlie discovered that he wasn't the has-been that he thought he was, that his life might have had a lot of low points, but it had at least five high points as well. And that was it for him. Shannon died moments after Sayid told her that he loved her and believed her story that she was seeing Walt, after a lifetime of no one ever showing her that kind of respect. Ana Lucia was killed by Michael when she realized she couldn't shoot her way out of a situation anymore, and that she'd moved beyond that mentality.

For Sayid, his epiphany is that he no longer wants to be a torturer. In season 1, he tortured Sawyer for information, and when he realized who he had become, he forced himself to separate from the group in "Solitary." He knows he doesn't want to be that sort of person anymore. However, unlike the other personal revelations on the island, Sayid cannot fulfill his. He doesn't want to be a torturer, but every time he tries to walk away, his training — or perhaps his nature — pulls him back in. In season 2, he enters the armory where Ben is being held, and when he leaves, Ben looks like his face has gone through a paper shredder. In season 3, we saw a flashback where the husband of a woman Sayid had tortured decided to turn the tables on him ("Enter 77"). By the end of the season, he had killed a man with his bare hands . . . er, legs.

Sayid can barely live with himself at times, but sometimes in the *Lord of the Flies* climate that reigns on the island, his skills are needed by the others. Just as Jack wants someone else to take over as leader, but is simultaneously reluctant to give it up, Sayid wants to walk away from his past but returns to it whenever the situation calls for it. Where the other characters had epiphanies that made them change their lives, Sayid has never made that commitment to change. In the end, he's always going to be a torturer; he can't seem to escape that.

In this flashforward, we see that Ben was paying attention to Sayid's moral vacillation, and he has somehow used it to turn Sayid into a hitman in the future. Through a long con, Sayid tricks a woman, Elsa, to get to her boss, who for some reason is on a list of people he needs to kill. Elsa, however, is running a con of her own. The only thing that keeps Sayid from being a cold-blooded killer is his heart; in fact, that has always been his fatal flaw. Sayid always falls in love deeply and completely, and even when he enters a relationship in a fraudulent context, he can't help but be swept away. He knows he must stay vigilant, but the moment Elsa begins talking about love, Sayid is done for. Ben says to him that he needs to think with his gun and not his heart. Despite Sayid's life as a torturer, he always lets his heart get in the way.

While the Sayid flashforward was interesting, the scene that really had fans discussing this episode for days afterward was the experiment Daniel does with the payload and the beacon. One theory that arose online was that island time moves at a different speed than time off the island. Fans wondered if, to the outside world, the survivors had been gone for decades, or on the flip side, for minutes (see page 63 for a more detailed analysis).

Just as Daniel's experiment suggested that time on the island might be fluid, Ben's secret hideaway showed us that he is not as island-bound as we might have thought he was. The clothes, passports, money, and suitcases would suggest he's been coming and going at his leisure. The photo that Miles was holding in the previous episode showed Ben in what appeared to be 1970s clothing, yet he looked the

I think a lot of viewers would sell their souls to spend a moment in the water with Naveen Andrews. (MARIO PEREZ/© ABC/COURTESY: EVERETT COLLECTION)

same age as he is now — is it possible that he's not only traveling, but time traveling?

Lost has long been a series obsessed with cons, and in this episode, Sayid is tricked by that most innocent of survivors, Hurley. The central meaning of the con is that what you see is not necessarily what you get: no matter how trustworthy he or she may seem, everyone has a hidden agenda. The freighter folk don't appear to be here to rescue anyone. Ben always has something up his sleeve. Even Hurley, when pushed, will trick someone if he believes that to do so is vital to his own welfare. But in this case, when Sayid is locked up in the recreation room with Ben, it puts these two disparate characters together to foreshadow what will happen in the future. Sayid despises Ben. He sneers at him, saying, "The day I start trusting him is the day I sell my soul." By the end of the episode, the viewer understands the dramatic irony in that statement.

As Sayid pulls away from the island in the helicopter and the music swells, he appears to have left the island and everything it stood for behind him. But in the future, he will work for the island's leading con artist, he will be conned by another person who appears to be innocent — just like Hurley — and he will once again see someone die in front of him. When he glances down to see the bracelet on Elsa's wrist, it reminds him of the same one he'd seen on Naomi's, and in that moment, Sayid realizes he will never leave the island.

Highlight: This was definitely Miles's episode, from his snarky comments about Frank tweezing his goatee and the Others having daycare, to Hurley's reaction to Miles calling him "Tubby." ("Oh. Awesome. The ship sent us another Sawyer.")

Timeline: The events on the island are happening on the same day as the previous episode, so it's December 22, 2004.

Did You Notice?:

- Sayid is playing golf in the Seychelles, which is a group of islands off the coast of Africa. In season 2, after Eko's brother's small plane landed on the island, some fans suggested that maybe the island is off the coast of Africa, since that plane wouldn't have had enough fuel to have gotten to the Pacific. These islands were approximately where some fans speculated the castaways really are.

- Frank says that if Sayid brings Charlotte back safe, he will take him off the island. That, of course, could mean plopping him into the ocean. He chooses his words as carefully as Ben does.

- Miles is a complete dick, and yet he's hilarious — unlike a duo whose names rhyme with Rikki and Raulo.

- When Sayid finds Hurley locked in the closet, Hurley's eyes dart around and he pauses before saying, "They left me," as if he's not completely on board with the con he is pulling.

- As Sayid glances through the books on Ben's shelf, we can see *The Holy Qur'an*; *Red Man's Religion: Beliefs and Practices of the Indians North of Mexico* by Ruth Murray Underhill; *Kings of Love: The Poetry and History of the Ni'Matullahi Sufi Order* by Nasrollah Pourjavady and Peter Lamborn Wilson; *The Sheltering Sky* by Paul Bowles; *Caravan of Dreams* by Idries Shah; and *Fahrenheit 451* by Ray Bradbury. Since the last time we saw his shelf it held nothing but mass-market pap, it seems the prop team has decided to improve Ben's reading taste.

- Thank you, Sawyer! It's about time someone addressed the fact that in the outside world, Kate is a convict and would probably be looking at prison time. I've been waiting three years for someone to ask Kate why she wants to leave the island.

- Ben tells Sayid it's no use having friends you can't trust, foreshadowing what happens to Sayid with Elsa. Sayid then says the day he begins trusting Ben is the day he's sold his soul, foreshadowing who his boss will eventually be.

- Locke brings iced tea to Sayid. The last time Sayid was offered iced tea, it was from Mikhail, who was conning Sayid, the same as Locke tricks him here.

- Sayid shoots Elsa the same way Shannon was shot by Ana Lucia, which could be one of the reasons Elsa's death affects him so much.

Interesting Facts: The golf hole in the Seychelles where Sayid and Mr. Avellino are playing is actually the 17th hole at Hawaii's Turtle Bay Resort.

Elsa was the name of the lioness made famous by the book and film *Born Free*, by Joy Adamson. Similarly, Sayid is now "free," but also in captivity.

On one of Ben's passports, we see he uses the pseudonym Dean Moriarty. Dean Moriarty is the main character in Jack Kerouac's *On the Road*, based on his friend Neal Cassidy. Moriarty is the one who convinces Sal, the book's narrator, to follow him around on various adventures, much like Ben convinces others to follow him for better or for worse. Moriarty suffers from serious daddy issues. Also, Moriarty is the name of Sherlock Holmes's arch enemy, which makes it even more perfect for Ben.

When Elsa's boss rings her pager, she says he's at the Hotel Adlon. That hotel is the one where Michael Jackson famously dangled his son off a balcony in 2002.

When fans initially watched "The Economist," they wondered what the connection was between Elsa's bracelet and Naomi's. Did Sayid take it from Naomi's wrist and give it to Elsa? Were they both part of the same organization and the bracelet was a marker to show that? But in an interview with *Entertainment Weekly*, Damon Lindelof sounded surprised that fans would have made such a specific connection between the two pieces of jewellery. "I got some emails from people who wondered if there was a connection between Naomi's bracelet and the bracelet worn by the woman Sayid killed in his flashforward," he said. "There is no connective tissue. Sometimes a bracelet is just a bracelet. We just thought it would be a cool emotional touchstone for Sayid; Elsa's bracelet reminds him of Naomi. But some people interpreted that, 'Is there something more there?' We might need to address that." If they just wanted the bracelet to be a bracelet, maybe they shouldn't have used the *exact same* bracelet in the scene. However, his comment, "We may need to address that," could be an indicator that they will change gears and actually turn that bracelet into something bigger than it was originally intended to be.

The Economist is a British newspaper famous for not listing any bylines with the articles, which offers anonymity to the writers. This practice has been praised and criticized, since on the one hand it puts the story above the person writing it, but on the other it allows sometimes shoddy writing to run without the author of the piece having to be ashamed of the quality of his or her work.

Nitpicks: After Sayid shoots Avellino, the sprinklers on the golf course come on. While it lends drama to the scene, a sprinkler system on a golf course would never

Funny *Lost* on the Web

Here are a few fun sites for *Lost* fans with a weird sense of humor:

Keamy's Paradise
keamysparadise.blogspot.com
One of my favorite sites, this is a blog where the admin has taken a screen capture of Keamy's face as he screams before opening fire on the Others during the helicopter shootout, and Photoshopped that face into various famous pictures. Keamy is seen screaming in the graduation shot of Buffy and the gang, in the promo poster for the original *90210*, and jumping for joy on *The Price Is Right*. This site is unique and hilarious.

Waaalt!
www.waaalt.com
This site, which claims to be "keeping track of Michael's annoyingness since . . . yesterday," records the number of times Michael screams for Walt in each episode of *Lost*. It hasn't been updated since season 2, but it's funny anyway. (Well, for about 20 seconds, but it's worth it for that long.) Be warned: if you're checking this site in a public place, there's a soundbyte of Michael screaming for Walt that plays in a constant loop, just to annoy the heck out of everyone.

The Opening Act from the Original, Unused Teleplay of *Lost*'s Pilot Episode
www.mcsweeneys.net/2008/5/29bridgman.html
McSweeney's is one of the funniest sites on the Net, bar none (you should check it out every week). It features some of the edgiest writing in the world today, and it's often riddled with pop culture references. In this particular piece, author Andrew Bridgman constructs a laugh-out-loud pilot for *Lost* that would have ended the show after half an episode, with everyone introducing themselves by giving their complete backstories. For example, after Locke tells everyone he was paralyzed because his father threw him out of a window, he disappears into the jungle and returns a few moments later, saying he found a hatch and opened it. "[T]here was a Scottish guy in there, and I made him stop pressing some button. It just exploded and released a bunch of electromagnetic energy, so the island is visible to the outside world again. DESMOND: Hi, bruthas. I'm Desmond. I can kinda see the future. Charlie, you're gonna die."

The Ack Attack
www.theackattack.com/?tag=lost-recap
An exceptionally funny *Lost* recap site, this one is run by Rachel, who recounts each episode of *Lost* with a lot of screen captures and her tongue firmly planted in her cheek. I defy you to read these without laughing out loud at least once (per frame). She is brilliant.

spontaneously turn on if there was a possibility of dousing the patrons. It's obvious Sayid has sneaked onto the course (after all, if he'd signed in at the clubhouse and they later found a dead man on one of the fairways, it would be a tad obvious who the murderer was). Still, Avellino would have been playing a legitimate round, since he had a golf cart (and presumably, his tee time was how Sayid knew to find him there). If they knew he was on the course, they would have held off on the sprinklers until they knew he was done.

Why doesn't Sayid use a silencer on his gun? Are the walls so thick at the hotel that no one heard Elsa shoot him and then him shoot her twice?

Finally, if the payload had been traveling in the air on a rocket for 30 minutes, it would have been red-hot, yet Daniel grabs it the moment it lands.

Oops: Naomi's eyes are closed as Sayid walks over to her body, before he closes them. Fans have pointed out several spelling mistakes on the German menu board when Sayid enters the café at the beginning of the episode. Also, Ben's Brazilian passport should have had "Brasil Passaporte República" on the front of it, and not "Brazil Passport Republica," as it says.

4 8 15 16 23 42: When Sayid walks into the café where he first meets Elsa, the top item on the menu is **15**.95. She suggests they meet for dinner at **8**. The timer on the payload reads 03:**16**:**23**.

Any Questions?:

- Naomi's bracelet reads "N, I will always be with you. R.G." Who is R.G.? Is it someone significant?
- When Sayid tells the man on the golf course who he is, the man becomes unnerved. Is it because he knows Sayid is here to kill him, or does he know something about what happened on the island? Or both?
- When Sayid uses a cellphone at the beginning to say he's made contact, Ben is the one who answers, but he's purposely deepened his voice so we can't figure out it's him.
- What is the significance of the volcanic ash that surrounds the spot where Jacob's cabin should be? Is it keeping Jacob in, or keeping others out?
- Why does Frank tell Dan to hang up the phone if Minkowski returns? Where is Minkowski? Why would he have to hang up if he came?
- What was with that little room hidden behind Ben's bookshelf? What does he do in there? Why did he have so many suits? Money from other countries? Passports? Has he been coming and going from the island like Richard does?
- Why don't Locke, Rousseau, or Hurley seem interested in Ben's hidden room behind the bookshelf?

- Ben says Sayid must continue to do what he's doing to protect his friends. By "friends," is Ben referring to the Oceanic 6, or the people left behind?
- Why do Daniel and Charlotte decide to stay on the island? Have they been given a mission that's being kept secret from Frank? What are they there to study?
- Why does Daniel insist that Frank stay on a particular bearing when going to and from the island?
- Is Ben a veterinarian, or is he just using the O.R. of an animal shelter as a meeting place with Sayid? Does Ben have surgical experience?
- Why is Sayid working for Ben? Why are these people on the list? Who made the list? Is it another list by Jacob? Is the island still playing a big part in the lives of the Oceanic 6, even after they've left? Are the others in Ben's hold, too, or is he just lording it up over Sayid?

Music/Bands: When Sayid and Elsa are in the café, we can hear "Wann Ist Es Liebe" by Jazzamor, from their CD *Travel*. When Sayid and Elsa are in bed together, the song playing is Bonobo's "If You Stayed Over," from *Days to Come*. Both CDs were released in fall 2006, which would suggest this flashforward takes place during or after that time.

4.4   Eggtown

Original air date: February 21, 2008
Written by: Elizabeth Sarnoff, Greggory Nations
Directed by: Stephen Williams
Guest cast: Beth Broderick (Diane Jansen), Shawn Doyle (Duncan Forrester), Susan Gibney (District Attorney Melissa Dunbrook), William Blanchette (Two-Year-Old Boy), Traber Burns (Judge), Fred Q. Collins (Bailiff), Tania Kahale (Kate's Nanny)

Flash: Kate

Kate tries to find out if the outside world knows who she really is, while Jack wonders why they haven't heard from Sayid on the helicopter. The flashforward reveals that Kate brought back a blond-headed secret from the island (and no, it wasn't Sawyer).

"Eggtown" is one of those episodes that is great when you watch it the first

The *Lost* crew prepares to film the exterior of a house in Kahala, Hawaii, which will stand in as Kate's upscale home in "Eggtown." (RYAN OZAWA)

time, but less great when you go back to watch it in the context of the entire season. In Kate's flashforward, we see how elaborate was the lie that the Oceanic 6 told the media. In "The Beginning of the End," Hurley told Ana Lucia's partner that he'd never met Ana Lucia. Now we see that the partner accepted Hurley's lie quickly because the 6 had already told the world she'd died. In fact, only eight people survived the crash, according to the story, but not all lived. Unfortunately, in order to go into detail about how some of the dialogue in this episode contradicts what we will later know to be true, I'd be giving away future plotlines, and I don't want to do that. Thus, to read my objections to this episode, you'll have to flip to pages 88 and 92–93 (this is advised only for people who have already watched the entire season and know its outcome).

We've seen island cons in almost every episode, but by the looks of the flashforward and Jack's bald-faced lies on the witness stand, the biggest con is yet to come. The writers do a brilliant job in this episode of making us think Kate got pregnant by Sawyer. From the secrecy of her son (leading us to believe she was pregnant when she was rescued but kept it a secret from the press) to Jack not wanting to see the baby, it makes perfect sense she's now raising a child Sawyer fathered. The twist that comes with the final word uttered in the episode, however, instantly debunks that theory, and makes jaws drop to the floor.

If there's one person who can keep a secret better than just about anyone else (especially when it involves her), it's Kate. She can look anyone in the eye and lie to them, whether it's making up names and backgrounds for herself to keep her real identity a secret, or tricking people on the island to get her way, Kate knows how to fend for herself. Jack was never any good at lying (everyone seems to see through him when he tries), but on the witness stand, he becomes a very good liar. Kate, on the other hand, can't follow through. Even though what he's saying will benefit her in the trial, it's too much for her to live with. Why? Did something so terrible happen — worse than incinerating her own father, regardless of how awful the man was — that she can't bear for Jack to lie about it? By lying about the three months she spent with those people on the island, does she dishonor their memories by pretending she never knew them? (Or is the scene intended to further our conviction that her son is Sawyer's and she doesn't want to pretend Sawyer didn't exist?)

This episode also provides us with some closure on the "Diane Jansen is a horrible mother" story line. Diane took her husband's side over her daughter's, despite the fact he was beating her and making sexual overtones to Kate. Then she screamed for help when Kate risked everything to see her (twice!) and now she's testifying as the star witness against her own daughter. Huge surprise there. On the island, Kate makes a deal with sniveling little Miles to take him to see Ben if he gives her some answers. But it's a testament to Diane's lack of maternal love that Kate refuses to make any sort of deal with her — Diane will let her off the hook if she just lets her see Aaron, and Kate hisses at her that she'd rather go to prison than let Diane anywhere near the boy. Diane actually finds a tiny place in her cold, black heart for her daughter and decides not to testify against her, after all. Her decision to backhandedly support her daughter for once isn't exactly redeeming. After all, she tells Kate that everything changed for her when she thought Kate was dead, and yet it's taken her *two years* to bother to come and see Kate post-rescue. But it ends the Diane story line, and allows Kate to put her mother issues to rest (which is important, now that she's become one).

The flashforward was about withholding information and deceiving people to get what you want. The story on the island was the same. Locke declares a dictatorship (while insisting it's not a dictatorship); Jack tells the people on the beach that the people on the freighter are indeed coming to save them, even though he knows that's not true; Sawyer and Kate pull off a rather brilliant con against Locke; Miles promises to lie about Ben's whereabouts if Ben will pay him off. At this point, the "live together, die alone" motto seems to have become "every man for himself," which is Sawyer's motto. (Interestingly, Sawyer is the only person who is honest in this episode — especially when he comes out and tells Kate how thrilled he is that she isn't pregnant — and he's vilified for it.) Through Kate's deception of Locke, she discovers that the outside world knows who she is, and that she'll always be Kate the Fugitive. Yet something clearly makes her decide to go back. Perhaps, after Locke banishes her from New Otherton, she realizes that no matter where she goes, she'll be exiled, and she'd rather deal with her ostracism in a place where she doesn't have to worry about killing her own food.

Highlight: Locke reaching a whole new level of torture technique. Holy Gestapo, Batman!

Timeline: The majority of this episode takes place on December 22, the day after Sayid's helicopter leaves, and then Kate stays overnight with Sawyer and we see part of December 23.

Did You Notice?:

- The episode opened on Locke's eye; in previous seasons this always signalled the episode and flashback would be about him, but not this time.
- Locke sleeps in Ben's hospital bed.
- When Locke gives Ben the book, *VALIS* by Philip K. Dick, Ben says he's already read it, to which Locke responds, "You might catch something you missed the second time around." This seems like a comment on the viewers who watch *Lost* episodes over and over again, catching new details every time.
- The scene where Ben and Locke face off mirrors the same scene in season 2 when "Benry" was locked up in the armory. And just as he did then, when he walked out and smashed the dishes all over the Swan station, Locke falls for it *again* and lets Ben know that he's won this round, and has gotten to him. Locke, Locke, Locke . . . when will you learn?
- Kate's trial is being presided over by Judge Arthur Galzethron, whose name is an anagram of "get thru jungle or hazard."

- This is the first conversation between Jin and Sun we've seen all season. Interesting that so many fans were up in arms for the first six episodes of last season because we didn't get to see enough of the other characters, and this season we're seeing even less of the others, yet no one is complaining. Looks like the writers finally found the right balance.
- Jin suggests they go to Albuquerque, which is where Sawyer says his daughter Clementine is located in "Every Man for Himself."
- Emilie de Ravin looks like she's wearing a wig in this episode and in the rest of the season.
- The backgammon is back, but it's so different now. In season 1, when Locke was playing it with Walt, he seemed like a generally good guy. Now he's . . . not.
- Everyone seems to be referring to Hurley as Hugo these days.
- Kate's listening to Patsy again.

As we see in "Eggtown," Kate (Evangeline Lilly) cleans up well. (STHANLEE MIRADOR/SHOOTING STAR)

- Kate has a very devoted nanny if she took over Aaron's care full-time for several weeks (or even months) while Kate was in custody.
- Now we know who Kate meant when she told Jack in the flashforward in "Through the Looking Glass," "He'll be wondering where I am."
- In "Raised by Another," the psychic Richard Malkin tells Claire that she must raise Aaron, and he cannot be raised by another. Does that mean Kate is not supposed to be raising him?
- Is Kate pretending that Aaron is her birth son or that she adopted him?

Interesting Facts: The box office flop *Xanadu*, starring Olivia Newton-John, is about the nine Greek muses entering the modern-day world through a mural, which is a portal for them. Newton-John's character, named Kira (who has adapted to the modern-day world through headbands and roller skates), inspires two down-on-their-luck men to open an old theater and turn it into a nightclub. When Zeus finds out Kira has fallen in love with one of the men, he forces her to return to him, but changes his mind, allowing her to take a mortal form and stay with the guy she's fallen in love with. "Xanadu" is used in Samuel Taylor Coleridge's famous poem, "Kubla Khan," and is the "pleasure-dome" that housed Kublai Khan, the ruler of Yuan China. In Orson Welles's 1941 film *Citizen Kane*, Xanadu is what Charles Foster Kane names his giant estate, where he eventually dies alone.

After this episode aired, fans were baffled by its title. Some suggested it's a reference to a door-to-door sales term during the Great Depression: an "eggtown" was a place where they'd pay you with eggs, which would go bad pretty well immediately. It became a term meaning "a bad deal." Other fans postulated that it referred to a children's book called *The Easter Egg Adventure* where a group of bunnies live peacefully in a place called Egg Town until a group of mean roosters shows up and steals all their eggs. But the producers weren't actually being that complex with the title. Carlton Cuse explained in an official podcast that the title simply referred to Locke making eggs for Ben at the beginning of the episode, and Kate's worry about being pregnant.

Nitpicks: I'm disappointed with the lack of mourning over Charlie. Claire finds out he's dead just before midnight on December 21. The morning of the 23rd, a little over 24 hours later, she's rocking on the porch, enjoying the breeze, joking with Kate, and making Sawyer coffee. Hurley's gone from inconsolable to being the butt of everyone's jokes again as he sits and watches *Xanadu*.

Oops: When Ben pushes Locke too far, Locke throws the food tray against the wall, and the "concrete" wall moves. Also, in a criminal trial, the prosecution would present its entire case first, including all witnesses, and then the defense would be given the chance for rebuttal by presenting *its* case. But Jack takes the stand before Diane, which wouldn't have happened. Finally, when Kate is talking to Sawyer on the bed the morning after her sleepover, his hair flips back and forth between tidy and disheveled.

4 8 15 16 23 42: When Kate's lawyer sees her in jail, he suggests she'll probably be given a **15**-year sentence, serving seven years. Diane says she's been hearing she's had six months to live for **4** years. In the settlement negotiation, the DA first offers Kate a **4**-year sentence. Miles asks Ben for $3.2 million, which is the number **23** in reverse.

Lost in Translation: When Kate enters the courtroom, there's a crazy bearded guy yelling in her face, and it's not clear what he says to her. One fan isolated the audio, and it still didn't make any sense . . . until he ran it in reverse. Then you could hear the man quite clearly yelling, "We hate you!"

Any Questions?:

- When Kate arrives at the boathouse to see Miles, he is hunched over in the chair. Could he have been communicating with the ghosts of the island? I'm convinced that Miles has been talking to them since he got there . . . if so, he's possibly talked to Dharma victims from the Purge, natives who have died over the years, other survivors who didn't make it, which could be why he's so angry. Could he have been talking to the dead on the flats when Jack and Co. first came upon him?
- What did Miles mean when he said he's right where he wants to be?
- Why has Jack maintained that Kate was the real hero in the crash? Was it out of love? Was it to deflect attention away from himself? He's clearly been doing that since the rescue (she mentions that she's heard him say it over and over). Was it simply to get her off the hook in the trial?
- Why does Miles ask for $3.2 million specifically?
- Miles tells Ben not to treat him like one of them, and says he knows who he is and what he can do. Who is Ben? What can he do? Miles talks to him with a lot of hostility. Does it have anything to do with Miles being a ghost whisperer? Are the dead telling him things that Ben has done?
- Charlotte and Dan seem to be playing a memory game with the cards, where she's showing him the cards and he tries to remember them a few minutes later, but he can't. What's wrong with him? Does he suffer from memory loss? Why?
- What happened to the helicopter? Did they not follow the same bearing Dan gave them?

Music/Bands: Hurley listens to "Xanadu," sung by Olivia Newton-John, from the movie soundtrack. Kate listens to "She's Got You," by Patsy Cline, available on any greatest hits compilation. It's an interesting song choice for her; like most Patsy Cline songs, it's a sad song about how she's lost her man to another woman. Yet in Kate's case, she has two men after her and is never at a loss; no matter what she does to one, he'll always be there with arms open when she comes bouncing back to him later. It would almost be more apt for Sawyer and Jack to be listening to Cline.

✍️ *VALIS* by Philip K. Dick (1981)

It's weird, it's mind-bending, and it's a little baffling at times, but there might have been a good reason why Locke chose Philip K. Dick's autobiographical novel *VALIS* as the book to give to Ben in "Eggtown."

VALIS is the story of Horselover Fat, who is actually Philip K. Dick. ("Horse lover" is the English translation of the Greek word *philippos*, which means lover of horses, and "Fat" is the English translation of the German word *dick*.) Dick explains early on that he's going to refer to himself as Horselover Fat, even though for most of the book Dick also features as a separate character who hangs out with Fat. Fat is a man who has been having strange visions and hearing voices. He begins seeing faint outlines of another time overlaid upon his own time, as if Ancient Rome were trying to break through to modern-day California. He is hit with a beam of pink light, a shade of pink he's seen nowhere else, and believes he's been contacted by God, who is trying to impart some important information to him. The moment he's hit, he immediately knows that something is wrong with his five-year-old son, who seems perfectly healthy. He takes him to a doctor to say his son has a birth defect, and the doctor sees nothing. Fat explains that his son has a hernia, and after much pleading, convinces the doctor to do some tests. Fat's prognosis is completely correct, and had the condition been left untreated, it would have killed his son instantly once it had manifested itself within his body.

Fat becomes a believer, and the book contains long passages where he argues with his friends — Philip K. Dick, Kevin (based on sci-fi writer K.W. Jeter), and David (based on sci-fi writer Tim Powers) — about the existence and meaning of God, whom Fat refers to as Zebra. Kevin is the most vehement nonbeliever and David is a devout Catholic, but Fat has proof that he's been contacted by God. He knew of his son's serious condition when there was no way he could have known; he's seen modern-day California and Ancient Rome superimposed on one another; and one day he begins speaking in a language no one can decipher, and when they transcribe it, they identify it as *koine* Greek, an ancient language that hasn't been spoken since 60 A.D. Fat believes that he is the reincarnation of Thomas, a man who lived in 60 A.D. and who begins to take over Fat's consciousness for periods of time. Thomas learned to transfer his essence to another person so he can keep regenerating through time, and has been reincarnating himself through various forms for 2000 years. Fat also has visions of a being with a third eye that gives him information, and he wonders if that person is his own descendent, contacting him from the distant future.

When Kevin excitedly tells everyone he's just seen an experimental film called *Valis* and urges them to come see it with him, they indulge him. The movie contains dozens of symbols that Fat had described to them from his dreams and visions, and there is a pink beam of light and a character with a third eye. The music contains subliminal messages that Fat recognizes. Afterwards, Kevin becomes a believer. "VALIS" stands for Vast Active Living Intelligence System, and in the film, VALIS is the entity that sends out the intelligence. They all travel to meet the filmmaker and his wife, who explain that they're all onto something, that the Savior does exist and walks among them, and its current incarnation is their two-year-old daughter, Sophia. When the foursome meets Sophia, she speaks words of wisdom to them, tells Dick he no longer needs Horselover Fat (upon which Dick looks to where Fat had been sitting and Fat is gone), and that they must get away from the filmmaker and his wife immediately, to speak out and gather wisdom, and to await their commission. By the time they return home, they begin to wonder if it is they or the filmmakers who are insane. The others admit to Dick that they've been wondering when his split personality would heal, and they're happy that he seems to have realized Horselover Fat was a bad part of his personality he had to let go. They get word that Sophia has been killed, and Horselover Fat returns to Dick before embarking on an international quest to find out more about the source of his visions.

In real life, Philip K. Dick had encountered some mental problems. Much of the book is based on what he believed to be true, including being hit by the beam of light, and learning of his own son's hernia in time to save his life. In an interview Dick gave in 1980, he explained the strange occurrences that had happened to him and described *VALIS*, a book he was then still working on. "It's the theological study of the inbreaking of futuristic technology, established by supernatural intelligence, into the life of an ordinary, present-day man," he said. "It basically deals with this invasion from the future into the present and man's attempts to cope with it."

Throughout *VALIS*, Horselover Fat jots down his thoughts as part of his "Exegesis," which he reads out to friends. Dick kept a similar journal, to which he'd contributed over one million words by the time he'd died. One recurring phrase, "The Empire never ended," was a phrase that Dick not only put in several of his notes (as does Horselover Fat), but inserted into a few others of his

"Well . . . it's better than *The Brothers Karamazov*." Ben ponders whether or not he'll reread *VALIS*. (MARIO PEREZ/© ABC/COURTESY: EVERETT COLLECTION)

books. *VALIS* is the first of a trilogy, and the third book remained unfinished when he died suddenly of a heart attack in 1982, four months before *Blade Runner*, a film adaptation of his brilliant book *Do Androids Dream of Electric Sheep?*, would have turned him into an international literary sensation. To this day Dick is considered a seminal science fiction writer, and *VALIS* is possibly his greatest literary achievement.

The main philosophy of the book is Gnosticism. Derived from the Greek word *gnosis*, meaning knowledge, Gnosticism maintains that God is not necessarily the creator of the world, but that human beings are in the material world and the only way to escape it is through knowledge. Knowledge is derived from a direct contact with God (Horselover Fat uses the example of Adam and Eve and the fruit of knowledge). Many of the theological discussions in the book are descriptions of Gnosticism and incorporate many of the basic tenets. "I believe you have a direct relation with the divine or you have no relation with the divine," explained Dick in an interview. "It has nothing to do with faith or dogmatic creeds. The initiative comes from the divine side. There is nothing you can do. All you can do is live an honest life, be brutally honest with yourself, and hope to become an object of interest with the divine beings . . . I guess you could call me a neo-Platonist with Gnostic overtones."

The name of the man from 60 A.D. who contacts Fat — Thomas — is mentioned in the *Nag Hammadi*, a collection of books Fat talks about in *VALIS*. In 1945, a peasant discovered 12 leather-bound books that contained many of the earliest writing on Gnosticism, much of which was written by a man named Thomas. Sophia, the name of the two-year-old "Savior" in *VALIS*, is also the Greek word for wisdom, and the name Sophia is very important to Gnosticism. In the

Nag Hammadi Library, Sophia is described as the lowest emanation of God, the Holy Spirit of the Trinity. She is the creator of the material universe and its god.

Ben Linus and John Locke are both very spiritual people, but they don't subscribe to a particular dogma or read the Bible or follow religion in the traditional sense. If Jacob is the divine, they have both been contacted by him, the same way Fat/Dick was contacted by VALIS. Gnosticism is dualistic in nature, believing that there are two opposite elements that are constantly in conflict. Fat talks about light versus darkness or yin versus yang and that one side will eventually prevail over another. Sophia not only created the world, but could destroy it. Similarly, on *Lost*, light and dark have been metaphors from the first season, and while Ben talks about Jacob's good deeds, he also shows a certain fear of Jacob, as if he could also destroy all of them. As the fourth season of *Lost* progresses, we will see more and more similarities between Ben and Locke, almost as if theirs is a similar relationship to that between Horselover Fat and Philip K. Dick.

The most important similarity between this book and the themes of *Lost* is that of time. Again, throughout this season, we will begin to see hints that time doesn't exist, or that characters are existing in more than one time plane at once. In a scene in *VALIS*, Horselover tells his psychiatrist, "Time does not exist. . . . The universe is contracting into a unitary entity which is completing itself. Decay and disorder are seen by us in reverse, as increasing." Dick comes to the startling realization at one point that the reason Fat is seeing one time superimposed on another is because Fat is living in both times at once, and that both times are existing at once. "Horselover Fat is living in two different times and two different places; i.e. in two space-time continua," he writes. On *Lost* we see flashbacks, flashforwards, and present-day experiences all happening simultaneously. Some of the things on the island seem futuristic, while others are archaic (like the IBM computers) and still others are ancient (like the *Black Rock* or the four-toed statue).

Fat's visions happen after he takes a particular kind of drug. Similarly, in the first two seasons of *Lost*, we saw Desmond had been taking a "vaccine," which was also administered to Claire. Will these two characters have a connection to Jacob or the divine as well? We've already seen in "Flashes Before Your Eyes" that Desmond returned to the past, whether in reality or in his mind, and can also see into the future. In much the same way, Fat has time traveled in both directions: "Horselover Fat is able to travel through time, travel back thousands of years," says "Dick" in the novel. "The three-eyed people probably live in the far future;

they are our descendents, highly-evolved. And it is probably their technology which permitted Fat to do his time-travelling. In point of fact, Fat's master personality may not lie in the past but ahead of us — but it expressed itself outside of him in the form of Zebra." Perhaps just as the three-eyed people who appear to Fat are from the future, so too is the four-toed statue that is on the island.

Throughout the book, Horselover is constantly trying to help people who don't want to be helped. He tries to avert his friend Gloria's suicide, but she eventually finds another way to kill herself. He asks his friend Sherri to move in with him during her cancer's remission, as she awaits its return, but he can't keep her from dying either. Fat is a lot like Jack in these scenes, always trying to fix the situation, but usually either making it worse or simply sinking deeper within himself as a result.

The film *Valis* that the gang goes to see is reminiscent of an episode of *Lost*. The main plot is complex, but it's the Easter eggs and hidden messages in the background that get the gang riled up. Kevin sees it multiple times, and keeps urging them to see it again. "'[W]e'll all have to go see the picture again,' Kevin said. 'I'm going to; ninety percent of the details are designed to go by you the first time — actually only go by your conscious mind; they register in your unconscious. I'd like to study the film frame by frame.'" The film has a huge impact on the group, and it's not only because of what is in the film, but also because of how it is presented to them. The strange electronic music is aggressive and annoying, yet it too contains the seeds of what they've been looking for. There are moments that aren't part of the plot, but simply flash at them and enter their subconscious. It sounds like a description of Room 23, where Ben was bombarding Karl's conscious and subconscious with loud music and rapid-fire images. Ben might have gotten the idea from this book (and a VHS copy of *A Clockwork Orange*).

When the group meets with the filmmaker and his wife, they also meet the man who created the music for *Valis*, named Mini. He explains that VALIS programs people from birth, sending encoded messages to babies that will eventually move into their consciousness, whereupon they can act on the instructions. He says that the world is a living maze and we spend our lives trying to get out of it. When Kevin asks what would happen if we ever escaped the maze, Mini responds, "We're freed from space and time. . . . Space and time are the binding, controlling conditions of the maze — its power." In other words, anyone who makes their way out of the maze will find salvation. When Desmond tries to escape the maze of the island, he turns around and comes right back, as if he is unable to conquer space and time.

When the gang meets Sophia, her mother Linda explains that she was an immaculate conception, born of Linda and VALIS. Interestingly, Locke's mother told him that he'd been born of an immaculate conception. Just as Locke finds confirmation of his mother's mental instability, the Rhipidon Society begins to question Linda's sanity. After the group search for a long time for the "Savior," they are surprised to discover it is a two-year-old girl. There has been a lot of speculation among *Lost* fans that Aaron could play a much larger role by the end of the series and could be a savior of sorts. Sophia explains to the group that they were all chosen, and that she'd called for them four years earlier, despite the fact she wasn't yet conceived, just as most viewers would agree that the people on Flight Oceanic 815 were chosen to be on that flight, and their fates had been sealed several years earlier.

At the end of the book we read some of Fat's "Exegesis," which are passages from Dick's own journals (interestingly, we see Ben keeping copious journal notes at the end of season 3). He writes, "The universe is information and we are stationary in it, not three-dimensional and not in space or time. The information fed to us we hypostatize into the phenomenal world." In other words, we create the material world around us based on the information that is given to us, but that world doesn't exist. It could just be one of the best explanations for what the heck is happening on that island.

 ## *The Invention of Morel* by Adolfo Bioy Casares (1940)

In "Eggtown," when Hurley asks Sawyer if he wants to watch *Xanadu*, Sawyer is so engrossed in Casares' masterpiece, *The Invention of Morel*, he can barely look up from it to tell Hurley to turn the television down. There's a good reason — the events of the book share many similarities with *Lost*.

The story is told through diary entries by an unnamed narrator who is a fugitive from Venezuela. We never discover what he did, but he fled to a deserted island on which he discovered a museum, a swimming pool, a chapel, and a mill, and he has been living peacefully there ever since. He assumes no one will ever come to the island, because it is apparently disease-ridden. He explains that a rug merchant had told him about the island, saying that the disease "attacks the outside of the body and then works inward. The nails drop off the fingers and toes; the hair falls out. The skin and the corneas of the eyes die, and the body lives on for one more week, or two at the most. The crew of a ship that had stopped there were skinless, hairless, without nails on their fingers or toes — all dead, of course — when they were found by the Japanese cruiser *Namura*. The horrified Japanese sank their ship."

As the fugitive is sitting by the pool one morning, a group of socialites suddenly appears. He leaps up and runs away, down to the marshy lowlands of the island. Here he lives in naked misery, constantly keeping track of the tides so he can move to the side of a hill and not drown. The socialites meanwhile play loud music (the same music over and over) and move in and out of the museum. At one point they appear to ready themselves for a swim, and the fugitive thinks to himself they wouldn't dare, since the water is fetid, but to his shock, they all jump in. He lives in fear of discovery, assuming the people are there to find him and bring him back to face his crimes. Soon, however, he realizes they don't seem to know he's even there. He notices one woman who often comes and sits on the edge of the cliff, looking out over the water, and after several days of watching her, he falls in love with her. A bearded tennis player, named Morel, refers to her as Faustine, and they speak French to one another. The narrator becomes bold, approaching Faustine to tell her that he loves her, but she doesn't respond at all, and he runs away, terrified that he'd done a stupid thing and now they'd come after him for sure. But they don't.

One day, they all disappear. He's heartbroken, thinking Faustine has left him. He walks up to the museum and looks around, and sees everything exactly as he'd left it before they'd arrived. He can't understand where they could possibly have gone, or why they haven't left any trace of their presence behind, but suddenly they all appear in the museum again, and again he runs and hides. Slowly, the narrator begins to venture closer to them, paying attention to their conversations, and he begins to notice strange anomalies. The fish in the aquarium are exact replicas of the dead fish he'd seen upon his own arrival, but now they're swimming around and are very much alive. There are two suns in the sky during the day, and two moons at night. He notices certain conversations repeating themselves exactly every week, to the point where he can anticipate what they're going to say. Fiercely in love with Faustine, the fugitive becomes jealous of Morel, and keeps trying to get her to notice him, to no avail.

One night he enters the museum while everyone is bustling around talking about Morel making a big speech. Morel announces that he's an inventor, and has created an invention that will be astounding to anyone who hears of it. He says that, to date, technological advances have been in the realms of sight — "television, motion pictures, photography" — or hearing — "radio, the phonograph, the telephone." But he has invented something even more marvelous. He has been recording the people as they've been spending their week at the museum, and the recording will live on as if they are real people, constantly showing them as a loop. One man, Stoever, mentions that he's heard of the previous tests Morel had done with his invention, and that all the people he recorded died soon after of terrible side effects. Morel leaves the room in a rage. The fugitive steals Morel's notes and runs away with them. In Morel's notes he sees that they are all being run by a machine that uses the energy of the tides. In fact, the reef system surrounding the island has kept intruders away. The strange light on the island has allowed the images to remain preserved and unharmed.

The fugitive realizes that the tourists are not present on the island, and instead had all been figments of Morel's invention, moving around the island in a constant loop. However, far from being empty holographic images, Morel's machine has turned them into something else. As he says in his notes, "If we grant consciousness, and all that distinguishes us from objects, to the persons who surround us, we shall have no valid reason to deny it to the persons created by my machinery. When all the senses are synchronized, the soul emerges." He adds that if a person "exists for the senses of sight, hearing, taste, smell, and touch," then that person is actually there.

Now the narrator can put everything together. There are two suns and two moons because he's seeing the real sun and the one that had been recorded by Morel that is projected alongside it. Unusually hot days were the result of the narrator experiencing the regular spring temperature of the island overlapping with the hotter summer temperature of the recording. The fish in the aquarium were dead, but came back to life simply because they were projections of Morel's machine. The fugitive makes his way into the room that houses Morel's machines by breaking a hole in the wall of the basement of the museum, but when he turns to leave, the hole has been fixed because the machines are projecting the intact wall that had been there during the recording. He panics and tries for days to get out, despite the fact he is rendered almost speechless by the heavenly blue atmosphere that exists in the room with the machines. One day, he stares at the machines long enough to figure out how to disconnect them. Once he manages that, he is able to leave. Walking around the island he sees certain vegetation that had previously seemed to be alive and is now dead, yet other flora that had appeared dead in the projection is now blooming. He realizes Morel's machine had caused a certain immortality for everything around him, and that's when he decides what he needs to do.

Going back into the museum, Morel turns on the machines again, and goes outside and holds his hand in front of the projector. That same hand is now in that spot, disembodied and moving slightly. He watches the recordings of everyone going through their routines, and decides to insert himself into the scenes so he can make it look like he and Faustine were in love. When she talks, he answers, becoming an actor in the drama. His next step is to try to figure out how to remove Morel from the scenes, but he doesn't manage to do that. After a few days, his hand begins burning and the skin peels off, and soon after recording his scenes with Faustine his hair falls out and his skin begins to peel. He knows he is going to die just like the others had after Morel had recorded them — and realizes they must have been the people the Japanese seamen had discovered on the island. So, the fugitive leaves behind his diary of what happened to him. He hopes that someone will discover that recording some day and learn the inner workings of Morel's invention, developing it further so they could manipulate the recordings and bring back the consciousnesses of those who have died. In his dying hours, he makes one final plea: "To the person who reads this diary and then invents a machine that can assemble disjoined presences, I make this request: Find Faustine and me, let me enter the heaven of her consciousness. It will be an act of piety."

Bioy (as he was called) has written a book that is a remarkably tight 103 pages, and can be read quickly (though you'll want to read it through a second time as soon as you finish). In the prologue to the original edition, Bioy's friend and mentor Jorge Luis Borges wrote, "To classify [the book] as perfect is neither an imprecision nor a hyperbole." The science-fictional element was surprising for the time, and while Bioy is far from a household name, this one book is upheld as his masterwork, and was the inspiration for the 1961 experimental film *Last Year at Marienbad*. Bioy said he based the character of Faustine on American actor Louise Brooks, the 1920s pinup girl known for her sleek, black bob, with whom he was obsessed at the time.

If the *Lost* writers have been influenced by this book, then many things click into place. Just like the survivors of Flight 815, the narrator is on an island (though he is the one who put himself there), and the island is not as deserted as he originally thought. He worries about a disease on the island, just as Desmond and Inman had been giving themselves a vaccine to protect against an illness on the island, the same one that Rousseau says killed her people. Early in the book, the narrator begins to wonder why the people on the island don't respond to him or don't see him, even when, at one point, he accidentally walks right in front of them. He begins to come up with theories, just like viewers of *Lost* do after every episode. The narrator refers to himself as a dead man in his diaries (which, on *Lost*, reinforces that early notion among fans that the survivors were in fact dead and dwelling in purgatory). At one point, he attempts to convey to Faustine the message, "You have awakened me from a living death on this island," and "You have kept a dead man on this island from sleeping." He begins to wonder if he is somehow invisible to her. As I read this book, thinking of it in the context of *Lost*, I began wondering if he was invisible to the other people just as the whispering people in the jungle are invisible to the survivors.

There are smaller, more subtle links to *Lost* as well. When the people first arrive, the narrator believes they are from Australia. The number 15 recurs throughout the book. There are 15 tourists who come to the island. He jumps out of a window 15 feet above ground. There are 15 rooms in the museum. He refers to time in increments of 15 minutes.

The key section in the book for *Lost* fans, though, is when the narrator begins to pull out all possible theories to explain the anomaly of the visitors on the island. He wonders if he could have the sickness they spoke of and it's creating hallucinations; perhaps the bad diet and putrid air have rendered him invisible (then he remembers he's not invisible to the mosquitoes); the people are aliens and their eyes can't actually see; he is in an insane asylum and is merely dreaming everything that is happening, including his own presence on the island; he and the other people are dead, and "this island may be the purgatory or the heaven of those dead people"; he is in hell. When the narrator begins to theorize, it calms him, because if he only had an explanation for these baffling occurrences, it would help put his mind at ease. "Thinking about these ideas left me in a state of euphoria," he writes. "I had proof that my relationship with the intruders was a relationship between beings on different planes." From here we get one of the only flashbacks in the book, where he talks about his childhood and how it could possibly relate to him now being in this place.

Perhaps Jacob is Morel, who has captured all of the Others on the island and has put them into this little play, and the survivors are now the spectators, as confused as Bioy's narrator is when watching the tourists. It would explain why certain people, like Richard Alpert, never age. However, unlike the people in Morel's invention, the survivors can actually interact with the Others. Perhaps Jacob has achieved what Morel couldn't — has he created images with consciousness?

The Invention of Morel is a fascinating book filled with possible explanations for the mysteries in *Lost*, and I highly recommend checking it out.

4.5   The Constant

Original air date: February 28, 2008
Written by: Carlton Cuse, Damon Lindelof
Directed by: Jack Bender
Guest cast: Sonya Walger (Penelope Widmore), Chris Barnes (Suited Guard), Edward Conery (Auctioneer), Chris Gibbon (Soldier), Darren Keefe (Billy), Graham McTavish (Sergeant)

Flash: Desmond

As Frank, Sayid, and Desmond are flying to the freighter, Desmond experiences strange side effects where his consciousness begins jumping through time.

Episodes like "The Constant" are the reason I watch *Lost*. When stories like this happen — ones that alternately make my brain and heart ache — I know I'm watching a television series unlike any other. This was the sort of episode that would separate the casual viewer, who might have gone, "Huh?! Okay, next episode" from the diehard one, who stayed up all that night discussing it with other online fans, and continued hammering out the minutiae of the episode for a week.

When it comes to the Desmond episodes these days, audiences can be sure of two things: the format of the episode will be unique and nontraditional (i.e., not a straightforward flashback or flashforward), and it will always come down to love. Thanks to the essential nature of the Desmond-centric episodes, we've seen his story completely out of order. What we know is that he was engaged to a woman named Ruth whom he left at the altar ("Catch-22"). He became a monk, thinking he'd been given a sign from God, until Brother Campbell understood that Desmond's destiny was outside the monastery. Desmond met Penelope Widmore, they fell in love, and eventually moved in together ("Flashes Before Your Eyes"). He wanted to get engaged to her, but her father told him he was no good for his daughter, and Desmond believed him. He dumped her and enrolled himself in the Royal Scottish Army, all the while still pining for her (and her him). Eventually, he was dishonorably discharged ("Live Together, Die Alone") and discovered upon his release that all the letters he'd written to Penelope had been stolen by Widmore before she could read them, and that she'd moved on. Anxious to regain his honor, Desmond began training for a race around the world. He began running in stadiums (where he met Jack), and he met a woman named Libby in a coffee shop, whose husband had recently died, and she gave him her sailboat. He entered the race, went adrift on the island, was "rescued" by a man named Kelvin Inman,

Even on the red carpet, Desmond (Henry Ian Cusick) will be waiting for Penny. (CAMILLA MORANDI/REX FEATURES)

and spent the next three years stuck in the hatch pushing a button. When he realized the electromagnetic energy would consume the island and everyone on it, he turned the key to diffuse the energy, knowing that to do so was suicide, and his "last words" were "I love you, Penny." But he survived. Meanwhile, in the outside world, Penny discovered her father had been keeping Desmond from her, and she began searching the world for him, certain that he was still alive, even though he'd never returned from the race. She seems to have found out something about the island from her father (it's still unclear what she knows or how she found out) and she hired two men to watch for any sign of the island. When they saw one during the hatch explosion, Penny tried sending out messages to the freighter docked near the island. She finally made contact with Charlie in the Looking Glass station ("Through the Looking Glass") and that's when she realized Desmond was still alive.

In "Flashes Before Your Eyes," we saw that when Desmond turned the key he was thrown from the hatch with the force of the explosion. In that episode, his present-day consciousness travels back to 1996, and when he's in the past, he has all the memories of the present. In "The Constant," Desmond's 1996 consciousness travels forward to 2004, meaning he has none of his future memories, and his past self takes over his present one. The way the time travel was handled in this episode left some fans scratching their heads. But 1996-Daniel's explanation of what had happened to Desmond — that his consciousness had become "unstuck in time" — not only provided the clarification of what was happening in "The Constant," but also what had happened in "Flashes Before Your Eyes." An argument among fans has always been whether or not Desmond physically time traveled in "Flashes Before Your Eyes," or whether he was just imagining it like a dream right before dying. Turns out, it was a bit of both. His consciousness time traveled, but not his physical self. The things his present-day self did in 1996 were actually happening in 1996, but he never physically left the island.

The term "unstuck in time" comes from Kurt Vonnegut's *Slaughterhouse-Five* (see page 69 for a more thorough analysis of the book). In that book, a character named Billy becomes unstuck in time, but as he explains it, while he will zip back and forth in time, he cannot actually change any events. Damon and Carlton have insisted that there is only one timeline in *Lost*, and that assertion is strengthened in this episode. In *Slaughterhouse-Five*, the past, present, and future are always happening at the same time, and will always happen the same way. Events cannot be changed (in "The Constant," Daniel says bluntly, "You can't change the future"). Mrs. Hawking told Desmond in "Flashes Before Your Eyes" that you cannot change things, because if you try, the universe will course-correct to put things right. Desmond can keep trying to save Charlie from certain death, but eventually he'll lose energy or become distracted and Charlie will die. Charlie was a hero who sacrificed himself, but at the same time he was always going to die, and his fate was outside of his control. Similarly, Desmond will never get engaged to Penny in 1996, he will always leave her and go into the army, and he will always get on that boat. In 2004, he will always travel back in time to his 1996 self to give Daniel the very coordinates he needs to help Desmond and himself. For the next eight years, Daniel will always know those coordinates despite the fact that technically, Desmond hadn't traveled back to give them to him, simply because those two time periods are

Wormholes and Time Lags and Course Bearings, Oh My!

So what is causing all these time delays on and off the island? In "The Economist," we saw Daniel conduct an experiment with a payload, where he asked Regina to send out a payload from the freighter to the island. She knew the rate at which it was traveling and began counting down the seconds until it would arrive. When it should have arrived according to her calculations, it wasn't there. Daniel sat and waited, and eventually the payload crashed near the beacon. He opened up its clock and saw a discrepancy of 31 minutes, with the payload having a time reading 3:16:23, and the beacon having a time of 2:45:03. Why did the rocket show a time of 31 minutes more than the beacon?

One of the most popular theories at this point is that the island is surrounded by an invisible bubble. Imagine a tiny hole in the bubble, and if you pass through it to the other side and don't touch any part of the bubble, you'll be safe. But if you miss that hole, and actually penetrate the bubble (which is thick), you'll be stuck in the wormhole that surrounds the island. It'll feel like you were only in there for a few minutes, but your perception of what is happening outside of that bubble is skewed. Outside, hours are passing, so when you finally emerge on the other side, it's the next day. The outside world is therefore not moving at a different speed than the island. Both are happening at the same time (hence Desmond's computer printout in "Live Together, Die Alone," that showed it was September 22, 2004 on the island, which was the same date as the crash), but it's what happens inside the bubble that causes all the problems.

In this case, perhaps the opposite is true when one comes toward the island. That's why the clock in the rocket showed a time that made it look like it had been in the air much longer than it should have; in the world outside the bubble, time moved by more quickly, and the world inside the wormhole moved more slowly, allowing more time to accumulate on the clock.

Therefore, in this theory, the bubble that surrounds the island is affecting time. So if the bubble is, in fact, a wormhole that can change time, what happened when Desmond took off in the boat and came right back? Or when Michael and Walt disappeared at the end of season 2? Ben gave them a bearing of 325; is that another hole in the bubble that Daniel didn't know about? What about the raft at the end of season 1? Walt, Michael, Jin, and Sawyer seemed to be out on the raft for a long time, but they never hit the wall of the bubble. Were they on the same course as Desmond? Could the bubble have a different effect on someone traveling by boat? George Minkowski said that he and a friend went out in the boat and were affected by the bubble, but again, maybe it has a different effect on someone outside the bubble trying to come in, toward the island.

In any case, the situation cannot be too complicated. While *Lost* is an intelligent show written for and by intelligent people, they can't expect all of us to have PhDs in physics. This theory seems to be a valid one, however; if I can understand it, most people can.

existing simultaneously, just like all time periods are. Just as Daniel is sitting in Queen's College Physics Department in 1996, he is simultaneously sitting on an island in 2004, eight years older. If we take *Slaughterhouse-Five* to be a framework for *Lost*, then time on *Lost* isn't linear but made of fractured timelines all happening at the same time. (For those who wonder why 2004-Daniel can't remember Desmond visiting him in 1996, it's because the years of radiation have affected his memory so badly that he barely recalls anything, and there were a few references to his memory loss in the episode to make that clear.)

Does your brain hurt yet?

When Desmond first appeared on *Lost*, he seemed to be a peripheral character. After all, his story existed separately from the other Losties, and although he'd had a brief encounter with Jack a few years earlier, it certainly didn't seem to be a meeting for the ages. Yet we saw Libby give him a boat, which hinted that maybe Libby was a recruiter to get people onto the island (remember that she also showed an interest in Eko getting on the plane at the airport, and she was in Hurley's mental institution, almost as if she were watching him). With this detail, Desmond suddenly became more important. When Naomi dropped from the sky holding a photo of Desmond and Penelope, the other survivors seemed to recognize they'd been underestimating good ol' Des.

In the end, it all comes back to Desmond's constant, which is Penny. At no point in Desmond's post-monastery life has Penny not been an integral part of it, even if she's only in his dreams. Unlike so many of the other people who have been brought to this island, Desmond has hope, and that hope rests with Penny. The love story between these two is one for the ages, and I defy anyone to watch that final scene where they finally make contact via telephone with a dry eye. Henry Ian Cusick and Sonya Walger perform that moment beautifully — he quiet, she amazed, and both eventually finishing each other's thoughts and sentences. It was an amazing moment, a flash of pure romance, but one that never triggered our gag reflexes. Penny will always be Desmond's constant, someone who will be a part of his life no matter what timeline he is in, and as long as he has her, he can continue to hold onto something. Desmond is not shattered like the rest of these survivors, and so far, he's the closest to salvation.

Highlight: Daniel's nervous chuckle when he puts on a radiation vest and Desmond says, "So what do you put on your head?" That suddenly explains a lot.
Timeline: Desmond's consciousness travels back to 1996; but in the present day, as referenced in the episode, we're on December 24, 2004.

Did You Notice?:

- Desmond's friend in the army is named Billy, which is presumably a wink at the protagonist of *Slaughterhouse-Five*.
- There's something seriously creepy about that doctor on the freighter.
- We already knew the *Black Rock* was a slave ship, and that the Hansos had something to do with it. In *The Lost Experience* (see *Finding Lost — Season 3*, page 22), it's established that Magnus Hanso owned the ship, and in the season 2 blast door map, we could see a spot pinpointed where Magnus Hanso is buried on the island. Now we know it had left Portsmouth, England, for Siam, and was lost at sea.
- As Widmore leaves the room with Desmond, you can hear the auctioneer say the next lot is a collection of Charles Dickens books, which is interesting since Desmond has read every book except one, which he's saving for when he's about to die. Also, Portsmouth, England (where the *Black Rock* departed from), is Dickens' birthplace.
- At the end of the episode, after his consciousness moves back to 2004 and he's talking to Penny on the phone, we see Desmond in 1996 walking away from her apartment, rather than going comatose, which would suggest the zipping back and forth has come to an end because he's found his constant. The smile on his face is more likely caused by the fact he's just seen Penny and has stopped feeling confused, rather than that he retains any memory of the future.
- Desmond tells Penny he's been on an island, and refers to Sayid by name at the end, which is our indicator that he's got all his memories back.
- In "The Beginning of the End," Jack had said to Kate that he feels like 100 years have gone by since the crash. Maybe time is passing differently on the island.

Interesting Facts: On Daniel's chalkboard, you can see two written notations. The first is "Relative Quantum Mechanics. Temporal Sloshing. Temporal Double Well." The second is "Kerr might work! Can it evade Hawking's chronology protection conjecture?" The second is a reference to Roy Kerr's discovery in 1963 of a possible solution to Einstein's black hole theory, which is that if a black hole is spinning fast enough to create a naked singularity, one could technically pass through the black hole to the other side, which would be in another time, and hence, one could time travel. Hawking's "chronology protection conjecture" was Hawking's declaration that the laws of physics prevented time travel.

The auctioneer states that the first mate of the *Black Rock* kept a journal, which was found among some pirate's loot seven years after the ship went missing, on Île Sainte-Marie off the coast of Madagascar. The writers have done their homework . . . Île Sainte-Marie was a popular place for pirates to stop over in the 17th and 18th centuries because it was close to the trade routes the other ships were following. Today, pirate lore still dominates the island.

This is the episode where we finally see George Minkowski. The character was named after Hermann Minkowski, who is most famous for his concept of Minkowski spacetime. In his concept, he takes the three spatial dimensions — length, width, and height — and adds to them the dimension of time, creating a mathematical formula for spacetime in Einstein's theory of relativity.

Penny lives on Cheyne Walk, a posh street in the Chelsea area of London. Several artistic types have lived there over the years, from George Eliot and James Whistler to Keith Richards and Mick Jagger.

Find815: "423 Cheyne Walk," "020 7946 0893," "campmillar," "Queen's College," and "Southfields" were all clues in the game (Camp Millar is where Desmond is stationed; Southfield's is the name of the auction house where Widmore is bidding on the journal).

Nitpicks: There's an inconsistency with what happens to Desmond when he's time traveling. In every instance, his consciousness goes back to 1996 for only a few minutes — when he's in the army yard, when he's on the phone to Penny — but when he jumps back in time and he's slumped in the telephone booth, he has instructions from Dan to leave Glasgow and get to Oxford, a trip that would take, at minimum, six or seven hours.

Meanwhile, later Daniel says that Desmond's consciousness is traveling exponentially, that he was out for 75 minutes in the chair but only lasted five minutes in 2004, as if it's increasing in length, but there's no constancy with any of the times that Desmond has been time traveling, so Daniel's formulae wouldn't have much of an impact on what Desmond is experiencing.

Also, in the earlier alternate reality games, the *Black Rock* was said to have set sail in 1881, but in this episode, the writers changed it to 1845. One would definitely take the episodes to be canon over the reality games, but the *Black Rock* was filled with sticks of dynamite . . . which wouldn't have been invented until 1866. Were the sticks placed there after it had crashed?

Oops: Frank is told to stay on the bearing of 305. But the beach is on the south side of the island, and therefore the freighter would be further south. If he were bearing 305, he would be flying north, over the island. He should instead be flying 125, and only staying on the bearing of 305 to come *back* to the island.

If it's true that the past, present, and future are all happening simultaneously, and there's no way you can change the future by what you do in the present, then Eloise the mouse shouldn't have died when she did. She is able to run the maze because Dan said he was going to teach her to run it an hour later. Desmond passes out, Daniel puts him in the chair, and 75 minutes go by. When Desmond awakes, Eloise is already dead, and presumably has been for a while. The chalkboard is covered in numbers, so Dan had been preoccupied with writing, not teaching Eloise how to run the maze. If Dan didn't teach her how to run the maze in the future, there's no way she could have run it in the past.

4 8 15 16 23 42: Desmond travels **8** years back in time. The sergeant tells the soldiers to be in the yard in **4** minutes. Dan's machine has to be set at **2.342**. The *Black Rock* painting is in auction lot **2342**; the bidding opens at £**15**0,000. Penny's new address is **423** Cheyne Walk. The numbers in Penny's phone number add up to 46, which is **23** x 2. Penny picks up on the **15**th ring.

It's Just a Flesh Wound: Sayid slams Doctor Ray against the wall. George probably incurs a headache when he passes out and his head bangs heavily on the table . . . not that he stuck around long enough to notice. Both George and Desmond get nosebleeds. George dies of an apparent aneurysm.

Any Questions?:

- Throughout season 3, Desmond could see flashes of the future, and that was how he knew Charlie had to die. Why doesn't he see the future anymore? Were his flashes given to him by the island only to make him help Charlie find his destiny, and now that ability has been taken away?

- When the helicopter was coming to the island in the storm and Daniel was ejected, was he experiencing any consciousness time traveling at the time, or was Frank better able to keep the chopper on course?

- Frank's "cheat sheet" says he has to go North bearing 305. Michael was told by Ben that he had to bear 325. If going outside of 305 means you'll cross the barrier and possibly begin to time travel, why wouldn't Ben have given Michael the same coordinates? Is there another wormhole at 325 that's a safe one?

- Frank tells Keamy that Desmond and Sayid are both survivors of Flight 815, but he knows Desmond isn't (in "Confirmed Dead" we find out he memorized the flight manifest and knows the name of every person on it). Why didn't Frank ask any questions about who Desmond was? Why did he lie to Keamy?

- Omar says their last port was off the coast of Fiji. Is he telling the truth?
- Daniel says that Desmond is the one who is affected on the helicopter because he had been exposed to a large dose of radiation. But both George and his friend in the dinghy experienced the same situation as Desmond; could they have somehow been exposed to a dose of radiation or electromagnetism the same way Desmond was?
- Could Daniel have had a residual memory of Desmond coming to see him in 1996 and mentioning that he'd end up on an island by 2004, and that's why he was crying at the beginning of "Confirmed Dead"?
- Why is everyone on the freighter so dismissive of Daniel?
- George says that Penny was constantly trying to contact the boat and he'd been under strict orders not to answer the phone. Why? Secondly, what does Penny know, and how would she know to contact this boat?
- Why was Widmore keen to get the *Black Rock* journal?
- Once Desmond learned about the importance of a constant, why didn't he tell George to find one in his past? Was George too far gone? Or was Desmond so wrapped up in solving his own problems he didn't have time to deal with George?
- On the calendar where you see the days marked off with X's, there are no X's over the dates October 20, 21, 22, or 23. The Boston Red Sox won the American League Championship Series on October 20, and went on from there to win the World Series. Could that have caused some seismic reaction in the world that made four days go missing on the calendar?
- Daniel clearly made the note in his journal that Desmond would be his constant should anything happen to him because he knew he would run into Desmond in the future and that Desmond would still be alive in eight years (something he couldn't be sure of for anyone else he knew). But in the present, did he know that notation was there? Was the note just for the viewer, or did it serve a higher purpose? Will this note take on a greater significance? In other words, will Daniel find himself in a position where he will need Desmond to be his constant?
- If it's possible that all time periods are happening at the same time, could the whispers in the jungle be conversations from another time that have somehow broken through the time-space barrier?

Ashes to Ashes: George Minkowski was the ship's communication officer on a freighter currently sitting somewhere off the coast of Fiji (if Omar is to be believed). He was curious to see the island, so he and a friend took a boat out to see it, but hit the wall of time travel and returned to the freighter, where both his friend and he succumbed to the consequences of their curiosity.

✍ *Slaughterhouse-Five* by Kurt Vonnegut (1969)

In "The Constant," Daniel Faraday tells Desmond that the experiment he is working on at Oxford is to "unstick Eloise in time." The opening line of the narrated section of Kurt Vonnegut's classic antiwar novel, *Slaughterhouse-Five*, is "Listen: Billy Pilgrim has become unstuck in time." Perhaps it was this novel that set Daniel on his course.

Slaughterhouse-Five is Vonnegut's attempt to describe the massacre that occurred during the firebombing of Dresden, Germany, during World War II. The air raid by the Allies, which took place between February 13 and 15, 1945 (three months before German surrender), has always been a controversial event in the history books. On the one hand, Dresden was a communication center for the Nazis during the war, and it housed several factories that were creating munitions for the German army. On the other, the city was known for its baroque architecture and was considered one of the true gems of Europe. When the bombing was over, the city center had been completely consumed by flames, and the death toll estimates have typically hovered around 135,000, more than Hiroshima and Nagasaki. (Today, several historians are arguing the number was closer to 35,000, but it's hard to say how many people were there, simply because the city housed thousands of refugees.)

Kurt Vonnegut was an American soldier during WWII, and he was a prisoner of war held in Dresden. He witnessed the firebombing from the ground, and he only survived because he was in a meat locker. Afterward, the Germans forced him to help dig in the rubble for bodies, but when they discovered just how many bodies there were (and found hundreds of mass graves under the rubble), the Germans used flamethrowers shoved down the holes to incinerate the dead instead.

Vonnegut was traumatized by what he'd seen, and he struggled for many years after the war to find a way to describe the horrors of Dresden. The result of those struggles is *Slaughterhouse-Five*, a largely autobiographical novel about a man who witnesses the same carnage that Vonnegut did. The format of a traditional novel has its limits, however, and Vonnegut realized it was nearly impossible to describe in words how horrifying it was. So he uses the device of time travel, and the protagonist of the book (which is narrated by Vonnegut himself, who introduces himself in the first chapter) is Billy Pilgrim, a man who is unstuck in time. He can't stay put in one place for long, and instead zips from one time frame to another, from infancy to death, constantly.

Billy is a quiet man who was a POW during World War II. After the Germans capture him, he is put in a boxcar along with the other prisoners and forced to stand night and day. When they arrive at the camp, the captured British soldiers treat them as clowns, but invite them to a feast and a play. Billy suffers a breakdown before the prisoners head to Dresden, where they are paraded through the streets before being confined to a meat locker with the address, "Slaughterhouse-Five." Like Vonnegut before him, Pilgrim lives through the firebombing and is forced to try in vain to clean up the bodies. When he is finally let go once the end of the war is announced, he rides away in a green cart shaped like a coffin, being pulled by two horses. When an elderly couple stops the horses and clucks at him that the horses' mouths are bleeding from the bit and their hooves have cracked, causing agony with each step, Pilgrim cries for the first time, finally realizing what has been done to the horses, to him, and to the world around him.

After the war Billy Pilgrim settles down as an optometrist in Ilium, New York, with his boss's obese daughter, Valencia. He has a nervous breakdown and ends up in a veteran's hospital alongside another man, Eliot Rosewater, who introduces him to the science-fiction novels of Kilgore Trout (often thought to be Vonnegut himself). Eventually Billy and Valencia have two children and he becomes very wealthy after opening a string of optometry clinics. He believes he has fully recovered from the war until his eighteenth wedding anniversary, when a barbershop quartet begins singing to the wedded couple. Billy feels sick to his stomach, and needs to leave the room to lie down, and only then he realizes that when he first emerged from the meat locker to see the devastation that had been wrought upon Dresden, he looked up at the German guards, whose mouths were O-shaped, like the singers in a barbershop quartet.

Immediately following his daughter Barbara's wedding, Billy is abducted by an alien race called the Tralfamadorians, a species of beings shaped like toilet plungers, with little green hands sticking out of the top of the poles. They take him to their planet millions of light years away and put him in a dome where they can all watch him, like a zoo animal. They introduce an Earthling movie star to the environment named Montana Wildhack, who is terrified at first, but soon warms up to Billy, and eventually they produce a baby. The Tralfamadorians believe in fate, that there is no such thing as free will, that what will happen to us is preordained and there is nothing we can do to change it. They believe that all time — past, present, and future — is happening at once, which is why Pilgrim keeps jumping around to various points in his life. When a person dies, Tralfamadorians simply shrug and accept it, because they know that this being is still alive on another time plane somewhere. (Think of Charlie saying to Hurley in "The Beginning of the End," "I am dead. But I am also here." Put into a Tralfamadorian framework, it could mean he is dead, but he's also still alive at another point in his life, which is happening simultaneously.)

Billy returns to Earth and doesn't tell anyone about his experience. He boards an airplane full of optometrists that crashes into a mountain; only Billy survives. He is rushed into surgery. Valencia, who "adores" him, as the narrator tells us, rushes to the hospital, but she gets into a major fender bender on the way over that obliterates her exhaust system, and ends up dying of carbon monoxide poisoning. Once out of the hospital, Billy is under home care, but sneaks away to New York where he announces on a radio program that he'd been kidnapped by aliens, and he begins to reveal the secrets of the Tralfamadorians. A friend of Barbara's calls her, and she rushes to New York to get her father and bring him home. Then Billy writes a letter to the local newspaper explaining his experiences, and Barbara considers having him committed. To prove he knows what he's doing, Billy records a message explaining that he knows when, where, and how he will die, and explains it to the last detail: he will be shot after making a public speech.

This is a linear description of the plot of *Slaughterhouse-Five*, but the plot is by no means presented in linear fashion. We learn of all of these events out of order, as Billy closes his eyes in World War II, ends up with the Tralfamadorians, then closes his eyes as he watches Montana breastfeed their baby, and ends up in 1967. The book has several tropes, the most oft-repeated one being the laid-back, "So it goes," that Vonnegut writes after every single mention of death in the book (from that of an animal to the massacre in Dresden). By using this three-word phrase, Vonnegut not only manages to explain Billy's detachment from things as brought on by his alien friends, and his belief that somewhere these creatures are still alive, but he also highlights just how much death happens in the novel. Every time the reader hits another "So it goes," it emphasizes that another person has died, and readers add each death to the mental tally.

The debate between free will and fate is constant in Billy's explanation of the Tralfamadorians. Billy knows when he steps onto the plane full of optometrists that it's going to crash into the mountain, but he believes there's nothing he can do to change that fate, so he gets on the plane anyway, and doesn't warn anyone. He knows how he's going to die, but he doesn't shy away from actually going to the speech he needs to make, knowing that a man, Paul Lazzaro, who cursed him during the war would choose that moment to reap his revenge.

The horrors of war are preeminent throughout the book. Like *Catch-22* before it (see pages 140–144 of *Finding Lost — Season 3* for the analysis of that book), *Slaughterhouse-Five* uses absurdity as its only means to show just how insane war really is. In *Catch-22*, Yossarian is a loon, and Billy Pilgrim experiences a similar detachment from the events going on around him. Just as the officers seem to speak gibberish and all act like they're crazy, Billy Pilgrim tells people he was abducted by aliens, who have given him clarity into what the world is really like. By suggesting there is no free will, he absolves the Allies of what they did to Dresden, and the Germans for the atrocities they committed during the war. After all, if everything they did was preordained, was it really their fault they committed such crimes?

Billy Pilgrim shares a lot in common with Desmond Hume. Not only are they both unstuck in time, but they both believe in fate. In "Flashes Before Your Eyes," Mrs. Hawking explains to Desmond that no matter what he tries to do to alter fate, the universe will course-correct to make sure the initial events still manage to happen. He can try to save Charlie all he wants, but if Charlie is meant to die, he'll die. Similarly, Billy Pilgrim gets on the plane that is about to crash because he doesn't believe *not* getting on that plane is an option. Vonnegut's mantra of "so it goes" is an acceptance of fate in the world. Someone passed away in their sleep. So it goes. Over 100,000 people were reduced to ashes in a day. So it goes. The idea of fatalism comes off as little more than a shrug.

In Billy's description of his own death, which he has seen and experienced many times, and will do so again, he is blinded by a violet light that is accompanied by a loud hum. This description matches what happens at the end of season 2, when Desmond turned the key, thus causing the hatch to implode/explode, the sky turned violet and a loud hum nearly deafened everyone on the island.

At one point in the book, Billy becomes worried about the effect all this time travel is having on him. "Billy was starting to get worried about it, about his mind in general. He tried to remember how old he was, couldn't. He tried to remember what year it was. He couldn't remember that, either." In "Eggtown," we see Daniel and Charlotte playing a memory game with cards, as if Daniel's memory has been affected by his time traveling as well. In "The Constant," Minkowski dies of a brain aneurysm caused by the effects of the time travel, and Desmond almost follows him.

On Billy's wall is the serenity prayer ("God grant me the serenity to accept the things I cannot change, courage to change the things I can, and the wisdom always to tell the difference"), and the narrator adds, "Among the things Billy Pilgrim could not change were the past, the present, and the future." This prayer is also on a locket around film star Montana Wildhack's neck. In season 3 we see Christian attending an AA meeting in "Tale of Two Cities," and the serenity prayer is the mantra of every recovering alcoholic. Like Billy, Christian believes things are meant to be and cannot be changed, and "that's why the Red Sox will never win the series." Jack often takes him to task for that belief, saying it just allows him to shirk his responsibility.

Free will versus fate is one of the main themes in the book, as on *Lost*. At one point a Tralfamadorian says to Billy Pilgrim, "If I hadn't spent so much time studying Earthlings . . . I wouldn't have any idea what was meant by 'free will.' I've visited thirty-one inhabited planets in the universe, and I have studied reports on one hundred more. Only on Earth is there any talk of free will." A Tralfamadorian tells Billy they know how the universe will end someday, which will be when they accidentally blow it up while testing their fuels. Billy asks if they know this already, can't they prevent the test pilot from hitting the starter button that will cause the massive explosion? The Tralfamadorian replies, "He has *always* pressed it, and he always *will*. We *always* let him and we always *will* let him. The moment is *structured* that way." Similarly, Darlton has insisted that there is only one timeline for *Lost*, and even if we see people moving backward or forward in time, they were acting on a timeline where they always did those things. In "The Constant," Desmond will always go back to Oxford to visit Dan and tell him the codes, and Dan must ensure in the present that Desmond will find a way to go back and do that.

When Billy is staying in the veteran's hospital, Rosewater turns him on to the novels of Kilgore Trout, but before Rosewater does that he tells him that everything he needs to know about life can be found in Dostoevsky's *The Brothers Karamazov*. Interestingly, that is the novel that John Locke gives to "Henry Gale" when he's locked up in the armory. One of Kilgore Trout's novels is *Maniacs in the Fourth Dimension*. There is a lot of talk of the "fourth dimension" in this book, mostly because Tralfamadorians can see things four-dimensionally, rather than three-dimensionally, as we do. (The fourth dimension is time.) This is a reference to Hermann Minkowski's spacetime (see page 66), which added the fourth dimension to the three ordinary dimensions of space.

Slaughterhouse-Five is a brilliant book, and has clearly influenced the character of Desmond and many of the themes of the third and fourth seasons. The book is actually very similar to Philip K. Dick's *VALIS* (see page 50) in that both protagonists see a bright light that gives them messages, both believe that aliens have spoken to them, both books feature the author as an actual character (Vonnegut not only speaks in the first person in the prologue, but he appears in two scenes in the book), and both involve time travel. The writers have once again turned *Lost* viewers on to some superb books, and we are the richer for it.

4.6   The Other Woman

Original air date: March 6, 2008
Written by: Drew Goddard, Christina M. Kim
Directed by: Eric Laneuville
Guest cast: M.C. Gainey (Tom), Brett Cullen (Goodwin), Alan Dale (Charles Widmore), Andrea Roth (Harper Stanhope)

Flash: Juliet

When Juliet receives a message from Ben that Charlotte and Daniel are going to a Dharma station to kill everyone on the island, she must stop them before they succeed.

"What light through yonder window breaks? It is the east, and Juliet is the sun! *And she is MINE, all MINE!*" I'm a big fan of Juliet, and I loved her two flashbacks in season 3. But "The Other Woman" was a major letdown after "The Constant," mostly because the flashback rehashed things we already knew, and the island plot seemed to be a one-off throwaway story that had nothing to do with the overarching season arc. If you cut this episode out of the season, you can *almost* get by without having watched it.

We discovered through flashbacks in season 3 that Juliet came to the island at Ben's behest to try to discover why the pregnant women were dying and to put a stop to it ("Not in Portland"). As a fertility doctor, Juliet had accomplished the impossible: helping her sister Rachel get pregnant after Rachel had undergone harsh and invasive treatments to cure her cancer. Juliet's husband, the sniveling Edmund Burke, was a scientist who wanted to exploit her sister-in-law's test case to bring him and Juliet worldwide fame, but thankfully, he was flattened by a bus before he could go any further with that thought ("One of Us"). Once on the island, Juliet's optimism quickly faded into frustration and hopelessness as one woman after another died, and Ben refused to let her take them off the island to save them. The insanity of her situation began to dawn on her, and she also realized she was trapped — no matter what,

Juliet continues to do Ben's bidding in "The Other Woman," a disappointing and confused episode. (DAVE ALLOCCA/STARTRAKSPHOTO.COM)

Ben wouldn't let her go. She had made a deal with the devil to save her sister after Rachel's cancer returned (how Jacob/Ben saved her is still not known) and now she remains a prisoner on the island, beholden to Ben to ensure her sister's continued safety.

So when Harper comes a-callin', Juliet goes a-runnin' in this episode. There are several reasons why the story line doesn't work. First, if Ben really were planning some nefarious island explosion, he certainly doesn't seem to be too worried about it as he hangs out with Locke and they chat about his man on the boat and who owns the freighter. He doesn't have a gas mask handy, he's not madly checking the clock, and it seems to be the last thing on his mind. Second, Daniel manages to stop the gas only one second before it's about to blow, which seems a little too convenient for my liking. There's a chance Ben has set everyone up, and he's rigged the station so the gas will become inert one second before it blows just to mess with everyone's head, which is why he's not worried.

But the freighter folks' involvement doesn't make any sense either. Why lie about their mission? Why not just tell Jack that they know about the Tempest station and ask everyone to help them, rather than having a knock-down, drag-it-out fight on the floor of the station because they made it look like they were the bad guys? Why clock Kate in the head with the butt of a gun and render her bloody and unconscious? And how did the freighter folk know about the gas anyway? We now know that Widmore is the man behind the freighter, which is the major revelation of this episode, but if so, how could he possibly know Ben has rigged the Tempest station to blow if he doesn't even know where the island is? Why didn't Charlotte and Daniel try to get there earlier? One would think a possible poison gas leak would be cause for an Olympic-style race to the other side of the island, but Dan and Charlotte have been hanging out on the beach like they're not in any rush until the last possible moment. It's like the episode was inserted into an already finished season, and to make it worthwhile they moved the Ben and Locke conversations over to this episode.

Another question might be how Ben was able to communicate to Harper Stanhope a message that would be passed on to Juliet, but it's likely that Harper was simply a manifestation of Old Smokey, who in turn is either a pawn of Ben or Jacob or acting of its own accord. Even Juliet and Jack's kiss at the end of the episode felt out of place, since he doesn't act romantically toward Juliet in any other way. The only thing new that we seemed to learn from Juliet's flashback is that her affair with Goodwin was an adulterous one, and that Ben is crazy for her (crazy being the operative word).

The most interesting part of this episode involved Ben and Locke. Locke is still one of the most fascinating characters on the show, because he's been riding a rollercoaster of joy and tumult since he got to the island, and the ride never seems to let up. At some point, however, it would be nice to see him learn from a mistake. Just as Ben got to Locke when he had him imprisoned in the armory, now Ben manipulates him from his new cell. Locke trusted Ben, and Ben turned out to be a traitor. Later, Locke trusted Ben again, and Ben shot him in the gut. Locke rose from the ashes, one hoped a stronger, harder character, but instead we see that his leadership is mostly swagger and based on an unbending belief in the island's godlike nature. He is inflexible when anyone approaches him, whether it be Kate or, in the case of this episode, Claire. Kate eventually got her way anyway, and now that Claire comes to him, she simply shows the weakness of Locke's plan . . . or, lack of plan. He reminds her that Charlie had said the freighter wasn't Penny's boat, a fact Locke's been clinging to as his proof that the freighter folk are lying to them, but when Claire retorts, "All Charlie said was whose boat it isn't. Don't you want to know whose boat it is?" she makes him realize he's been asking the wrong questions.

Locke has no idea what he's doing, and everyone knows that. Jack was an annoying leader with a holier-than-thou complex, but at least he knew how to get the job done. Locke says his leadership is a utilitarian one, but so far it isn't. He may claim he's working for the greater good, but he's starting to come off as a religious fanatic. Locke's fatal flaw is his trusting nature. No matter how many times Anthony Cooper stabbed him in the back John Locke was ready to give him another chance. Locke is also extremely sensitive, which is bad in a leader, but good in a regular person. Watch how many times in the series he'll stop what he's doing to suddenly turn to a person, no matter how much he hates him, and tell him he's sorry for something terrible that's happened to him. When Ben begins to taunt him from the cell, Locke doesn't slam the door shut. Instead, he listens to the taunts, because he never knows when Ben might say something useful. The fact that Locke keeps returning to this one person who's proven to be a liar time and again shows that even Locke knows he's not doing a very good job as a leader. But it also shows that Locke knows how to listen to the one person who knows the island better than he does.

Through Ben, we discover that not only does Ben know about Widmore, who previously was only connected to Desmond, but that Widmore seems to be his mortal enemy. He reveals to Locke that Widmore will do anything to find the island, perhaps because he knows of its healing and supernatural properties. But in an interesting twist of "we're not so different, you and I," the scene where Widmore has one of the Others beaten up in an alleyway parallels Juliet's flashback where we discover Ben was behind Goodwin's death. Ben has attachments to the island, and he clearly has developed an attachment to Juliet.

"The Other Woman" seems like a standalone episode now, but the one thing that might make it important later is the subtle comment Harper makes at the beginning to Juliet: "You remind him of her." Who is this *her* she is referring to? Could it be Ben's mother? (Leave it to the therapist to bring Oedipus into the situation; after all, Ben's already killed his father, so why not marry his mother?) Ben has been struggling with some serious mommy issues all his life (and these complement his severe daddy issues nicely). In what appeared to be an innocuous scene where Ben throws a dinner party for two, Juliet tells Ben that Zach and Emma (the two children Ana Lucia and Eko rescued who were taken by the Others and were seen last season with Cindy) are asking for their mother, Ben says they're just children, and they'll stop asking in time. But Ben was only a few minutes old when his mother died, and he still hasn't stopped asking questions. Ben's dismissive comment is ironic, simply because his childhood has been monumentally influential in his life, as have the childhoods of all the characters on this show.

Highlight: It's a tie between Juliet explaining to Jack the need for a therapist in New Otherton — "It's very stressful being an Other, Jack" — and Ben's reaction when Locke brings him rabbit for lunch — "This didn't have a number on it, did it?" Ha!

Timeline: The events of this episode take place on Christmas Day, 2004, although there is no mention of the significance of the date, sadly destroying my hopes of seeing Jack pull Locke's name for the Island Secret Santa exchange.

Did You Notice?:

- In "Through the Looking Glass," Ben is very upset when he's talking to Tom and realizes Juliet told the survivors about their plan to kidnap the pregnant women. Now we know why Ben was so hurt by her betrayal.
- In "The Economist," Desmond shows the photo of himself and Penny to Frank and tells him to look him in the eye and tell him he's never heard of Penelope Widmore. Frank and Dan share a knowing glance. They don't necessarily know Penny, but they know the name Widmore.
- Harper says Ben is exactly where he wants to be, which is what Miles said about himself to Kate.
- Goodwin mentions that a woman named Henrietta died that morning. She has the female version of the name Ben uses as his alias, Henry.
- Many fans noticed the footage of Ethan was missing in the scene where Ben sends him to the beach, but it's probably because they would have had to pay William Mapother for using his scene again, and it was more appropriate to use the shot of Harper and Juliet exchanging knowing looks instead.
- The material in the flashbacks happens concurrently with many of the same events in "One of Us," but it fills in some of the gaps for us. In that episode,

Juliet comes to Ben's house in a rage days before the plane crash because she's just found out he has a tumor, and she's begging him to let her leave the island. Now it's clearer that not only did she want to see her sister, but she was becoming increasingly worried that something could happen to Goodwin, and that she was being stalked by Ben. Then he shows her proof that her sister is alive and well and has a son, and Juliet is eternally grateful. When Juliet goes to Ben's house for ham in this episode, it explains why she's kind to him.

- The tape of the Red Sox game that Ben showed to Jack was unmarked, yet this tape says RED SOX on it. If this really *is* the same tape that he showed Jack, it means the video of Widmore was recorded in the last month, since he showed Jack that tape a month before the events here.
- Now we know that Widmore was buying the journal of the first mate of the *Black Rock* because he was trying to find clues to get to the island.
- The symbol for the Tempest station is a wave, which is a reference to Shakespeare's play, *The Tempest* (see page 82). Fans have long drawn parallels between that play and the magical events on the *Lost* island.
- The title of this episode refers not only to Juliet being the other woman in the relationship between Harper and Goodwin Stanhope, but to Jack and Kate. Interestingly, however, while Juliet was the other woman who came between Harper and Goodwin, it seems more like Kate is the other woman who will come between Jack and Juliet.

Interesting Facts: The psychiatrist's name is Harper Stanhope. Her name is a reference to the Orchid video Darlton showed at Comic-Con (see pages 3–4). The Stanhopea is a genus of the orchid family, and the flowers appear to be upside-down. The flower blooms for such a brief period (three days at the most) that it has developed a way to spread its pollen quickly to avoid extinction. The flowers usually die on the second day, which is interesting . . . on the island, the pregnant women die in their second trimesters.

Find815: The combination on Ben's safe, "36-15-28," and "Red Sox" are clues in the game.

Oops: As Juliet is fighting with Charlotte at the Tempest, there's a moment where you can clearly see the face of the stuntwoman.

4 8 15 16 23 42: On Daniel's map, there's a notation marking a spot that is 8° N. The combination on the lock behind Ben's picture is 36-**15**-28. (If you subtract the third number, 28, from the first, 36, you get **8**.) On the computer where Daniel is typing, it keeps repeating the same warning about an overpressure alert, using the number **16**.

It's Just a Flesh Wound: Charlotte knocks Kate unconscious with the butt of a gun; Charlotte and Juliet fight each other and throw punches while in the Tempest station.

Lost in Translation: On Daniel's map, we can see the letter C inside a circle on the south end of the map (probably a notation of where the survivors' camp is) and to the northwest of it, an H, which could be an indication of where to land the helicopter. The notation beside the H reads: "8° N, 33° E Follow the river to the east end of the grotto + head due east towards the smaller mountain range. Helipad found just north of mountains." Along the top of the island is a spot marked that reads, "Possible pass through northern mountains." There is another long notation on the west side of the island, but Daniel's thumb is obscuring it.

This episode features those famous whispers we hear in the jungle right before an Other appears. Once again, those barely audible whispers were transcribed on the-odi.blogspot.com. Here is their translation:

Right before Juliet runs into Harper in the jungle:
  "Sarah is having another . . ."
  "Is that the other woman?"
When Juliet runs into Harper in the jungle:
  "Look out."
  "Sarah is having another . . ."
  "Did you hear that?"
  "If she won't save us then who is . . . ?"
  "Sarah, somebody's coming."
  Male: "There is somebody coming."
  Female: "Hold on one second."
  Male: "There is somebody coming."
After Jack runs into Juliet and Harper:
  "Look out."
  Male: "Sarah, it's someone we know. Sarah, it's someone we know."
  Female: "I'm not answering."
  Male: "Answer them."
  "We have our answer."
  "Can we trust her?"
Finally, a very faint whisper can be heard right before Juliet uses the pulley door

contraption at the Tempest station.

"It's Juliet."

Any Questions?:

- Could Juliet bear some resemblance (or more) to Ben's childhood friend, Annie? We saw a glimpse of Annie in "The Man Behind the Curtain," and fans have been clamoring for more about her ever since.

- Where has Harper been all this time? Will we see any of the remaining Others who vacated New Otherton when Juliet was left behind? How could Ben have communicated with her? Could she be a manifestation of the smoke monster?

- Juliet asks Harper how Ben could possibly know what Dan and Charlotte are up to if he's being held prisoner, and Harper says, "Ben is exactly where he wants to be." What does this mean? Is it possible that Ben has figured out how to astrally project himself in some way similar to Walt? Or has he also figured out how to move his consciousness around like Desmond did in the previous episode? Could he have time traveled and created more than one of himself?

- Now that we know the freighter folk were sent by Widmore, does that mean the map that Dan is holding could have been from the *Black Rock* journal that we saw Widmore buy in the previous episode?

- Daniel looks surprised when Kate tells him Locke has Miles, but he was right there when Sayid returned without Miles, saying he traded him for Charlotte, and Frank said he never liked Miles anyway. Did Daniel forget this happened?

- Charlotte says that Ben has gassed everyone on the island before. How did she know about the Purge?

- In the flashback where Juliet is showing Ben the microscope, she says the white blood cells are dropping in women who have conceived on the island, and adds, "which makes me wonder . . ." but doesn't finish her sentence. Was she going to suggest they bring an already pregnant woman to the island?

- Is Ben telling the complete truth about Widmore? Why does Widmore want to find the island? How did he find out about it in the first place?

- Who is the Other whom Widmore is beating up? Who was shooting the video? Was it Richard again?

- The revelation of the man on the boat is something that Ben thinks would make Locke need to sit down. Who is it?

- Why is Ben so obsessed with Juliet?
- What was the original purpose of the Tempest station?

Music/Bands: When Juliet is at Ben's house for dinner, he is playing "Un bel dì vedremo" from Giacomo Puccini's *Madama Butterfly*.

The *Tempest* by William Shakespeare (1623)

It's no coincidence that the latest Dharma station — the very one that holds within it the power to kill everyone on the island — is named the Tempest. Several fans have pointed out parallels between Shakespeare's final play and this show.

The play opens with men on a ship that is being torn apart at sea. The ship is carrying Alonso, the King of Naples; Sebastian, his brother; Gonzalo, a councillor to the king; Antonio, the Duke of Milan; Ferdinand, Alonso's son; Adrian and Francisco, two lords; Trinculo, a jester; Stephano, the drunken butler; and several mariners, a boatswain, and the shipmaster. The shipwreck is being watched on the shore of a nearby island by Miranda, who has lived on the island from the age of three, and her father, Prospero, a magician who is the rightful Duke of Milan. He sits Miranda down and tells her how his brother, Antonio, had usurped him. Prospero had been paying more attention to his occult books than he had to his post, and his brother made a deal with the King of Naples to make him duke, putting Milan under the rule of Naples in return. He turned Prospero and Miranda over to Gonzalo, who was given instructions to take them far out to sea and throw them onto a raft where they would most likely die. Gonzalo took pity on them and gave them food, water, clothing, and some of Prospero's magic books, and eventually they landed on an island.

Prior to their arrival, the island had been inhabited by a witch named Sycorax. She had been exiled to the island from Algiers, and was pregnant when she arrived. Soon after her arrival, she gave birth to a son, Caliban. Annoyed by the mischievous spirit Ariel, she imprisoned him in a tree, but died before she could reverse the spell. When Prospero arrives, he frees Ariel from the tree, but forces him to be his servant, constantly promising Ariel's freedom, but always at a later date. Prospero initially adopts Caliban, and he and Miranda attempt to educate him and teach him to read, but when Caliban attempts to rape Miranda, hoping to people "this isle with Calibans," he is turned into a base servant for Prospero.

Prospero has orchestrated the storm and the shipwreck, and with the help of Ariel, Ferdinand lands alone (believing his father is dead); Alonso, Gonzalo, Sebastian, Antonio and the lords wash up together (with Alonso believing his son is dead); Trinculo and Stephano are separated but near each other; and the seamen remain on the boat, asleep. Prospero then shows Ferdinand to Miranda, and because she has never seen a man other than her father or Caliban, she immediately falls in love with him. The love is mutual, but Prospero becomes cruel to Ferdinand to test his love for Miranda, ordering him to fetch wood so Miranda will take pity on him and try to help him, and through the trials the two of them fall deeply in love.

Meanwhile, Gonzalo tries to comfort Alonso to no avail, and Sebastian and Antonio conspire to kill them in their sleep. Ariel overhears their plan and wakes them before the deed can be carried out.

Caliban roams into the jungle, grumbling to himself about his hatred for Prospero, and when he sees Trinculo he believes him to be one of Prospero's magical spirits, here to taunt and hurt him. He hides under his cloak, and Trinculo, hearing a storm coming, hides under the cloak with him. Stephano stumbles onto the scene, drunk on the wine from a crate he was clutching to stay afloat, and believes the two men under the cloak are actually a four-legged monster. He pours some of his wine into Caliban's mouth, and Caliban begins to worship him as a god. Caliban tells the two men about Prospero and tells them if they could kill him, Stephano could have Miranda and the two could reign as king and queen of the island, with Caliban as their subject. Ariel, who is nearby, returns to Prospero to tell him of the conspiracy on his life.

Ariel leads Alonso and his companions to Prospero, where the spirits lay a banquet before them. As they are about to eat, Ariel appears before them as a harpy, causes the food to disappear, and tells them all that Ferdinand is now dead as a revenge for what they did to Prospero. He leaves, and Alonso wallows in his own guilt, accepting that he'd done the wrong things years before by allowing Antonio to become duke of Milan.

Convinced that Ferdinand really does love Miranda, Prospero welcomes him to the family, but warns him that Miranda must remain a virgin until their wedding night. He then invites the spirits to put on a play for them that celebrates marriage, until he remembers that Caliban will be making an attempt on his life. He hurriedly shoos the spirits away and calls on Ariel. Ariel tells Prospero that

Caliban, Trinculo, and Stephano are standing up to their necks in a stinking pond outside Prospero's bedroom, so they lay out sparkling clothes that Caliban and his new friends attempt to steal, and then they send the other spirits to attack them and try to drive them mad.

Ariel brings Alonso and his men to Prospero, who lectures them all on what they'd done to him years earlier. Alonso repents, and asks for his forgiveness. Prospero hisses at Antonio that he's not worth his time, but forgives him. Alonso asks him where his daughter is, and Prospero tells him he lost her during the storm. Then he pulls back a curtain, revealing Ferdinand and Miranda playing a game of chess. When Miranda turns and sees all the men, she is enraptured: "How beauteous mankind is! O, brave new world,/ That has such people in 't!" Alonso restores Prospero as the Duke of Milan, and they all decide to leave for Italy the next day after Prospero reveals that the ships were unharmed by the storm. Prospero calls Caliban, Trinculo, and Stephano in, and they enter wearing the clothes they had stolen. He orders them to return them and tells Caliban to go clean out his cell. Caliban apologizes, pledges his allegiance to Prospero, and admits he had been following fools. Prospero tells Ariel to guide the ships safely through the water, and once he completes his task, he will be free. Everyone but Prospero leaves, and Prospero turns to the audience and begs their forgiveness for his wrongdoings, and asks the audience to free him by clapping: "As you from crimes would pardoned be,/ Let your indulgence set me free."

The Tempest is a play that has become more revered as time goes on. When it was first performed, it was called a comedy, and later a romance. Today critics have re-evaluated it and consider it among Shakespeare's greatest plays. Its complexity is one of the things that make it a favorite among critics. The "good guy," Prospero, is actually a cruel tyrant, where the monster and fool, Caliban, has good reason to rebel the way he does. Postcolonial theorists have adopted Caliban as a favorite subject: he represents the native who has been colonized by a more powerful entity and who must succumb to the wills and pleasures of his ruler. Caliban never asked for the treatment he receives in the play. Even Miranda, who for the most part is soft-spoken and feminine, speaks with Caliban in harsh tones at one point. In fact, her hostility is so out of character that in some productions, the director has assigned her words to Prospero instead.

Prospero is far from a sympathetic character. He's egomaniacal — in the second scene of the play, as he recounts his tale of being usurped, he constantly interrupts himself to tell Miranda she's not paying attention to him, and she fawns over him and creates new hyperboles to stroke his ego: "Your tale, sir, would cure deafness." He's rude and harsh to Ferdinand, he makes promises to Ariel and keeps breaking them, and he treats Caliban like an animal. At the end of the play, we leave Caliban cleaning Prospero's cell, not realizing that everyone is about to set sail the next day, leaving him behind as the sole inhabitant of the island. There have been many revisionist versions of *The Tempest* in the twentieth century that paint Caliban as the hero and Prospero as the villain.

The parallels with *Lost* are fairly clear. We could see Ben as Prospero; he came to the island against his will (his father having brought him there) and Alex is his Miranda. Ben has vowed his revenge on Charles Widmore, a man who, like Antonio, knows about the island and presumably knows about Ben, but who is living his life in the outside world. Ben probably had something to do with the plane crash, just as Prospero created the shipwreck. And just as Prospero manipulates the island spirit to do things at his bidding, so too does Ben use the Others to carry out his tasks. In Shakespeare's play, Caliban is given some beautiful dialogue where he describes the wood, earth, and berries on the island, and is often associated with the island itself. As well, he is often referred to as black, dark, or dirty; in many ways, he could be the smoke monster, doing Ben's bidding. Juliet could be Ariel, flitting about from one group to another, fulfilling Ben's wishes because he keeps promising her a way off the island.

One could also think of Jacob as Prospero — Jacob is trapped in the cabin, much like Prospero was trapped on the island. Each believes his salvation might come from the people who have recently landed on his island. Ben could be Caliban, doing the bidding of Jacob. Like Caliban, Ben lost his mother at an early age. He is knocked around a lot on the show, but he keeps coming back for more, and continues to stay steadfastly devoted to the island. Ariel could be both the smoke monster and the mysterious whispers in the jungle. In one scene in the play, Ariel confuses the characters by flitting around and whispering in their ears until they think it is the other person in the scene mocking them.

Or, the island itself could be Prospero, and everyone else is a pawn or prisoner that the island holds in its thrall. Locke and Ben both believe the island is a living thing, and both do its bidding, like twin Calibans. The magic and sorcery that Prospero possesses are similar to the mysteries on the island.

Any way you look at it, Shakespeare's timeless play has undoubtedly had an impact on *Lost*.

4.7   Ji Yeon

Original air date: March 13, 2008
Written by: Edward Kitsis, Adam Horowitz
Directed by: Stephen Semel
Guest cast: Sam Anderson (Bernard), Marc Vann (Doctor Ray), George Cheung (Ambassador), Lynette Garces (Nurse), Lanny Joon (Doctor Bae), Christina Kim (Admitting Nurse), Sun Hee Koo (Delivery Room Nurse), Simon Rhee (Shopkeeper), David Yew (Security Agent), Tess Young (Maternity Nurse)

Flash: Sun, Jin

When Sun realizes Daniel and Charlotte are not there to rescue them, she plans to defect to Locke's camp . . . unless Juliet can stop her. Meanwhile, Sayid and Desmond meet the captain of the freighter, who tells them some surprising news. The flashforward reveals the final member of the Oceanic 6.

We've seen flashbacks, flashforwards, time traveling, and consciousness shifting. Finally, we get both a flashforward and a flashback in the same episode, but the writers construct it in such a way that we're tricked into thinking it's the same flashforward. The twist of this episode came in the ending: while we knew we were seeing Sun give birth in the future, it turns out Jin was on his way to the hospital in 2000, delivering a present on behalf of his tyrant employer, Mr. Paik.

Was it manipulation? Some fans certainly thought so. They didn't like their emotions being played with, or being tricked into a false sense of security, thinking that Jin was one of the Oceanic 6. But the writers included a lot of hints — some of them pretty obvious — to let viewers know we were, in fact, in the past. First of all, Jin uses a large cell phone (and if you weren't paying attention to it when he was taking calls, you couldn't have missed the size of the thing when he dropped it in

Daniel Dae Kim waits for the rain to stop between takes of the taxicab scene in "Ji Yeon." (RYAN OZAWA)

the street and the camera zoomed in for a close-up). Secondly, the shopkeeper tries to convince Jin to buy a dragon instead of a panda, telling him it is good luck to give a dragon toy in the Year of the Dragon. The last Year of the Dragon was 2000, and there won't be another one until 2012. There were more subtle hints you would catch on a second viewing of the episode: Sun refusing to let the nurses remove her wedding ring in the hospital; the knowing nod the nurse gives the doctor when Sun calls for Jin, as if she knew through Sun's celebrity status that her husband was dead; Jin reassuring her on the island that she'll never lose him (that's never a good sign); Bernard telling Jin that if you do bad things, bad things will happen to you. We all know Jin has done his share of bad things.

Hurley, Sun, and Ji Yeon visit Jin in one of the saddest scenes ever on *Lost*. I'm welling up just thinking about it. (MARIO PEREZ/© ABC/COURTESY: EVERETT COLLECTION)

And he's not the only one. On the freighter, Sayid and Desmond have been slipped a note telling them not to trust the captain, and then the captain begins telling them that the outside world believes everyone on Oceanic Flight 815 is dead, and they have solid proof in an actual plane that was found that was not only a replica of the plane, but contained all 324 dead bodies. Who would go to that length? he asks them. The scene elaborates on the media messages we saw in "Confirmed Dead," but what the captain says is also received with suspicion because of the note that Sayid and Desmond got. It's like the age-old trick question: if a man walks up to you and says, "Everything I say is a lie," is he lying? Gault's declaration that the freighter belongs to Widmore (the look on Desmond's face was worth the wait), followed by his revelation of the black box, and his story of the fake 815 plane, are topped only by his final line: "[It's] just one of the many reasons we want Benjamin Linus." What could that mean? Did Ben stage the fake plane?

What was so great about this episode were the many new questions it raised, while making us feel that we're much closer to discovering the answers. What is the link between Widmore and Ben? Who staged the plane crash? And bringing that revelation back to the shocking end of this episode (if you did not weep, you are made of stone), is Jin really dead? His tombstone lists his death date as September 22, 2004, which is the date of the crash. Who erected it? Is Sun telling people he died in the plane crash? Did a family member erect the stone when the media reported they'd found the plane and everyone was dead? Is Sun lying? Or is he really going to die before she gets off the island and for some reason she's telling them he died in the crash? Either way, the end of this episode was so beautifully done . . . but I'm holding out hope that Jin might still be alive.

In "Eggtown" Jack takes the witness stand and tells the jury that only eight people survived the crash, so there seems to be a pervading lie among the survivors that most people died in the crash. Perhaps they're saying that Jin is one of them. But the other major talking point among fans after this episode aired was who the final Oceanic 6 were. The producers said we'd know who they all were by episode 7, which is this one. The writers of the episode clearly wanted us to think Jin and Sun were the final two, which means they recognized there were theoretically two spots still open. But when Sun was revealed as the penultimate member — sans Jin — it meant the final member of the Oceanic 6 was Aaron. Some fans argued that he couldn't have been one of the Oceanic 6 because he wasn't on the manifest, but because Darlton established in podcasts that the "Oceanic 6" moniker would be a media construct, it made sense that Aaron would be counted among the six. What throws it off is Jack's story. He says eight people survived the crash. Then he says two people died, and then Aaron was born, which leaves seven, not six. The only way around this crack in the logic is the fact that Kate cuts Jack off when he's on the stand. All he says is, "She tried to save the other two, but they didn't . . ." and Kate cuts him off, as if she realizes he's really lousy at math and needs him to stop talking before he gives them all away. Either that or Jack believes a baby is a person before it is born and is counting Aaron as one of the eight before his birth.

One person who is not one of the Oceanic 6 is Michael. What was originally intended to be a giant *gasp!* moment in the episode — Michael walking toward Sayid and Desmond and introducing himself as Kevin Johnson — was probably the most anticlimactic moment of the season. Ben told Locke he'd better sit down; Sayid and Desmond were getting mysterious notes; George Minkowski said some strange person was sabotaging the ship; and all the while fans at home were saying, "Um . . . I think it could be Michael, Michael, or . . . Michael." And then it turned out to be — gasp! shock! horrors! — Michael. It's an inevitable pitfall in the Information Age: word will leak, and everyone will know Harold Perrineau is back. (Well, that and the fact he'd been listed in the cast at the beginning of every single episode the entire season. That was kind of a giveaway.)

So what are Michael's intentions, and how did he return? Stay tuned to the next episode, when we meet Kevin Johnson.

Highlight: Hurley looking at baby Ji Yeon and saying, "She's awesome."

Timeline: On the evening of Christmas Day, Jin tells Sun that he wants their daughter to be named Ji Yeon. The next morning, Sun asks Daniel if he's there to rescue them, and the rest of the events take place on Boxing Day. Presumably, the events on the freighter are taking place the same day. Incidentally, the devastating Indian Ocean tsunami that killed over 300,000 people happened on Boxing Day, 2004.

Did You Notice?:

- In the first flashforward, when Sun is packing a suitcase, that episode of *Exposé* that featured Nikki is on the television (it's at the scene just before the Cobra shoots her, and it's been dubbed in Korean).

- Jin tells Jack that Sawyer has taught him some English. He's referring to a scene in "Tricia Tanaka Is Dead," when Sawyer taught Jin to say, "I'm sorry," "You were right," and "Those pants don't make you look fat."

- There must have been other pregnant women on Flight 815. Claire would have used all her prenatal vitamins over the month she was still pregnant on the island, and presumably Sun's been taking them for a couple of weeks at least. If there's still at least one more bottle left, they must have found them in more than just Claire's suitcase. It's also possible Juliet took them from the Others, or they were in the suitcase of pharmaceuticals that Jack got from Ethan (see page 139).

- Bernard finally opening up to Jin and telling him about Rose's cancer was a moment where one character actually tells something personal to another. It almost never happens on this show.

- When Bernard is explaining karma to Jin, he doesn't finish the sentence, and says, "You make bad choices, bad things happen to you; you make good choices, good . . ." By not actually saying good things will happen to you, it foreshadows that no matter what you do on the island — good or bad — bad things will happen to you.

- Bernard says to Jin, "We must be the good guys, huh?" which is an echo of Ben saying to Michael at the end of season 2, "We're the good guys, Michael."
- The blood spatter on the wall of the quarters looked like the one Radzinsky left in the Swan station.
- Sayid is apparently good at acting on his feet, and pretends he doesn't know Michael, but when Desmond acts like he doesn't know Michael, that's because he doesn't. When he first came out of the hatch, Michael was with the tail section survivors. By the time Michael had returned, Desmond had run away and taken off in his sailboat. Michael killed Libby and Ana Lucia and then convinced Jack, Sawyer, Hurley, and Kate to come with him to the other side of the island. Desmond only returned in his boat after Michael had left. Michael got to the other side and left in the boat. Their paths never crossed.
- On the tombstone, you can clearly see Sun's name and birth date on the left hand side, carrying out the tradition that a husband and wife be buried together. It also makes it possible that the tombstone had been erected as a monument for both of them when they were believed dead, and Sun's death date was later removed.
- The episode ended with a close-up of Sun's eyes. In the past, episodes of *Lost* have traditionally opened with this image.

Interesting Facts: The book Regina was holding upside-down was Jules Verne's *The Survivors of the Chancellor* (1875). The book is about 28 people who set off on a voyage, and one by one they commit suicide (one by jumping off the boat) until there are only 11 left. After the ship sinks, those who make it onto the raft begin to cannibalize the people who die, and eventually decide to draw lots to see who will be killed and eaten next.

The captain's name, Gault, could be a reference to a series of short stories written by William Hope Hodgson. Published between 1914 and 1916, the Captain Gault stories featured a captain who smuggled various jewels and was eventually revealed to be part of a secret society. Many of the stories involved deception.

Not only is there a superstition about naming babies before they are born in Korea and other Asian countries (not to mention it is a common belief in Jewish culture), but the naming of a baby is a very important task, one that involves both the parents and paternal grandparents. It is believed a child's name helps determine his or her future, so it is treated with the utmost importance. "Ji Yeon" means "flower of wisdom."

Get *Lost* on YouTube

YouTube and other comedy video sites are full of *Lost* parodies. I've seen dozens of them, but so far, these ones are my favorites.

Lost Parodies
www.ravenstake.com
Go to the above URL and click on the box on the right that says "Lost Parodies." These are short films you can watch through YouTube where *Lost* action figures are used to mesh *Lost* stories with other pop culture icons. In one, the *Lost* gang is chased by Voldemort. In another, Darth Vader. Michael shows up in one but they use a Michael Jordan figure (there is no Michael figure). The voices and dialogue are spot-on, including Sawyer with his crazy nicknames. Hurley takes on the role of Kenny in *South Park*, dying in each episode.

Losticil
www.collegehumor.com/video:1723243
Do you have friends who are becoming increasingly obsessed with discussing the finer points on *Lost*? Are you starting to feel left out of the conversations? You might have *Lost* Discussion Deficiency Syndrome. But don't worry . . . there's now a medication for that.

Previously on *Lost*: What?
www.youtube.com/watch?v=GcatQSyRK6c
If *Lost* has ever left you with one of those, "Wait . . . what?!" feelings, you're not alone. Turns out everyone on the island is just as baffled as you are. This is a recap of the first three seasons of *Lost*, simply showing each person on the island saying, "What?" Or in Ben's case, "Whaaat?" and in Charlie's, "Wha?"

Lost in 8:15
www.youtube.com/watch?v=QIuXZ37GQIs
If you're looking for a real recap of the first three seasons, this one is brilliant. Told with a deadpan hilarity, this recaps the first three seasons of *Lost* in 8 minutes, 15 seconds. It's really only for the *Lost* fan who's seen the show, though; it's not meant to catch anyone up (seriously, could you possibly follow season 4 without having watched the previous seasons?).

Lost Theme Song
www.collegehumor.com/video:1739531
This is what the *Lost* opening credits could have looked like if the show had been broadcast in 1986.

The Kirk and Skylar Show
kirkandskylar.blogspot.com/search/label/Lost
All right, it's more action figures, but hey, action figures equal funny. This is a father-and-son team (yes, Dad has wonderfully brought his precocious and very funny eight-year-old son over to the Dark Side of Fandom) who use the *Lost* action figures (and many, many other action figures) to reenact several *Lost* episodes, mostly from season 1.

The panda costs Jin 50,000 Korean Won. That's the equivalent of about $35 U.S. Also, "Panda diplomacy," something that's no longer practiced, describes when China would give a live panda to another country as a show of friendship, because of the extreme rarity of the animals. This is probably why it's important to Paik to give a panda, and not another animal.

Blogger DarkUFO posted the following casting note that appeared for "Ji Yeon" for Regina: "Late-20s to early 30s, any ethnicity. Tough, formidable, someone who could take an order and execute it flawlessly but who is now a shell of her former self; nervous and paranoid. NICE CO-STAR. WOULD PREFER TO HAVE A STUNT WOMAN BUT NOT CRUCIAL." Regina is played by Zoë Bell, who is in fact a stuntwoman, best known as the double for Lucy Lawless on *Xena: Warrior Princess* and Uma Thurman's character in the *Kill Bill* movies. Bell did her own stunt in the scene where Regina commits suicide.

Nitpicks: Juliet clearly told Jin about Sun's infidelity because she would do anything to keep Sun safe, but was that really the best way to go about it? She eventually convinces Sun by giving her an impassioned description of what would happen to Sun in the following weeks. Couldn't she have given that speech earlier? Now Sun is safe in their camp, but her husband knows she had an affair. Knowing Jin, we can see that Sun ran the risk of being a single mom if he abandoned her out of anger.

Also, when Bernard is talking to Jin he asks him if he knows the word "karma," and Jin says yes. When would Sun have taught him that word? "Shoe . . . tree . . . mango . . . karma . . ."

To continue my nitpicks of "Eggtown" (which I couldn't print there without giving away that Jin was not one of the Oceanic 6), if Aaron is one of the Oceanic 6, he would have been in the media spotlight, and everyone would have known that either Kate adopted this baby from another survivor who died after giving birth, or she's telling the world he was her baby. Either way, everyone knows that she has a child. So when the DA suggests Kate be held as a flight risk, the obvious comeback for her lawyer would have been to say she is a single mother to a toddler and can't be away from him. Her lawyer later says to her that she needs to have Aaron in the courtroom, like he's a big secret who needs to be let out, and she refuses, saying she won't let her lawyer use her son. Yet when Jack takes the stand, the lawyer jokes that he'll introduce Jack only for those people who have been living under a rock and don't know who Jack is. So if Jack is world-famous, then it stands to reason that Aaron is, too. It makes sense that Kate wants to shield her toddler from the same scrutiny she allowed of the baby, simply because a baby wouldn't know what was going on and a toddler might. But even if she doesn't want anyone to see Aaron, the world knows that *he exists*. Therefore all of the scenes where everyone talks around Aaron are simply built up for the huge reveal at the end of the episode, rendering the rest of the episode a little over-the-top in retrospect.

Oops: Right before and immediately following Sun slapping Juliet, the big gash under Juliet's mouth is gone, as is the bruise on her cheek. The wounds reappear a few seconds later. Also, another production error: when Sun pulls her wedding ring out of the hospital bag, it says Kwon Sung Hieh (instead of Kwon Sun-Hwa, which is the correct spelling).

4 8 15 16 23 42: The license plate on the taxi that drives away with Jin's first panda is 2369. (First number is **23** and the second is **23** times 3.)

It's Just a Flesh Wound: Sun slaps Juliet.

Any Questions?:

- If the Oceanic 6 consists of Aaron, Sun, Kate, Jack, Hurley, and Sayid, why in season 3 did Desmond have flashes of Claire climbing onto a helicopter?
- What was going on between Keamy and Frank at the beginning? Frank looks squirrelly when Keamy asks him if he's ready, adding he'll be up to meet Frank later. For what?
- What's the problem they had in the kitchen? (Oh, and if all there were to eat were lima beans, I'd starve.)
- Why is Sun packing a bag at the beginning of her flashforward? Is she readying her bag for the hospital? If so, why does she act like something is wrong when she goes into labor? Is she not at full term?
- Dan says rescuing the survivors is not his call. Whose call is it?
- Was there something strange about the doctor who was on call when Sun went into labor? There must have been a reason, story-wise, that Sun's real doctor wasn't in the delivery room and Sun was attended to by a stranger. First he medicates her without asking her permission (typically in labor, medication is a woman's choice, though perhaps that's a North American thing), and then he wants to rush her into a C-section when the baby is actually crowning, meaning a natural birth would have been far easier on everyone at that moment. Was he trying to take her baby?
- Who was banging on the pipes in the freighter?
- What's up with that creepy doctor on the ship? Is he really a doctor? When

they're walking to their new "quarters" Sayid says the ship isn't moving, and the doc says, "Well, if you say so." What did that mean? Is it moving? Is that some reference to time travel?

- How did Gault know that Desmond knew Widmore?
- Whose blood splatter is on the wall in Sayid and Desmond's quarters?
- Why did Regina commit suicide? Could she have been the R.G. on Naomi's bracelet?
- What is on the island that could be causing madness on the ship? How long has the ship been there? You don't develop cabin fever by being on a boat for a week. Could it be proximity to the bubble around the island (the one that affected Desmond when he passed through it) that's causing a fast descent into madness?
- Who staged the elaborate Flight 815 hoax? Was it Ben? Why did Gault immediately assume Ben had something to do with it? What does he know about Ben?
- Is Michael Ben's man on the boat? Or does he just happen to be on the boat?
- When Hurley asks Sun if the others are coming (presumably meaning the rest of the 6) and she says no, he says, "Good." Why? Are the others putting the pressure on them to keep quiet and he'd rather not be around them?
- Why didn't the other Oceanic 4 come to see Sun? Have Sun and Hurley cut ties with them?
- Who erected that tombstone? Why are the Oceanic 6 lying about what really happened?

Ashes to Ashes: Regina committed suicide by stepping off the side of the *Kahana* freighter for reasons unknown. She worked on the freighter in various capacities, whether it be as a sentry guard or as a backup communications officer when Minkowski went mad.

4.8   Meet Kevin Johnson

Original air date: March 20, 2008
Written by: Elizabeth Sarnoff, Brian K. Vaughan
Directed by: Stephen Williams
Guest cast: Cynthia Watros (Libby), M.C. Gainey (Tom), Anthony Azizi (Omar),

Starletta DuPois (Michael's Mother), Galyn Görg (Nurse), James Locke (Jeff/Mechanic), William P. Ogilvie (Gus/Pawnbroker), Francesco Simone (Arturo), Jill Kuramoto (Female Anchor)

Flash: Michael

When Sayid and Desmond discover Michael on the freighter pretending to be Kevin Johnson, Michael has some 'splaining to do. His story fills us in on what happened to him and Walt after they left the island, and why he's back. Meanwhile, Ben sends Alex, Karl, and Rousseau off to the Temple to find refuge.

In the Bible, Job suffers the deaths of his 10 children, along with boils, pestilence, and the destruction of all his possessions. Yet there are times when it feels like he's got nothing on Michael Dawson.

Michael has had a difficult life. An artist by trade, he barely makes ends meet, but is happily married to Susan ("Special"). When they find out she's pregnant, Michael embraces his future as a father wholeheartedly, wanting only the best for his son. But

In "Meet Kevin Johnson," we finally find out what happened to the long-suffering Michael Dawson (Harold Perrineau) after he made it off the island. (MARIO PEREZ/© ABC/COURTESY: EVERETT COLLECTION)

when Susan decides the best things for Walt are expensive — and overseas — Michael is abandoned, left behind as she marries another man and takes Walt away. Michael devotes his life to trying to reconcile with Walt and be a presence in his life, but eventually he gives up his rights to the child, allowing Susan's new husband to adopt him ("Adrift"). It's not clear whether he had his own father issues or not, but he acts like a man whose own father wasn't there for him, and now he wants to make it up to his son by being the father he never had. When Susan dies, her husband dumps Walt on Michael, because Walt's "specialness" is a bit too much for Brian to handle.

On the island, Walt is sullen and has no relationship with Michael. Michael works hard to build one up, and eventually gains the child's trust. The father/son bond lasts about two days before Walt is taken by the Others. Michael's life on the island is a microcosm of what the rest of his life has been: he spends all his time searching in vain for Walt. The story of Michael's life in the last 10 years has always come down to one thing: what wouldn't he do to save Walt? In the case of the island, it involves killing two women and betraying four friends. But karma has it in for him. Days after being reunited with his son, Michael has apparently confessed his sins to the boy, and now it's Michael's own mother who is keeping Walt away from him. Worse, she's acting on Walt's decision.

All Michael's lived for is Walt. He tries to give a good life to Walt. He wants to always be available should Walt need him. And now that Walt is irrevocably out of his life, he has nothing to live for. Desmond tells Penny in "Live Together, Die Alone," that he's trying to get his honor back. Similarly, Michael is searching for redemption; not for himself, but so that Walt can think of his father after his father is dead and not despise him. He sold his soul to the devil, and now he'll do anything to get it back.

The Michael story strayed from the more exciting plotline of Ben, the freighter folk, the non-rescue, and what was about to happen on the island. The parts of the episode that take place in New Otherton rehash information we already knew, as even Miles is aware that Ben is playing everyone, much to Locke's chagrin. Ben reveals some useless information to the group (that the freighter folk are looking for him) and to the viewer (that Michael is the man on the boat). One of the more interesting parts of the episode is when Tom tells Michael about the elaborate cover-up Widmore staged for the fake Flight 815. Fans had been wondering how exactly Widmore (or whomever staged it) had come up with the 324 dead bodies. While digging up 324 graves seems pretty nefarious, it's the lesser of two evils when the other option is killing 324 people. Tom's assertion in this episode turns the whodunit story into a "he said, he said" argument. Gault suggests that Ben is the man behind the cover-up, where Tom says it's Widmore.

The single most important revelation of this episode is Tom's assertion that if someone has a task to complete on the island, the island won't let them die. This not only explains why Michael couldn't kill himself, but why Locke has healed so many times, why Ben can take horrible beatings and keep on walking, and why several other key characters have survived what they did, including a horrific plane crash. (It also makes the victims seem like people the island didn't need.)

What makes this episode stand out, however, is the brilliant performance of Harold Perrineau. Many of the scenes have no dialogue, so Perrineau has to silently carry them out, registering all emotion in his face. The entire opening with Michael attempting to kill himself in a car crash is done with virtually no words, as is the scene with him on the bed with the gun, and him alone in his berth with Ben's "bomb." We see him hopeful when he goes to his mother's house to see Walt, desperate when he points Tom's gun at his own head and begs him to pull the trigger, casual when he's first meeting the crew of the *Kahana*, terrified as he attempts to set off Ben's bomb, guilty as he hears Libby's voice tell him not to do it, and utterly defeated when he realizes it's Ben's voice on the other end of the phone, not Walt's. Perrineau's performance in this episode is one of the best of the series, as he displays the agony and desperation a parent feels when they want to do right by their child.

Which brings us to the episode's cliffhanger. Fans finally get their wish and see Rousseau profess her undying love to Alex . . . and then she appears to be shot. Is she really dead? ABC ran previews before this episode, saying, "Someone. Will. Die!!!" in melodramatic overtones. It would seem a little anticlimactic if that someone turned out to be Karl (no offense, Karl). But to kill Rousseau would deny fans that long-awaited Rousseau flashback we've been promised since season 2, something that is undoubtedly integral to the series. Rousseau is the one truly independent character on the island — she's not affiliated with the survivors, with Dharma, or with the Others. She managed to give birth on the island without dying, showing the Others that women die only if they conceive on the island. Her daughter is her link to the Others. But there seems to be so much more to her. Here's hoping that what hit her was a tranquilizer dart; or if it did kill her, that we are still granted that flashback in some way.

Highlight: Hurley once again becomes the mouthpiece for the fans when Miles points out that the freighter folk are here for Ben, and Hurley replies, "Uh, we kinda like, knew that forever ago."

Timeline: Locke holds a meeting in the barracks on Night 96, which is December 26, 2004. The next day, Rousseau, Karl, and Alex are surrounded by snipers in the jungle.

Did You Notice?:

- Several background characters on the island followed Locke when he split away from Jack, yet they weren't in the room when Locke came clean to "everyone."

- Sawyer's line about which "Michael" Ben was talking about seemed to be there to catch up all the viewers who have somehow forgotten who Michael actually was.
- Michael kept his hood up like Charlie used to do whenever he was taking drugs.
- The Temple is marked as a Dharma station on Ben's map. It's the same place he told Richard Alpert to take the Others at the end of season 3.
- When Michael dreams that he sees Libby, she's bringing him extra blankets. That's what Libby was holding in her arms when Michael shot her.
- When Michael wakes up from his dream, the hospital room is the same but has some differences — the man beside him has an oxygen mask on and the equipment is different.
- Malcolm David Kelley said in a television interview that the kid standing in the window was definitely played by him, but because he answers the question hesitantly, as if he's been told to say that, some fans believe it was not him. A close-up of the child shows that he looks like season 1 Walt (see http://lost.cubit.net/archives/4x08_WaltReturns1.php). Kelley was almost 16 when this scene would have been filmed, which would have made it difficult for him to portray a 10-year-old.
- The pawnbroker who takes Michael's watch is William P. Ogilvie, who also appeared in the season 3 episode, "Left Behind." In the scene where Cassidy is trying to sell necklaces at the gas station, Ogilvie is the man who threatens to call the police.
- When Michael tries to shoot himself in his apartment, there's an old game show on the television and a woman correctly answers the question, "Who is the author of *Slaughterhouse-Five*?" (See page 69.) The host says she'll make triple the points if she can name the book's protagonist, but the news bulletin cuts in before we see if she can.
- In season 3 Tom tells Kate she's not his type, and I asked in my book, "Is he gay?" And sure enough . . . he is.
- If you look closely at the records for the 777 plane, Widmore's "shell company" is Widmore Industries. Not exactly incognito there, Chuck.
- The passport for Kevin Johnson has Michael grinning on it, which would appear to be wrong, but the issue date is 1999, a time when people were still allowed to smile in passport photos. Also, if you look closely, you'll see Kevin Johnson's passport number is the same as Ben's fake one that we saw

in "The Economist." Maybe Ben has a loophole in the airports where he can always get through using this number? (Or perhaps the prop department just used the same template.)

- Michael immediately recognizes Naomi's Mancunian accent, probably because it's so similar to Charlie's.
- Creepy Miles is eating an orange when he first meets Michael, just like Creepy Locke was eating an orange on the beach when we first encountered him.
- Minkowski references *The Shining*, yet another in a long line of Stephen King allusions on the show.
- Ben tells Michael in his wonderfully self-righteous way that he'll do what he has to do but he won't kill innocent people. He seems to have conveniently forgotten about his role in the Purge — or he didn't regard members of the Dharma Initiative as innocent.
- Ben tells Michael to consider himself one of the good guys. In Ben's world, that's akin to welcoming him to the Others.
- Sayid goes ballistic on Michael when he finds out he's working for Ben . . . some major dramatic irony given Sayid's future.
- When Sayid tells the captain everything about Michael, Gault has a look on his face like he already knew.

Interesting Facts: Tom says he'll be at the penthouse of the Hotel Earle. This is the name of the hotel in the Coen Brothers film *Barton Fink*, where Barton goes to write a screenplay, deals with writer's block, and then somehow encounters a serial killer and begins to go mad himself. By the end of the film, the Hotel Earle has become Hell. A fitting place for Tom to be staying (in the penthouse, no less). Also, right before Karl is shot, he says, "I've got a bad feeling about this." This line is spoken in every *Star Wars* movie (in some cases, more than once), to the point where it's become a running joke. Now it's pretty much mandatory to insert it in everything related to *Star Wars*, and it's been spoken in dozens of *Star Wars* comics, novelizations, and cartoons.

Nitpicks: There may be a problem with the timing of the flashback, but it's possible to explain it away, which is why it's a nitpick and not a blooper. Michael and Walt leave the island on November 27, according to the Lostpedia timeline. Considering they're in a small boat, probably in the South Pacific, it would have taken more than a couple of days to get back to Manhattan. (Not to mention, how did they manage to do it covertly? How did they enter the country without

The *Kahana* docked at the Port of Suva in Fiji, where Michael boards it along with the rest of the freighter folk. (RYAN OZAWA)

showing a passport or saying who they were?) At Michael's mother's house, there are Christmas decorations, so it's December by that point. In season 3, we saw Tom in "The Man from Tallahassee" when he comes to talk to Ben in his bedroom (that episode occurs on December 11), and then we don't see him again until "The Man Behind the Curtain," when he's in Ben's camp as Locke walks into it (that episode is December 21), so presumably that was when he was off the island. Naomi is found on the island on December 17. So Tom could have left the island on December 11 (and knowing the island, he could have teleported) and immediately contacted Michael. He tells Michael the *Kahana* will be docking in Fiji in two days, then tells him to wait a couple of days until the boat is out at sea before setting off the bomb. Even if Tom somehow managed to get to Michael on December 12, the boat would have docked on December 14, probably would have left on December 15, and by the time they're two days out, Naomi has already been found on the island. Keamy does say in "The Constant" that they're close to Fiji, so maybe it wasn't a couple of days out, though we see Michael on the freighter for some time before he finally decides to detonate the bomb.

The other timing issue occurs when Michael sees the breaking news of the discovery of Flight 815. If he sees that news program on December 12 or 13, that's the same time Daniel, Charlotte, Miles, and Frank would have heard about it. Wouldn't they have found out about it much earlier than two days before getting on that boat? What Michael sees is "breaking news," meaning it's brand new, and Daniel and Frank saw it on the television at the same time as Michael. Miles heard it on the radio, and Charlotte read about it (which means she would have been reading it the day after). How quickly was Abaddon able to assemble this team? Did they get absolutely no notice before they were whisked away to the freighter?

Also, we see one large chopper on the deck of the freighter when the boat leaves its port. Just before Frank comes over to chat with Michael on the deck of the freighter, we see him arguing with Naomi about piloting the helicopter to the island, and she says she's going to the island first, and makes it sound like she'll be piloting it herself. But if she ejected from the chopper and it crashed into the ocean, where did they get a second chopper for Frank and the other three Losties to take to the island? Is there another chopper hidden on the freighter somewhere?

Finally, if Widmore had really dug up 324 bodies in a Thailand cemetery, wouldn't *that* have made the news? And wouldn't he have had to have found 324 bodies in similar states of decomposition? Digging up plots next to each other wouldn't have done that — some bodies would have been skeletons, some would

Downtown Honolulu dresses up to look like New York City for Michael's flashback. (JOEL ALPERN)

have been in advanced stages of decomposition, some would have been newly buried, and some would have been dust.

Oops: The last two letters of the name of the freighter, the *Kahana*, is scratched out in this episode, yet the name is painted on clearly in earlier episodes (in case you think someone went mad on board and began scratching out letters, they're also scratched out when it's docked near Fiji on the port side of the boat). Also, if a sniper bullet hit Karl's water container, it would have gone right through and we would have seen water spouting out of both sides of his water container, not just one. Finally, when Alex is sitting over Karl's dead body, you can see an earplug in his ear, which was probably put there to protect his ears during the gunshots.

4 8 15 16 23 42: Michael tries to kill himself **4** times in this episode (once in the car, once in the alley, once in his apartment, and once on the ship with the bomb). The code to "detonate" the bomb is 71776, which is divisible by **4**, **8**, and **16**.

It's Just a Flesh Wound: Captain Gault beats the snot out of two of his crew members. Sayid slams Michael against some pipes and twists his arm hard behind his back. Karl is shot and killed, and Rousseau is shot.

Lost in Translation: According to Lostpedia, the Korean inscriptions on the back of Michael's watch (which he'd acquired in "House of the Rising Sun," not realizing at first that it was Jin's) translate as "congratulations," "mutual cooperation," "business transaction," and "Mr. Paik."

Any Questions?:

• In "Through the Looking Glass," we see in the flashforward that Jack is standing on a bridge, about to jump, when a car accident happens behind him. Did the island cause that accident so he wouldn't jump? Is Jack needed, too?

- Sawyer finds out somehow that Miles asked Ben for money. Who told him? Ben?

- When Ben is glaring at Alex and Karl, Alex has her hand on her belly while Karl seems to be putting his hands on her tenderly . . . could she be pregnant? Or was the scene merely showing us Ben's greatest fear?

- Could the Temple be the place with the four-toed statue? Ben says the Temple isn't for "them," meaning the survivors, it's only for "us," meaning the Others. Why is that? Is he telling the truth?

- Michael sends the mechanic working with him off to get a pressure valve when Sayid shows up, and then he says to Sayid that the guy will be back really soon. So are we to assume Sayid got a very truncated version of the story we just saw? "So . . . uh . . . I made it back to New York and then Tom showed up and recruited me to come here, and I just have to screw around with the engine every once in a while and then talk to Ben a bit. I might have attempted suicide a couple of times. So how's Sun doin'?" If we saw all the details, but Sayid got a shortened version of the story, it would help explain why Sayid is so unsympathetic to Michael.

- How did Michael not go through the windshield if he wasn't wearing a seatbelt? Can the island defy physics?

- How did Tom get to New York from the island?

- Tom says they've been keeping tabs on Michael. How? With what resources? Is Jacob all-seeing and reporting back Michael's whereabouts?

- How is it that the island won't let Michael kill himself? Is this true? Notice that when it looked like Locke was going to die in "Through the Looking Glass," Walt appeared to him and told him he still had work to do, just like Tom tells Michael here.

- Did Widmore really stage the fake Flight 815? It wouldn't be hard for the Others to generate a fake photo to show Michael (after all, the prop department managed to do it).

- How did Miles know Michael was lying? Was it just a hunch or did he know for sure?

- Why does Keamy and crew have such heavy weaponry? (And why are they wasting so many of their limited number of bullets?)

- Why did Ben give Michael a fake bomb? If he really believes these people are coming to torch the island, why not let Michael get rid of all of them and nothing more would have happened? Why have him instead compile lists, disable engine and communications rooms, and risk letting these people onto the island anyway?
- Who was shooting at Rousseau and company at the end? Did Ben recruit someone to do it? Was it Keamy and crew using sniper rifles?
- Is Rousseau really dead or was she shot with a tranquilizer dart? You can see a bullet hole in Karl that goes right through him, whereas we don't see a similar mark on Rousseau.

Ashes to Ashes: Karl was an Other who was in love with Alex, Ben's adopted daughter. He enjoyed being in love with Alex, and his dislikes included being strapped to a chair while a sensory overload plays around him. He was known to spout strange non sequiturs like "God loves me as He loves Jacob." It is unclear how, why, or when he came to the island. He was shot and killed while trying to get to a place of refuge with Alex and her birth mother, Rousseau.

Music/Bands: When Michael attempts suicide in the car he's listening to "It's Getting Better" by Mama Cass Elliot. When season 2 opened, Desmond was listening to Mama Cass's "Make Your Own Kind of Music."

The 2007–2008 Writers' Strike

When ABC announced in March 2007 that *Lost* would officially have 48 episodes left, spread over three seasons running without breaks from February to May, fans hoped this new plan would put an end to the long hiatuses that broke up the momentum of the show. Everything seemed to be going perfectly well in fall 2007, as *Lost*'s production was in full swing and episodes were being finished and readied for their February premiere. And then . . . the Writers Guild of America reached an impasse in its negotiations with the studios, and called a strike, which began on November 5, 2008.

The reasons for the strike were simple: in the 1980s, the writers had been asked to take an 80 percent pay cut on residuals for VHS tapes to try to boost the home movie market. Writers agreed to it with the understanding that once that market

The Writers' Strike generated a lot of support within the arts community. Both Damon and Carlton took to the picket lines with their colleagues. (AP PHOTO/REED SAXON, FILE)

was booming (which it soon was) they would be given the money back. At the time of the pay cut the cost of a movie was between $40 and $100, but by the 1990s, home movies could cost less than $10, and that percentage writers now received was next to nothing. With the advent of DVDs, the residuals weren't renegotiated, and writers were simply given the same small percentage. But in the early 2000s, a new medium reared its futuristic head: the Internet. Between television shows for sale on iTunes and various sites streaming video off the network, studios were figuring out ways to get their shows directly to the Internet generation.

The problem was the writers weren't seeing any of the money generated by these media. The networks instead argued that the streaming video and iTunes sales were purely promotional, despite the fact they got $1.99 for every iTunes download and sold advertising with the streaming videos. With the advent of DVRs and TiVo, which rendered commercials — and in the near future, possibly television itself — obsolete, it appeared that more television was going to move onto computers and away from the traditional medium. If that were to happen, writers wouldn't get paid for their work at all. As Damon Lindelof wrote at the time, "[Cutting out commercials] probably sounds exciting if you're a TV viewer, but if you're in the business of producing these shows, it's nothing short of terrifying. This is how vaudevillians must have felt the first time they saw a silent movie; sitting there, suddenly realizing they just became extinct: after all, who wants another soft-shoe number when you can see Harold Lloyd hanging off a clock 50 feet tall?"

What writers asked for was an increase in the percentage of residuals they would make, from the current 2.5 percent (or 4¢ on every $20 the studios made) to 5% (8¢ on every $20). When the studios refused to budge, the writers went on strike, a month into the new 2007–2008 television season. The result was devastating to the television industry. Talk shows ceased production immediately. Network television ran through what had already been filmed and was ready to show, and after a few weeks, they had run out of new material and started broadcasting reruns. Reality television was everywhere. The brand new shows that had found an audience — like *Pushing Daisies, Dirty Sexy Money, Chuck, Reaper, Life, Journeyman* — were halted, and the word quickly came down that they'd be pulled for the remainder of the season and would start up again in fall 2008.

Soon after the strike had started, however, all eyes turned to *Lost.* Its fourth season hadn't yet begun. Damon Lindelof and Carlton Cuse said they had eight finished episodes, and the eighth one — "Meet Kevin Johnson" — would end on a small cliffhanger, but it certainly was not the stuff of a season finale. If the strike ended quickly, they'd be able to continue the season, possibly without interruption. But a few weeks into the strike, people were anticipating it would last three months or even longer. Carlton Cuse was part of the WGA negotiation committee, so his time was spent on the committee and away from *Lost.* Gregg Nations, writer and script coordinator on *Lost,* posted on the Fuselage in October that "if there is a strike, we will shut down immediately. Carlton is on the negotiating committee for the WGA, and there is no way that any of the writers would cross a picket line. We will not bank episodes or scripts. Depending on how many episodes are completed before a strike were to happen, it would be up to ABC to decide how to air them." How ABC would air them became the big question. Rumors began circulating that ABC was going to run the eight episodes and let them stand as the fourth season. There was also talk of pulling the season completely and starting season 4 in January 2009 instead of 2008. Both options had the potential of being disasters.

Damon Lindelof wrote an op-ed column in the *New York Times* where he explained why he was on strike and why he would continue to strike:

I am angry because I am accused of being greedy by studios that are being greedy. I am angry because my greed is fair and reasonable: if money is made off of my product through the Internet, then I am entitled to a small piece. The studios' greed, on the other hand, is hidden behind cynical, disingenuous claims that they make nothing on the Web — that the streaming and downloading of our shows is purely "promotional." Seriously?

At the time, audiences were generally supportive of the WGA's position, even if they didn't exactly understand it. But Lindelof worried how long that support would last. "Public sentiment may have swung toward the guild for now," he wrote, "but once the viewing audience has spent a month or so subsisting on *America's Next Hottest Cop* and *Celebrity Eating Contest*, I have little doubt that the tide will turn against us."

By late January, he was right. Some television fans began shouting for the writers to get back to work, suggesting they were whiners who were already being paid gobs of money (these outspoken folks weren't considering the 48 percent of the WGA that were unemployed at the time of the strike). When the Golden Globes were canceled, NBC co-chairman complained to E!'s Ryan Seacrest, "Sadly, it feels like the nerdiest, ugliest, meanest kids in the high school are trying to cancel the prom. But NBC wants to try to keep that prom alive." (I am not making that quotation up.) Newspaper columnists began making impassioned pleas on behalf of the writers, explaining to the public that the actors, crew, publicists, and caterers wouldn't have jobs if the writers weren't writing scripts. Many were glad the Golden Globes were canceled, because it showed how much Hollywood depended on these people to keep things going. "The writers are asking for the equivalent of a freaking cup of coffee," wrote Joanna Schneller of the *Globe and Mail.* "Give them this fraction of their due."

ABC had made the decision to begin airing the episodes of *Lost* that were finished, and fans crossed their fingers that the season wouldn't be halved. By the beginning of February, there was word that a deal had been reached, and on February 11, the writers voted to end the strike. After some discussion, Damon and Carlton announced on February 12 that *Lost's* fourth season would be extended to 13 episodes, and shortly after they said the finale would be two hours long, which would give them 14 hours. The remaining two hours would be rolled into the next two seasons, which would now be 17 episodes each.

In the end, the writers got a slightly fairer deal while showing the world just how dependent Hollywood was on them. Television returned to normal, even though some shows didn't fare as well in their post-strike lives. But because by February most other shows were off the air and writers were now scrambling to come up with new material, it meant *Lost* was one of the few shows airing first-run episodes (when the strike ended, *Lost* had just aired the second episode of the season). More viewers tuned in than in the previous season, and they stuck around after the hiatus. And it's a good thing they did, because the final six hours of the season were incredible.

4.9   The Shape of Things to Come

Original air date: April 24, 2008
Written by: Brian K. Vaughan, Drew Goddard
Directed by: Jack Bender
Guest cast: Faran Tahir (Ishmael Bakir), Yetide Badaki (Tunisian Desk Clerk), Nick Hermz (Bedouin #1), Sean Douglas Hoban (Doug), Kaveh Kardan (Iraqi Merchant), Michael Sadler (London Doorman), Sammy Sheik (Bedouin #2)

Flash: Ben

Keamy and his men invade New Otherton, and when Widmore "changes the rules" on Ben, things get ugly. Ben's flashforward explains some old alliances, introduces new ones, and raises even more questions.

If "Meet Kevin Johnson" was a slightly disappointing episode to end on before the forced hiatus, the writers make up for it with the brilliant "The Shape of Things to Come." This episode and "The Constant" have probably sparked more discussion than all other episodes this season combined. This episode had everything: action, drama, and intrigue.

First, the action. Sawyer fans everywhere emitted squees of delight as he dashed across the lawns to save Claire amid a hail of gunfire, then swooped her up in his arms and ran back over to the house. *Swoon . . .* (We decided to look past the typical Hollywood ridiculousness of everyone else getting shot with a single bullet, yet Sawyer escapes unharmed amid dozens of them.) But the Sawyer scene was quickly outstripped by the awesome return of Old Smokey, who hurtles into the camp like a gigantic angry pit bull to exact some serious revenge.

Without a doubt, it was the most amazing visual effect of the season. Ben says he knows nothing about the smoke monster, but we saw Ben enter an underground lair covered in hieroglyphics, and the next thing you know, the smoke monster screams its way into New Otherton, taking out everything in its path. Does Ben actually control it or did he just feel it coming?

Darlton have said that with every appearance of the smoke monster, we learn more about it. In the case of the believers, like Eko and Locke, it first showed itself to them as a harmless thing before returning and attacking them. It allowed itself to be seen by Charlie, also a religious type. It can be scared away by sudden attacks like dynamite or the sonar fence, yet in this episode it runs headlong into battle and isn't scared off by the machine guns. It appears to be called forth by someone, as it clearly was here, but does it ever act of its own accord? What about when it chased Juliet and Kate? Did it kill Eko for its own reasons, or did someone else tell it to?

If you were looking for a little sadness to go with the action, look no further: this episode had it in spades. First, we discover that not only did Sayid manage to find Nadia after his rescue, but he will marry her and then lose her, all within a year. We've watched Sayid pine for Nadia his entire time on the island, and knowing that, after everything he's gone through while searching for her, she will be killed so soon after their reunion is devastating. Now it's clear why he seems a shell of his former self in "The Economist." Just as with "Through the Looking Glass," we're once again reminded of how depressing the future will be. On the island, Sayid at least has hope: hope that he'll be rescued, hope that he'll find Nadia. But now, everything is gone. He's alone, the love of his life is dead, and he's a murderer. After the redemption he got on the island when he realized he no longer wanted to be the man he used to be, we see that he has become even worse.

We didn't actually see Sayid's discovery of his wife's murder, and can only imagine what his reaction must have been. But we do see Ben lose Alex in this episode, and it's heartbreaking. Ben is a consummate liar, and sincerity is something that usually eludes him. He's excellent at lying, and because of what we know about him, it's hard to trust him. Despite everything, though, he truly loved Alex. Alex was probably the only person he ever cared about in his adult life, and to watch her die is earth-shattering for him. The moment is made worse because the last words she heard him say were that she means nothing to him. It's one thing to lose your daughter; it's quite another to have her die hating you. Michael Emerson has always been a marvelous actor in this series, but he outdoes himself as he stands at the window, rendered immobile and speechless as his dead daughter lies on the lawn outside. As he drops down to her side shortly after and bends over to kiss her, there is no doubt we are seeing Ben in a rare moment of genuine emotion. There's no cover-up, no lies. His world has imploded.

Which leads us to the best parts of the episode: the intrigue. On the beach, the doctor's body washes ashore, but the freighter folk are acting like nothing happened. Jack is almost doubled over in pain from a stomach bug, but it seems to be far more serious than what he's letting on. Could the two doctors be linked?

While the beach mysteries keep us linked to the freighter, nothing compares to the flashforwards in this episode, which are baffling. Ben awakes in the Saharan desert wearing a winter parka, and it's almost a year in the future. He uses Sayid's desire for revenge to recruit him as a hitman. The circumstances of how he got to Tunisia, why he's been there before, and why he's dressed the way he is are not explained in the episode (but will become a little clearer by the end of the season; see page 182 for a more elaborate explanation of the flashback in this episode). But the most intriguing moment of the flashback is Ben's showdown with Widmore. So far we know that Captain Gault believes (or wants Sayid to believe) that Widmore is the man who owns the freighter, and Ben also knows Widmore is the man with the freighter. What we discover in this episode is that Ben and Widmore appear to be mortal (or immortal) enemies.

In this episode, we discover Charles Widmore (Alan Dale) is a lot more than just an angry potential father-in-law: he could be part of the key to the whole mystery. (TEAR TAN/SHOOTING STAR)

The face-off between Ben and Widmore never gets boring, no matter how many times you watch it. There have been many references to chess in this series (see page 187), but this scene suggests the entire series might be one elaborate chess game, and Widmore and Ben are the two players. In fact, the scene requires a close analysis.

Ben asks Charles when he started keeping scotch by the bed, and Charles says it coincided with when the nightmares started. He asks Ben if he's here to kill him, and Ben replies, "We both know I can't do that." Does he mean he *won't* do it, or he can't physically do it? Is Widmore immortal? Are they both immortal? Or as we learned in "Meet Kevin Johnson," could the island have greater plans for both of these men, so they can't be killed?

It's easy for us to watch this scene as if Ben is the victim and Widmore is the bad guy. We just saw Alex murdered execution-style in front of Ben, and Widmore has always treated Desmond like dirt. Widmore hisses at Ben in this scene, calling him "boy" in a condescending way, and ignores Ben's feelings of grief over the loss of his daughter. But try watching this scene as if Ben is pure evil, and Widmore is the victim. First, you can't help but notice that Ben is dressed all in black, with one side of his face completely swallowed up by the darkness, and the other side lit up in blue. Widmore is wearing white, with one half of his face bathed in light and the other half in shadows. Both men take on a Janus-like appearance if we look purely at the mise-en-scène.

When Ben says Widmore murdered his daughter, Widmore replies that they both know he did nothing of the sort, and that Ben was the one who killed her. He also refers to her as "that poor girl" and not "your daughter," as if suggesting that because Alex is not Ben's biological daughter Ben is putting on a show and Alex never did mean anything to him (*that* part I cannot believe). Ben maintains that it isn't true that he killed Alex, and Widmore repeats, "Yes, Benjamin, it is." He asks Ben how he has the nerve to pretend he's the victim, and then says, "I know who you are, boy." His sneering use of the term "boy" could stem from their different classes: Widmore comes from a higher class, either within British society or within the ranks of Otherdom, and he sees Ben as a lower-class peon. But it could also be an indication that Widmore is older than we think, and he knew Ben as a boy and Ben will always be such to him. (Perhaps Widmore's obsession with the *Black Rock* is because he was originally on it?) Again, Widmore says, "I know who you are, boy. What you are. I know that everything you have you took from me." Notice Widmore says he knows *what* Ben is, as if Ben is something other than human. And Widmore adds that Ben took everything from him, as if the island was his and Ben usurped him in some way. Ben replies that he's going to kill Penny, so that Widmore will know how he feels, and will regret that he'd "changed the rules." Widmore barely blinks.

If this isn't a signal to what's next to come, I don't know what is. I'm just hoping we get many more scenes with these two actors, because they are riveting to watch together.

Highlight: Super Sawyer. Between saving Claire and threatening Locke if he touches a hair on Hurley's head, Sawyer has come a long way from the dismissive self-centered pariah he was in season 1.

Timeline: Technically, it's Day 97 on the island, or December 27, 2004. But considering the freighter-doctor situation, time seems to be relative here.

Did You Notice?:

- In "Through the Looking Glass," Ben tells Jack that Naomi is with the people who work for a man who is trying to find the island. Now we know he was telling the truth, and because of his obvious history with Widmore, we understand why he was so adamant that Jack not make that phone call.

- In "The Economist" Sayid says the day he works for Ben Linus is the day he sells his soul. Apparently his soul was Nadia.

- Jack joking with Kate that he wrote his own prescription foreshadows what we saw in "Through the Looking Glass," where he attempts to write a prescription using his father's pad.

- Vincent, the dog of death, is once again at the scene when Ray's body washes ashore.

- The doctor has huge Frankenstein-like stitches on his face, yet in "Meet Kevin Johnson," the gash on his cheek was just a serious cut.

- Hurley, playing Risk, says Australia is the key to the whole game. Considering Flight 815 took off from Sydney, he seems to be commenting on the "game" that's being played on the island, with them as the pieces.

- When Keamy is holding Alex up to the sonar fence and telling her to enter the code, she begs for them to be careful because there's a baby in New Otherton. This line proves that Alex was never like the rest of the Others. Apparently the writers believe in Nature over Nurture.

- When Ben awakens in the Saharan desert, you can see a puff of steam blow out of his mouth, as if he had just exhaled cold air. The parka he's wearing had a Dharma symbol on it (Darlton referred to it as a "Dharka" leading up to the episode) and it says "Halliwax" under the symbol. In the Orchid orientation video (see page 3), Dr. Marvin Candle refers to himself as Dr. Edgar Halliwax.

- When the camera first shows Ben lying in the desert, he is lying in the same position as Jack was in the pilot when he first woke up after the crash, and the way we've often seen Locke flat on his back, most recently after Ben had shot him.
- We *finally* get a calendar date on one of the flashforwards: October 24, 2005. That's 10 months after the events we're watching now.
- When Daniel says he could construct a telegraph with strips of metal, a 9-volt battery clip, and some wiring he sounds like the Professor on *Gilligan's Island*. I suppose next he'll be making nuclear bombs out of coconuts and mangoes.
- The third redshirt to be killed by the hail of gunfire was actually wearing a red shirt. Ha!
- Sayid brings Nadia back to Tikrit to bury her. In an earlier episode he says he was born in Tikrit. Incidentally, it is the same city Saddam Hussein was born in.
- Ben tells Sayid that Bakir was seen speeding away from the corner of LaBrea and Santa Monica. In "The Beginning of the End," Hurley's car chase began at LaBrea.
- Miles holds up the walkie and says he was sent to them by "the people who gave me this," but doesn't say they're "his people," clearly because, at this point, he wants to distance himself from them.
- When Ben re-emerges from the hidden chamber, he is covered in soot, and the bruises on his face are faded, as if some time had passed while he was gone. Did he time travel to summon the smoke monster?
- When Smokey comes hurtling into the village, it looks like there's a face at the front of the plume. There are flashes within the "body" of Smokey, but it's too far away to actually see if they are images or just flashes of electro-magnetic static.
- Jack's resentment when he realizes the freighter folk were never planning to rescue them seems to be less about the fact they're not getting rescued than the fact that Locke was right.
- The bottle of scotch beside Widmore's bed is MacCutcheon whisky, the same drink he refused to offer Desmond in "Flashes Before Your Eyes."

Interesting Facts: The man Sayid kills is named Ishmael Bakir. Ishmael is the name of the main character in *Moby Dick*, who begins as an important character involved in the action, and eventually becomes a narrator who's not really part of it. Ishmael is also the name of one of Abraham's sons, and is the dividing point between Islam and Judeo-Christian religions: Muslims believe that Ishmael was Abraham's eldest son and therefore the true heir, while the Jewish religion believes Isaac to be the true heir.

The current Tunisian national anthem is based on a poem by Aboul-Qacem Echebbi, a poet who was born in Tozeur, where Ben's hotel is located. The lines of the poem that have been adapted to the anthem are filled with revenge and bloodlust for the hardships that have been done to the people. Considering Ben preys on Sayid's desire for revenge, it's appropriate that Ben was in Tozeur. The poem refers to the enemy as "lovers of the darkness" (light and dark are common themes on *Lost*), and says "Beware because there is a fire underneath the ash," which is interesting, because there is a ring of ash that encircles Jacob's cabin.

The scenes in London where Ben visits Widmore were actually filmed in London. Alan Dale, who plays Charles Widmore, was appearing onstage in *Spamalot* and couldn't leave to film the scenes, so the show came to him.

Find815: "Morse code" was a clue in the game.

Oops: During the shootout scene, Sawyer runs toward a barbecue that is standing upright, but when he reaches it, it's been flipped over onto its side. Ben's hidden room has a different layout in "The Economist" than it does in this episode. When Sayid enters it in "The Economist" and stops at Ben's desk, you can see a built-in shelving unit beside him, and beside that is more shelving that holds binders and suitcases. In this episode, the rack of suits is beside the built-in shelving. Also, where the trapdoor came down locking Sawyer out, there's just plain drywall in the previous episode, and not any indication there's an extra door.

4 8 15 16 23 42: On Sawyer's second roll of the dice, he rolls a **15**. The code on the sonar fence is **1623**. The date in Ben's flashforward is October 24 (reverse **42**). Sayid says he searched for Nadia for **8** years. The license plate on the taxicab that Ben rides in is R8**38** VLW. Ben tells the concierge that he's here to see Mr. and Mrs. Kendrick in **4**E.

It's Just a Flesh Wound: Claire suffers a concussion when her house explodes. Three survivors are killed by gunfire. Alex is killed with a single gunshot to the back of the head. Keamy and his fellow psychos are attacked by the smoke monster. Jack has a stomach condition. Daniel is manhandled menacingly.

Lost in Translation: When Ben first encounters the Bedouins, he first asks in Arabic if they speak Arabic, then in Turkish he asks if they speak Turkish. In

Arabic, they say to each other, "Look! There are no footprints around him!" and "Where did he come from? Did he fall from the sky?" When Ben enters the underground chamber, the ancient-looking door to the chamber has hieroglyphics on it that read, roughly translated, "to summon protection." That would seem to suggest he really did call Smokey.

Any Questions?:

- In "The Constant," we saw Widmore buy the journal of the first mate on the *Black Rock* in 1996, which means he's been trying to get back to the island at least since then. Did he figure out rough coordinates based on the first mate's description of the journey and then send Desmond out as a guinea pig in 2001 to try to locate the island?

- How could Ray be dead on the island, but alive and well on the freighter (assuming the message Dan receives is true)? It would make sense if, for example, he was dead on the freighter but got caught in the wormhole and took three years to wash up, showing signs of having been killed only the day before. But for his body to be found before the actual event occurs? If this isn't a testament to fate winning out over free will, I don't know what is.

- No one on the island ever seems to get sick — no colds, no flus — so what is the significance of Jack's "stomach bug"? What's wrong with him? Are we meant to assume some sort of connection between the freighter doctor dying and Jack feeling ill?

- How did Ben end up where he was? He's shaky and disoriented, wearing a thick coat, and cold air is coming out of his mouth. Is it possible he teleported to the desert? Could there be wormholes on the island and he knows how to slip through them to certain points in the world? Is he traveling normally in 2005, or did he also time travel? It would appear he has time traveled, since he had to check what year it was.

- Why do the Others seem to have super-strength? We see Tom overpower Michael easily in the alleyway in "Meet Kevin Johnson," and Ethan fought like a superhuman. Juliet has the strength to take out Kate easily when Kate tries to hit her in "Left Behind." And we've seen Ben on numerous occasions act with superhuman strength. Does it have something to do with their longevity on the island? Is there something in the Dharma fish-biscuits?

- How did Jack know that Bernard knew Morse code? He pulls him aside to ask him something as Dan is working on the telegraph machine, and he's

Once again, Hawaii stands in for another nation. Top left: The crew brilliantly dressed up the back gravel lot of the Honolulu Community College, and used the backdrop of a low-rise apartment building that was slated for demolition. The market was constructed against the apartments by the crew. Top right: The extras hang around on the set before appearing as the mourners following Nadia's casket. Bottom left: The Tikrit bar where Ben tails Omar was built inside a utility room or cooling annex on the lot. Bottom right: Michael Emerson is directed as he shoots the camera scene (and that is not actually Lapidus standing behind him, but a crew member who looks remarkably like him). (RYAN OZAWA)

clearly instructing him to listen to the code and tell him what it really means.

- The freighter folk shoot every single person who runs outside near Sawyer. Yet despite Sawyer running around in broad sight, they don't kill him with a single one of the dozens of bullets that come flying at him. Were they missing on purpose? A similar scene happened in "Not in Portland," when Sawyer and Kate were running through the jungle with Alex and Karl. Danny and other Others are chasing them and shooting several bullets in Sawyer's direction, but none of them hit him. Is the island keeping him safe?
- How did Claire survive that explosion? Is it possible the island has work for her to do, too, and it won't let her die?
- What was Ben previously doing in Tunisia? Could his repeated visits to the same remote place support the wormhole theory?
- Is there a link between Ben waking up in the Tunisian desert and Charlotte finding a polar bear in the desert near Tunisia wearing the Dharma collar?
- Why does the woman at the Tunisian hotel pause when she sees Ben's name in the register?
- How were Nadia and Sayid reunited? Why was she murdered?
- Were Sayid's parents at the funeral? He doesn't seem to have any emotional ties beyond Nadia herself.
- What made Sayid look up to see Ben taking his picture? Could he feel the presence of the island nearby?
- What was Keamy doing as a mercenary in Uganda?
- In "The Economist," Avellino tells Sayid that a wager makes everything more fun. Could Widmore and Ben have made a wager years ago and it's gotten out of hand? Are they playing a game and using other people as pawns?
- What does Ben mean when he says Widmore changed the rules? What were the rules? Ben seems so confident in everything he does, and always seems to anticipate how other people will react to what he does, yet Alex's death catches him off guard in a way we've never seen. Is it possible he time travels so often that he actually lives moments over and over, and he's lived through this one before and knows that Alex is supposed to survive?
- As Ben walks away from Sayid, he smirks. Was it all a setup? Did Nadia simply die because some random thief killed her in an alleyway and Ben saw his opportunity and took it, or did Widmore legitimately have anything to do with this?

- What did the person on the freighter mean by, "the doctor is fine"? Is he fine? Is it a lie? Are there two different time periods overlapping now, with the doctor simultaneously being fine on the freighter but dead on the island?
- In "The Beginning of the End," Hurley tells Jack in the flashforward that he never should have gone with Locke. Did he mean it was a mistake to have followed Locke in the first place, or it was a mistake to have gone with him later? Presumably, the worst is yet to come.
- Widmore says he's been drinking whisky since the nightmares started. Nightmares about what?
- Is Penelope on Sayid's hit list, or is Ben keeping her death for himself?

Ashes to Ashes: Alexandra Linus lived a life of constant uprooting. She was stolen from her birth mother, Danielle Rousseau, when she was only two weeks old, and was raised by Benjamin Linus. She watched her boyfriend (and possibly her mother) be killed in front of her the morning of her own death. She had a big heart, and never quite belonged with the Others.

Three background "socks" died, too. They will be remembered by no one.

Music/Bands: When Locke and Sawyer come to the house Ben is staying in to tell him about the phone call, he is playing Rachmaninoff's "Prelude in C# Minor."

"Let's Do the Time Warp Again!": The Time Loop Theory

It doesn't matter where you go on the Internet, you'll run into websites that are filled with theories about *Lost*. Maybe the characters are all dead; maybe everything is a hallucination or the dream of a single character. Are the Others immortal? Are people time traveling from one era to another? Perhaps the entire show is an allegory of one particular religion/philosophy/book. Even the book you're holding now strives to point out the possibilities of what *Lost* could be about.

But one of the most intricate and solid theories — mentioned on EW.com and averaging 25,000 hits a day while *Lost* is airing — is the time loop theory. Created by *Lost* fan Jason Hunter, the theory was first posted before season 4 began, and has been evolving ever since, yet surprisingly, the core of it still holds up. When Hunter first devised the theory in May 2007, he showed it to a few fellow fans and coworkers, and they asked him to develop it further. He then sent it out to the *Lost* message boards, and it got such a huge response he gave the theory its own website. What follows are the theory highlights. However, I suggest you check out the entire theory (including a section where Jason responds to criticisms and questions) at www.timelooptheory.com to get the full story.

In the 1960s, the Dharma Initiative, formed by the descendents of the people on the *Black Rock*, begins experimenting on the island, and one of those experiments uses the island's unique electromagnetic properties to create a time machine. They use polar bears as test subjects, sending them back in time to see the effects it will have on the animals. The main purpose of the machine is to test something that has been the subject of an ongoing debate among the characters on the show — the question of fate versus free will. If they go back in time, can they change what happens, or will things always turn out the same way, course-corrected to ensure no disturbance in the timeline? They begin sending people back in time, but find they can't change anything. So they release an airborne disease on one a part of the island, and tell the people who catch it that the only "vaccination" is stepping into the time machine, turning the inhabitants of that area into unwitting test subjects. By doing so, they are cured of the disease, which would make it appear they *can* change the course of their lives. However, the smoke monster suddenly appears as a course-correcting agent of the time machine, killing them so they no longer exist beyond when they should have. The group that is not infected by the virus realizes that people are being killed in the name of experiments, and in a rage, they break away from Dharma, becoming the Others.

Ben and his father come to the island (Dharma actually wanted Ben, but had to pretend it was his father they were recruiting). Ben grows up working for Dharma, trying to find a use for the time machine, continuing to use test subjects, and discovering the bubble that surrounds the island. Dharma learn certain things about the machine. You can only go back in time (not forward) and you can only go as far back as when the machine was created. When you go back you remain the same age you were when you stepped into the machine; in fact you don't age at all until you catch up to the moment when you stepped into the machine. If you have an illness when you step into the machine and go back to a time when you were healthy, you will indeed be healthy again, as the time machine will temporarily take the illness away, but the illness will return when you catch up to the moment when you got sick. You cannot change anything around you unless it is a small thing that doesn't influence your basic destiny; if you somehow die before you make it to the moment you stepped into the machine, you won't be totally dead, and your spirit can still communicate with certain people so you can continue to play the role you were supposed to have played. You cannot go back in time to have a child if you didn't have one when you stepped into the machine — however, the universe will make an exception if the mother dies during childbirth so that the natural order of things is maintained by not creating a life that wasn't supposed to be there. The rules are entirely determined by fate. (In Jason's explanation here, he gives several examples from the show to illustrate his theory.)

By 2007, Ben and the Others realize that the machine isn't doing anything and Dharma is just an evil organization that doesn't value human life. They use the machine to go back in time to the '90s and commit "the Purge," the complete destruction of the Dharma organization. Worried that Dharma still has proponents in the outside world who might be looking for the island, the Others synch the time machine with the bubble surrounding the island, and hold the island in 1996 in perpetuity, resetting the machine every 108 minutes so it's held in stasis. This keeps the bubble closed and the outside world cannot see the island, but it also means that only the island stays in 1996 while the rest of the world continues on. Now, with the island stuck in a certain time, the women find they can't get pregnant because in the original timeline, they didn't have babies. Those who do get pregnant die before they can give birth, which is the island course-correcting things. Ben and Richard discover a "special coordinate" that allows them to leave the island and return. When Ben and Richard went back in time, they were in cahoots with one of their colleagues, named Jacob. He died accidentally, therefore his spirit must stay alive until the moment when the island time reaches 2007, when he'd stepped into the machine. He communicates only with Ben.

On September 22, 2004 (outside world time), fate brings down a plane onto the island, either because these people will right the wrongs that have been done, or will simply repopulate the island. Jason suggests that in the original timeline these survivors had more normal lives without all the tragedy, but when Ben reversed time, their lives changed and gradually fate played out to bring them all to the island. The reason Ben seems so sure of himself all the time, by the way, is because he's lived through all of this once and knows what is going to happen. Richard and Ben begin traveling off the island to recruit people like Locke (at the age of five) or Juliet (after she successfully impregnates her sister). Perhaps in the original timeline Alex didn't die by Keamy's hand, and now that she has, Ben's shock stems from the fact that something has actually changed on a second pass through time.

Further, Charles Widmore, who had originally been one of the Dharma Initiative, was off the island when Ben orchestrated the Purge and set the island on a time loop, and he is desperate to return. He rigs a boat with the bearing needed to penetrate the island's bubble, and hires Libby's husband to be the guinea pig, but he dies, and later she gives the boat to Desmond. Desmond makes it to the island, and gets recruited to push the button that holds the island in stasis. When Desmond fails to press the button, it opens the bubble momentarily, and Oceanic Flight 815 is pulled in. All of the people on the plane are now in 1996, the year in which the island is frozen, and have effectively traveled back in time through the machine to that time. That's why Rose's cancer is gone and Locke can walk; they've returned to the health they had in 1996. Charlie appears to Hurley in "The Beginning of the End" somewhere in 2006/2007 because in the original timeline (the one that existed before Ben went back in time in 2007) he was still alive. The same goes for Boone, Ana Lucia, and everyone else who has reappeared after their death.

At the end of season 2, Desmond turns the key, which turns off the time loop, and because he turned the key, he gets to relive the last part of his life over again, though he cannot change anything in it. He also sees glimpses of the future because the island is effectively eight or nine years behind the rest of the world. Widmore stages the fake plane crash, explaining away the missing Losties; meanwhile, a group of people who are affiliated with Dharma — headed by Matthew Abaddon — put together a group that will go to the island ahead of Widmore's people and suss out the situation. Ben has already lived to 2007 and knows certain people will live through everything as well, so he's not surprised by anything that happens, and he anticipates everything.

The rest of the theory explains what remains of season 4, and I won't print it here because it would spoil future episodes. I urge you to check out the theory yourself, and see the sheer amount of detail Jason Hunter has put together, including: why Ben can take such a severe beating, why the Others don't celebrate birthdays, what Rousseau has to do with all of this, how the freighter folk are able to communicate between two different time periods, what really happened to Desmond in "The Constant," why Richard Alpert had an ultrasound of a youthful womb that appeared to belong to a senior citizen, and much more. What the theory boils down to is that the series is about fate versus free will, and while until now, everything on the island had tended toward fate, events in seasons 5 and 6 could push free will to the forefront.

I talked to Hunter about the theory. He explained that, while he's had his detractors, most readers support the theory and are fascinated by the many ways he pulls in tiny details and supports them through his theory. "I'd say that about 40 to 50 percent of the readers think that the theory is spot-on," he explains. "Forty percent are skeptical because they don't feel it answers certain questions well enough. About 10 percent of people absolutely hate it — usually because they can't get past what they perceive to be major holes in the theory." There are certain parts of the theory that Hunter needs to smooth out, and when I pointed out a few dates or details that might be off, he acknowledged that not absolutely everything in the series matches his theory. But he certainly covers a *lot* of ground with it. He posted the theory before season 4 began, and now he makes updates of a few paragraphs after each episode just to show how new events continue to support his overarching theory. He's only had to make one major revision — when Jack's story in "Through the Looking Glass" was revealed to be a flashforward. "In my initial theory," he says, "I thought that everyone had left the island in the past, and the characters were reliving eight years of their lives off the island (from 1996 to 2004)." He says he still hasn't come up with an explanation for that second island that was near the first one, and whether or not it exists in the same time bubble as the other island.

The producers on the show have no doubt seen this theory or heard about it, even if only in snippets. Maybe it's really close to the ending they had been planning; maybe it's not even in the ballpark. The chances of it being exactly what Hunter says it is are slim, and even he admits that, because his theory doesn't take into account certain details that are in the show. But I asked him, if his theory turns out to be true, will he be a little bit disappointed because he'd called it early on and it wasn't a surprise to him? He said no, he wouldn't be. "I spent way more time than I ever dreamed working on this theory. So if the theory turns out to be right, I'll feel like all this hard work paid off."

4.10 Something Nice Back Home

Original air date: May 1, 2008
Written by: Edward Kitsis, Adam Horowitz

Directed by: Stephen Williams

Guest cast: William Blanchette (Aaron), Bill Fiddler (Dr. Stillman), April Parker-Jones (Dr. Erica Stevenson), Traci Toguchi (Receptionist), Carla Von (Ms. Berenberg)

Flash: Jack

As Juliet performs an emergency appendectomy on Jack, Sawyer leads Claire, Aaron, and Miles across the island, but loses someone along the way. Jack's flashforward reveals the beginning of his downfall.

Family reunions: aren't they wonderful?

"Something Nice Back Home" focused on Christian Shephard and his descendents, the most prominent of those being Jack. Jack has long been cast as a man with a compulsive need to fix things. He needs people to be healthy, happy, and safe, but he often tries to make that happen to the detriment of his own happiness and health. Now, he risks his own life by ignoring his ready-to-burst appendix so he can continue to play leader and get everyone rescued. How, exactly, he plans on doing that is anybody's guess.

Jack is a classic type A personality, typified by a constant pressure exerted on oneself to do better, to achieve every goal, and to always be ready for anything. According to scientific literature, "Type A individuals can get a lot done and have the potential to really move ahead in the world. But there is a high price to pay. Certain components of such a personality can inhibit happiness and even threaten health. For example, the goals that type A folks set are often poorly defined and therefore hard to achieve — a perfect recipe for misery." In this episode, Jack knows he has appendicitis (he answers "no" very matter-of-factly when Juliet asks him if his appendix has ruptured) and he continues to push himself beyond the point of stupid. Type A people may be very successful, but they will often, at some point, lose control simply because of the immense pressure they've put upon themselves. "Type A folks experience a constant sense of opposition, wariness, and apprehension — they are always ready for battle. And anyone can imagine how this constant (and very exhausting) existence would deplete reserves of contentment and happiness and disrupt personal equilibrium." Any fan of *Lost* can immediately envision Jack's portrait beside this definition. Often, a type A personality has been formed by a parent who expected a lot from the child, and urged the child to always do better and never rest on his or her laurels, which is exactly how Christian raised Jack.

Throughout the four seasons of *Lost*, we've had more flashes of Jack's past and future than any other character's ("White Rabbit," "All the Best Cowboys Have Daddy Issues," "Do No Harm," "Man of Science, Man of Faith," "The Hunting Party," "A Tale of Two Cities," "Stranger in a Strange Land," "Through the Looking Glass"). He has immense daddy issues, having been raised by a man who expected the moon from him. Jack became a surgeon just like his father and ended up usurping Christian's throne by revealing his drinking problem and getting him fired. His father became a major alcoholic afterwards, but when he finally started to become sober again, Jack accused him of having an affair with his wife, Sarah. Christian fell to drinking again, went on a bender in Australia, and died (it would seem). Now Jack is on the island because he was escorting his father's body back to the United States, even though the body appears to have been lost in transit. Christian is Jack's

Matthew Fox opts for business casual on the red carpet. (STHANLEE MIRADOR/SHOOTING STAR)

nemesis, but he's also the man Jack wants to please more than anyone else. Jack believes he's seen Christian on the island, but always chalks it up to his imagination. Now that he's seen him in the future, walking around the hospital dressed in the suit and white tennis shoes he was wearing in the coffin, Jack's self-control begins to unravel.

The appendectomy that Juliet performs lacks suspense — she ominously declares to Kate that "he will DIE" if they move him, and the music swells to a fever pitch, while everyone at home utters, "Uh . . . yeah, but . . . he doesn't." We all know he's alive and mentally unwell in the future, so it's not like we're on the edge of our seats wondering if he could possibly make it through the surgery. Instead, the appendicitis is a sign of something else, something that Rose expresses to Bernard. If no one on the island gets so much as a sniffle, why would Jack's appendix suddenly become infected and threaten to burst at such a critical point?

In the final mobisode (see pages 140–141), we see Christian on the island communicating with Vincent, and he tells the dog that Jack has work to do. If Christian is linked to the island in some way, then clearly the island has a job for Jack to do, much like it has one for Michael. Michael can't die, no matter how many times he tries. When Jack makes it back to the mainland, he thinks at first that there's no amount of distance he can put between himself and that island that would be sufficient, but then he realizes he needs to go back. His obsession to return to the place of his suffering suggests the island was trying to keep him there with that appendicitis, and failed, and now it's figured out another way to lure him back. (Perhaps it could have come up with a kinder method than turning him into a freaky, paranoid pill junkie, but hey, you do what you can do.)

Jack's loss of control and downward spiral will be the character arc we will watch until we finally get an episode of him returning to the island, if that day ever comes (plot-wise, it seems rather necessary). Three short months ago, Jack was beginning to unravel a bit already (we saw him knocking back tiny vodkas and very quickly turning into his father when he was on the plane). The island seemed to give him a reprieve by allowing him to fix people and situations again. But now his control is slipping away, and even when he tries to run the "OR" as Juliet is operating on him, she overturns his decision and removes him from the process. It's interesting to see how the island is turning people into the opposite of who they used to be. In the future, Jack will seem to have it all — Kate, Aaron, a good job. He seems to be fine at work, and even asks Kate to marry him. As Hurley observes, it's like he's in Heaven. But, as usual, Jack is his own worst enemy, and he will let everything slip from his fingers. Jack will hurt everyone around him, will have a singular obsession that rules his life (returning to the island), and will end up alone. When we first watch him walk into the kitchen and step on a toy, muttering, "Son of a *bitch*," we can't help but realize exactly what character he's about to turn into.

And just as Jack becomes the old Sawyer, Sawyer is becoming Jack. He leads Claire and Miles across the island, becoming a hero along the way and making sure Claire and baby Aaron are safe. When he threatens Miles and orders him to stay away from Claire, Miles asks, "What are you, her big brother?" Which is, in fact, Jack's relationship with her (though he doesn't know it). While there's about as much love lost between Sawyer and Miles as there was between Jack and Locke, Sawyer still manages to stay on course and reassure Claire that everything will be okay. And just as Claire was somehow kidnapped right under Jack's nose in

"Raised by Another," she's gone again as Sawyer sleeps, unaware that the island apparently has a role for Claire, too.

Christian appears to Claire — and he is actually holding Aaron, something that would be a little difficult for a ghost to do. This scene sparked a lot of fan discussion: is he or isn't he dead? "Death" seems like a temporary or ephemeral thing when it's related to the island. Could Christian have died and the island has given him a ghost-like existence? When Jack sees Christian in the lobby, Dr. Stevenson comes up behind him and she clearly doesn't see anything there. In "White Rabbit," when Jack thought he saw Christian on the island, Vincent also saw him. Some people believe that dogs have a sixth sense. And . . . so does Miles. He tells Sawyer he saw Claire talking to a man, but he could have been seeing the ghost, and maybe he didn't realize Christian was a ghost and not a man. (Or he did know the difference and just left that part out of his explanation to Sawyer.) Why is Christian important to the island? Why was he in Jacob's cabin in "The Beginning of the End"? Charlie died on the island, and now he's appearing to Hurley and telling him things, just like Christian is appearing to Jack and Claire. Is Charlie really appearing to Hurley?

Sawyer has become Superman in season 4, fulfilling the fantasies of many viewers. (YORUM KAHANA/SHOOTING STAR)

Or has the island followed the Oceanic 6 to the mainland?

Highlight: Sawyer's hilarious interaction with Miles, from giving Miles his restraining order to calling him Donger (a reference to Long Duk Dong from *Sixteen Candles*) to waking up to see Miles stoking the fire and mumbling, "It's way too early for Chinese."

Timeline: The episode begins the morning of Day 98 (December 28, 2004) with the survivors yelling at Daniel and Charlotte. The end of the episode, where Sawyer awakes to find Claire missing, would be Day 99.

Did You Notice?:

- The episode opens on Jack's eye, but the view from it is foggy and incoherent, rather than a clear perspective. The scene foreshadows Jack's uncertain future.

- Jack walks into the kitchen and steps on Aaron's *Millennium Falcon* toy. The moment is a subtle nod to the many comparisons fans have made between *Star Wars* and *Lost* (for one of the better explanations I've read, see pages 159–164 in the book *Lost Ate My Life* by Jon Lachonis and Amy Johnston).

- The newspaper headline, talking about the Yankees beating the Red Sox, is a wink that Jack's world has gone back to normal, since in the world he's always lived in, the Red Sox would never win the series.

- Many fans (including myself) could not see the appendectomy scar on Jack in the opening flashforward, and because Jack spends so long shirtless, it seemed to be a hint that somehow the future could be altered. But fans with high definition television and very clear screen capture abilities were able to catch the scar as Jack leaned over to clean the wine glasses, and as he looks at the razor on the bathroom counter.

- When Kate is first talking from the shower, she sounds just like Juliet, the same way the writers tried to disguise Ben's voice at the end of "The Economist." (This was undeniably a fantasy episode for the Jater fans, those who wanted to see Jack and Kate end up together.)

- Jack tells Kate that his father read *Alice in Wonderland* to him as a child (see **Interesting Facts** below). Where Ben is aligned with *The Wizard of Oz*, Christian Shephard is always paired with the Lewis Carroll books. The first time Jack sees Christian after Christian's death is in the first full-episode Jack flashback, "White Rabbit." "Through the Looking Glass" was also a Jack flash. Is Jack in Wonderland? And is Ben in Oz?

- The people who cast the part of toddler Aaron have definitely found a child who looks a lot like Claire.

- In Aaron's room, there's a quilt draped over a chair with a dinosaur standing next to a palm tree on it.

- Every time we see toddler Aaron he always seems to be asleep in bed, or wearing his pajamas as if he's about to go to bed.

To film Hurley's flashforward scenes, this sign was erected at Windward Community College in Kaneohe Oahu, where they filmed the exterior scenes. (RYAN OZAWA)

- Spelling is not Juliet's forte: a close-up of the list of supplies she needs includes "gause pads" and "forcepts."
- Daniel says that he's done some animal autopsies . . . apparently Eloise wasn't the only rat who met an unfortunate end.
- In the flashforward scene where Jack first sees Christian walking through the hospital lobby, Dr. Stevenson comes behind him and hands him an X-ray of a patient, saying there's a problem with the L-4 vertebra in his spine. That's exactly where Ben's spinal tumor was.
- Charlie's message to Jack (via Hurley) is, "You're not supposed to raise him, Jack." This brings back what Claire was told in "Raised by Another" by the psychic, that Aaron must be raised by her and not another. Or is it possible that the message is referring to Christian, and Jack wasn't supposed to raise him from the dead?
- In season 2, when we see Hurley in the institution, it seems to be right

downtown, with a lot of cars going by. But now, it's an out-of-the-way place in the country.

- Despite hating Charlotte, Jin must have felt a bit of a thrill hearing someone aside from Sun speak Korean on the island.
- Bernard applied the freezing to Jack the way a dentist would, with lots of little needles around the spot. Which is appropriate, since he is a dentist.
- Jack walks out to the lobby when he hears the smoke detector beeping, and removes the battery. This could be a huge clue that Christian is a manifestation of Old Smokey, since he manages to get Jack to dismantle the one thing that could actually detect him in the building. (As a nitpick, however, I think in a hospital the smoke detectors would be a more elaborate alarm system, and not individual units like you'd have in your home.)
- When Christian is sitting in the lobby, he's wearing the same suit, tie, and white tennis shoes that he was wearing when Jack spotted him in the jungle in "White Rabbit." (Incidentally, it's the same suit he's wearing when he's sitting in Jacob's cabin.)
- Anyone who says engagements should reduce stress has never planned a wedding.
- Look closely at the artwork on Kate's refrigerator — it's the same ladybugs and butterflies that we see on the walls of the Santa Rosa psychiatric hospital's rec room in "The Beginning of the End."
- Jack shouts to Kate that she's not even related to Aaron. The way he says it insinuates that he knows that *he* is.

Interesting Facts: Jack reads to Aaron from the second chapter of *Alice's Adventures in Wonderland*, entitled "The Pool of Tears." The White Rabbit drops some gloves and a fan when Alice startles him, and he runs away. Alice has just arrived in Wonderland, and she is bewildered by everything around her. In this scene, she begins to wonder if she was somehow exchanged for someone else. "I wonder if I've been changed in the night? Let me think: *was* I the same when I got up this morning? I almost think I can remember feeling a little different. But if I'm not the same, the next question is, 'Who in the world am I?' Ah, *that's* the great puzzle!" Jack stops reading here, but the next line is, "And she began thinking over all the children she knew that were of the same age as herself, to see if she could have been changed for any of them." This line is interesting, because in some ways Jack seems to have swapped places with Sawyer. The line also has significance with Aaron — Clare was kidnapped at night, and Ethan injected

Aaron in utero. Rousseau later kidnapped him at night, as did Charlie, and now he's been "changed" for someone else in a sense; he used to be Claire's son, and now he's Kate's.

When Claire is walking through the jungle with Miles and Sawyer, she says "At least I'm not seeing things anymore." Jeff Jensen at *Entertainment Weekly* reported that in "The Shape of Things to Come," Claire hallucinates after the house explosion, but the scene was cut for time. Perhaps she's becoming clairvoyant like Desmond, or it could be an indicator that she's not exactly with us anymore (see page 150).

The scene where Sawyer and company are hiding from Keamy, and Aaron makes a noise is reminiscent of the classic series finale of *M*A*S*H*. In that episode, Hawkeye is seeing a therapist and recalls being on a bus with a group of wounded GIs who tell everyone the enemy is coming down the road, and they need to stay quiet. As the enemy approaches, a refugee baby begins wailing. Hawkeye turns to the mother and tells her in panicked tones to keep the baby quiet. The mother realizes that she can't quiet the baby, and if they are caught they'll all die, so she puts her hand over its nose and mouth and smothers it. His story is one of the most haunting television moments of all time.

Nitpicks: One of the confusing things about this episode was where it fell in the timeline of the flashforwards (see page 199 for an explanation of the possible future timeline). The definitive date we get in this episode comes when Jack picks up the newspaper at the beginning. The headline says, "Yankees Bludgeon Red Sox in Series Sweep." Fans at first wondered if that was a reference to the "Boston Massacre" of 2006, where the Yankees swept the series against the Red Sox in four straight games, but the article mentions the massacre from the year before, making this the Yankee sweep of August 2007. The problem with that date is it makes the newspaper obituary from "Through the Looking Glass" inaccurate. Fans have held on to the fact the newspaper date clearly seen on the obituary that Jack is reading is April 2007. But if that flashforward happens after this one, which clearly it does, then it couldn't possibly have been the correct date. I realize a prop department doesn't usually have fans dissecting background material, but after four years, you'd think *Lost*'s would have caught on.

Oops: On Jack's white lab coat his surname is misspelled as "Shepard."

4 8 15 16 23 42: Jack's patient, Ryan Laker, has a tumor on his L-4. There are 4 people who go to the Staff station. Jack mentions the nanny usually works until 4.

It's Just a Flesh Wound: Jack gets an appendectomy.

Any Questions?:

- Kate tells Jack she's happy he changed his mind about being around Aaron. What changed his mind? Why did he not want to be around Aaron initially? Is it because he knows Aaron's his nephew, and it's too difficult for him to look at him? Or is it something bigger?

- Jack tells Kate that his dad was a great storyteller. Could this be a clue about Christian? What stories has he told Jack that aren't true? What has he been hiding? Is he some sort of omniscient storyteller and the entire series is the story he's telling?

- Who buried Rousseau and Karl?

- The writers have promised a Rousseau flashback since the first season, and now that she is undeniably dead, how will that happen? Will her flashback be part of one of Ben's? (If so, it won't be from Rousseau's perspective, but from Ben's.) Is it possible we might see an actual "Island" flashback, where past events are shown from the point of view of the island?

- What has changed in Sawyer to turn him into a superhero?

- Why is Miles so interested in Claire all of a sudden?

- Is Rose on to something? Is the island trying to stop Jack from leaving?

- Is there any significance to the fact that Juliet shaves Jack two inches higher than the incision or is Juliet just being thorough? Is there any way each of the Oceanic 6 were tagged in some way so they could follow them? Jack is unconscious here (and Bernard leaves before Juliet closes him up, so technically she could have slipped something inside him). The Others knock Kate and Hurley unconscious with poison darts in "Live Together, Die Alone." Ethan gives injections to Aaron in utero. Sun is knocked unconscious by Charlie in "The Long Con," and while Charlie was certainly never aligned with the Others, he now seems to have a connection with the island. Could they all somehow have tracking devices on them now?

- Hurley has $150 million and a sizeable settlement from Oceanic. Why is he staying in such a bargain basement institution?

- Why does Charlotte know Korean? Is it from her work as a cultural anthropologist? Would that be a culture she would have studied? Why would she know a difficult language like Korean, but need a translator in "Confirmed Dead" when speaking to a French man?

- What favor was Kate doing for Sawyer? Did it have something to do with Sawyer's daughter Clementine? Why wouldn't she tell Jack?
- Is this how Claire is permanently separated from Aaron? Will she ever see him again? How will anyone feed him now? (Was there a can of formula in that pallet drop?) And won't the poor girl be in a lot of pain soon, since she'll still be producing milk but won't have anyone to give it to?

Ashes to Ashes: Danielle Rousseau, a scientist who is believed to be French (though she's never confirmed it), was on a research mission in 1988 when her boat crashed on some rocks near the island. She was seven months' pregnant at the time. Her team began getting sick, and died one by one. She killed her lover, Robert, when he became deathly ill. She gave birth to Alex alone, but two weeks later the Others took the baby, and Rousseau spent 16 years searching for her daughter. She was finally reunited with her on December 21, 2004, but was shot and killed by mercenaries on December 27. She was survived by her daughter Alex, who remained alive for only a few hours before being murdered as well.

Missing Pieces: The *Lost* Mobisodes

The *Lost* mobisodes were a long time in the making. Originally planned as early as November 2005, the idea had been to hire non-union actors to play out some scenes that had nothing to do with the actual canonical series, but might be fun to watch. Ultimately, the writers fought to have the actual cast and crew of *Lost* perform in the episodes, and there was a long negotiation for proper compensation. Ironically, the first episode debuted during the 2007–2008 Writers' Strike (see page 103), which was precisely about the issue of payment for exclusive online broadcasting. The episodes were written by *Lost* staff writers and directed by *Lost* director and executive producer Jack Bender.

The first episode aired on Verizon mobile phones on November 6 (followed by its ABC.com broadcast six days later) and the episodes ran until January 28, 2008, three days before the season 4 premiere. Fan response was less than stellar after the first handful of episodes failed to deliver anything new or shocking, but as the episodes went on, there was an increasing feeling that we were getting some big clues in these little one-act plays, which usually ran only a few minutes long each. And since the mobisodes are considered canon (i.e., we should treat them with the same importance as anything that happens within an episode), it pays to have seen them.

Episode 1: The Watch (November 6, 2007)

Written by: Carlton Cuse

Context: *This scene would fall within the flashback that we see in "Do No Harm."*

Jack is standing on the beach the morning of his wedding, throwing rocks. His father approaches him and says he wants to give him a gift of a watch that his father had given to him. When Jack says he's never seen it before, Christian explains that his father had given it to him as a wedding present while telling Christian he thought his bride-to-be was wrong for him, so Christian never wore it, out of protest. Jack wonders if the gift is Christian trying to warn him of the same thing, but Christian reassures him that he's making the right choice with Sarah. Before he leaves, he pleads with Jack that if Jack ever has a child to treat him better than Christian ever treated Jack.

A major theme of season 4 is that of time, and it's a theme that has run throughout the series, and is often associated with Christian and Jack. During Locke's hallucination in the smoke lodge in "Further Instructions," he sees Jack removing a watch at the airport, which is presumably the same watch that Christian gives to him here. Christian's appearance in the first mobisode also points to his importance in the series. In season 1 he seemed to be merely the albatross around Jack's neck, and nothing more, but as the series has progressed, and John Terry is appearing in more and more episodes, it's becoming clear that there's a lot more to Christian Shephard than we might have originally thought.

Episode 2: The Adventures of Hurley and Frogurt (November 13, 2007)

Written by: Edward Kitsis and Adam Horowitz

Guest star: Sean Whalen (Neil)

Context: *Hurley had prepared a picnic for he and Libby in "Two for the Road," and when she realized he'd forgotten drinks and blankets, she offered to go and get the blankets and told him to go to Rose and Bernard's tent, because she knew they had wine.*

Hurley sneaks out of Rose and Bernard's tent after getting the supplies that he was going to take to his meeting with Libby on the beach. "Frogurt," or Neil, begins to question him about where he's going. Hurley is evasive, and Neil asks him if he's going to make a move with Libby or not. He tells Hurley he's "holding up the line," and that everyone knows Hurley's never going to get past doing laundry with her. Hurley boasts that actually, he and Libby are about to go on a picnic right now. Neil tells him if he doesn't close the deal, it's "Neil Time."

While this episode is mildly funny, its humor is overshadowed by the fact that while Hurley was off getting the wine, Libby was in the hatch getting blankets . . . and being shot and killed by Michael. We know that Hurley will never see Libby alive again. "Frogurt" was actually mentioned previously to this mobisode; in "S.O.S.," Bernard asks Hurley to round up some people to help him out with his sign, and he tells him to grab "that Frogurt guy — the guy who used to make the frozen yogurt." Hurley corrects him by saying, "Neil?"

Episode 3: King of the Castle (November 20, 2007)

Written by: Brian K. Vaughan

Context: *This episode falls somewhere between "Stranger in a Strange Land," where Jack is freed from the cages and brought to New Otherton, and "The Man from Tallahassee," where Locke blows up the submarine.*

Jack and Ben are playing chess. Ben is in a wheelchair, and says it must be strange for Jack being there with them. He asks jokingly if there's anything he could do to get him to stick around, then tells him he intends to honor the deal they've struck together. Jack asks him if he *intends to* or *will*. Ben says it's not up to him, that if the island doesn't want Jack to leave, it won't let him. Jack asks if the island is going to sink the sub, and Ben says he won't do anything to stand in Jack's way, but if he does leave, there will come a day when he wants to return. Jack says, "Never." Ben counters, "I've learned never to say never." He adds that when that day comes, he hopes Jack remembers the conversation. He castles his king (a move where you transfer your rook in front of your king to save it from being taken), and tells Jack it was a nice try.

Chess is a recurring motif on *Lost* (see page 187), mostly because it's a game of intelligence, where each side is chasing the other to try to topple it, and only through skill and cunning can one both fend off attacks and try to launch an offensive in the other direction. In this clip, Jack attempts to make a move on Ben's king, but Ben moves another piece in front of his king to protect it, just like Ben is always moving other people around his own island chess game to preserve himself. Ben doesn't sink the sub, as Jack suggests he will — he goads Locke into doing it for him. And just as Ben predicts, a couple of years later Jack will want to return to the island.

Episode 4: The Deal (November 26, 2007)

Written by: Elizabeth Sarnoff

Context: *This moment would fall during the flashback we saw in "Three Minutes" of Michael being held hostage by the Others. Presumably Juliet enters the room right after Ms. Klugh has given Michael his list and his instructions on what to do if he ever wants to see Walt again.*

Juliet enters the hut where Michael is being held hostage by the Others. She tells him he can have the boat that he asked for. She says that she's spent time with Walt, and he's very special, and that she's glad he's going to get him off the island. Michael angrily responds that he doesn't believe they care about Walt. She tells him that the man he is going to free is named Ben, and he is very important. She reassures him that they'll help him get off the island, and confesses that she, too, made a deal, and Ben saved her sister's life in exchange for Juliet staying on the island. Michael asks what the point is of her sister staying alive if Juliet couldn't be with her. She counters, "Wouldn't you do anything to save Walt?" She wishes him luck and leaves.

This is actually the only scene that Elizabeth Mitchell and Harold Perrineau have together on *Lost*. While at this point she doesn't appear to hate Ben, and it seems like she actually cares about him, when Michael asks her if Ben will really let him go she closes her eyes and shakes her head (as if saying no) as she's saying yes. Any psychologist would tell you she's lying in that scene. Notice she refers to him as Ben, and not Henry Gale, an admission that could have blown both Michael and Ben's cover if Michael had repeated that name to anyone in his own camp after he got there and let Ben go.

Episode 5: Operation: Sleeper (December 3, 2007)

Written by: Brian K. Vaughan

Context: *This moment takes place during the early part of "The Brig." In the previous episode, "D.O.C.," Juliet and Sun see the baby on the ultrasound. At the end of "The Brig," when Juliet and Jack are sitting on the beach and Kate approaches, Juliet says enigmatically, "We should tell her." She's referring to the conversation in this mobisode.*

Jack wakes up in his tent with Juliet sitting there saying they need to talk. She admits she's still working for Ben, that he's asked her to test the women and find out which ones were pregnant so he can abduct them, and that he promised no one would get hurt. Jack gets angry and says he doesn't understand, and that she seemed to want to get on that submarine as badly as he did. She says she was foolish to think Ben would let them go. Jack looks confused and says Locke blew it up, and that Ben was in a wheelchair. "Did he?" she asks. Jack asks why she's telling him now, and she says last night she and Sun saw her baby on the monitor, and if Sun's still on the island in a month, she'll die. She says she's been living Ben's dream for three years, and it's time to wake up.

So far, this is the mobisode that most feels like a deleted scene, as if it were something plucked straight out of an episode. When we first saw Kate march up to Jack and ask to speak to him in private and Jack refuses to make Juliet go away, he comes off as a traitor, especially since no one else in the camp trusts Juliet at this point. However, this episode gives us the background to that scene, and we see why Jack now trusts Juliet. She didn't have to come clean to him, but she did. We know she's not telling Jack everything she knows yet, but by revealing her secret, she certainly comes off as more trustworthy than most people on the island.

Episode 6: Room 23 (December 10, 2007)

Written by: Elizabeth Sarnoff

Context: *This episode happens in the early part of season 2, shortly after the Others capture Michael in "Exodus, Part 2" and begin to realize the extent of Walt's "specialness."*

An alarm is going off, and Ben comes running in asking what happened. Juliet, standing in the hallway as other people rush by her, says he's done it again. Ben tells her to get him to stop, and she says she's not going in there and the others are scared of him. She says his father is looking for him, and he's Ben's responsibility. Ben counters that Jacob was the one who wanted him here. He says he's special, Juliet says he's dangerous. Ben says he's just a child, and she leads him outside the compound and he looks down the fire escape to see a dozen dead birds sitting below a boarded-up window.

The person Ben and Juliet are talking about is clearly Walt. In the season 1 episode "Special," Walt is reading a book about birds and as he stares at a picture of one, a bird of the same variety flies straight into the window. The suggestion is that Walt just needs to picture something in his head for it to happen. Why are there so many dead birds? The clue could be in the title of the episode. Room 23 is the famous room where Ben tied Karl to a chair and showed him hundreds of images to affect his subconscious. Perhaps some of those images are birds, or maybe as Walt is becoming agitated he's unwittingly using his powers to kill the only small things within his mental reach, which are birds. Birds are often a symbol of freedom, and his thoughts could be forcing one bird after another to fly straight into his boarded-up window. This missing piece suggests the reason the Others actually let Walt go. He may have been special, but his specialness was too dangerous for them to risk dealing with. Knowing that it was okay to let Walt go, Ben probably left this station and went to the computer to communicate with Michael in the guise of Walt, which lured Michael over to that side of the island.

Episode 7: Artz and Crafts (December 17, 2007)

Written by: Damon Lindelof

Context: *This episode happens during or shortly after "The House of the Rising Sun,"* *right after Sun has told Michael that she speaks English and Jack is trying to recruit people to come to the caves.*

Jin and Sun are going through things and Jin says he thinks Shannon and Boone are lovers, given the way Boone looks at her. Sun says they're brother and sister and he asks her how she knows that, and she says it's a good guess. Arzt shows up, yelling about how he's heard they're moving from the beaches to the caves. He asks Jin and Sun if they're going, but Hurley tells him they don't speak English. Michael and Sun exchange a knowing look. Arzt explains why he doesn't think they should go to the caves (the moisture will attract insects that would lay eggs in their mouths while they sleep). He tells everyone to vote no when Jack comes by, and suggests Jack is crazy because he saw him a few days earlier running through the jungle and yelling for his father ("White Rabbit"). Suddenly they hear the monster, and Arzt says he'll see them at the caves.

There is a continuity error with this episode: in "House of the Rising Sun," Jin is handcuffed to the plane. Jack is trying to recruit people to come to the caves, and Sayid asks Michael if he'll come to the caves with them. After that exchange, Sun approaches Michael, tells him in English what the watch meant to Jin, and Michael frees Jin from the plane with an axe. But in this mobisode, Michael doesn't seem to know anything about the caves yet, even though Jin has already been freed. (Not to mention, Arzt was never seen in the caves; but that could be explained away by the fact he wasn't actually a character until the season 1 finale.) It was great to have Arzt back for this episode; you can see even Harold Perrineau and Jorge Garcia are trying not to laugh as he rants.

Episode 8: Buried Secrets (December 24, 2007)

Written by: Christina M. Kim

Context: *This mobisode probably happens soon after the previous one. Sun and Jin are not at the caves yet, Jin still has the handcuff on him, and Sun and Michael's friendship is still awkward and new.*

This one is for the Sun/Michael shippers. Sun sees Jin getting his fishing rods prepared, and she goes into the jungle to bury her California driver's license, which she had on her before the crash. Michael comes through the jungle looking for Vincent and sees what she's burying. She tells Michael she was going to leave Jin and start a new life in America, but she changed her mind at the airport because she was afraid. He says not to worry, they'll get off the island soon, and she says the island is her punishment. He says maybe she should talk to Jin, but she counters that Jin is not the man she married. Michael touches her face tenderly, and as they move in for a kiss, Vincent shows up to spoil the moment. Sun rushes away.

There has always been speculation among the fans that there was sexual tension between Michael and Sun. This is probably the extent of their attempt at a physical relationship. At the end of "House of the Rising Sun," there's a suggestion that Sun didn't leave Jin because she still had some hope that he might change. He shows her a flower and she joins him at his side. But in this missing piece, she says that she stayed with him because she was afraid.

Episode 9: Tropical Depression (December 31, 2007)

Written by: Carlton Cuse

Context: *This episode happens near the end of "Born to Run," a few hours after Arzt has announced the monsoon season is coming, and before the boat leaves and Arzt accompanies the expedition to the* Black Rock *in the following episode.*

Arzt is trapping spiders. Michael asks him what the wind will be like the next day, and he admits the stuff he'd said about the monsoon season was entirely made up so he could speed up the raft-building process and get off the island quicker. He confesses that he'd fallen in love with a woman from Australia whom he'd met on the Internet, but he'd used his friend Nick's photo, and when he got there, she was very beautiful, but she ditched him at the restaurant. Arzt says the worst part is that he was meant to leave later, but he got himself on an earlier flight out and it crashed. Michael says he doesn't feel sorry for him because everyone on the beach has a similar story, and no one wants to be there. Arzt apologizes for lying about the winds and says when Michael comes back with rescue he'll be the first one on the beach waving hello.

This mobisode makes Arzt more of a tragic clown by adding depth to his character and explaining the sad circumstances that led to him being on that flight (also, we know he won't be waving hello because he'll be dead by then). Perhaps those people who weren't meant to be on the flight were disposed of by the island. The episode puts to rest the fan nitpicks that the monsoon Arzt had predicted never happened.

Episode 10: Jack, Meet Ethan.
Ethan? Jack (January 7, 2008)

Written by: Damon Lindelof

Context: *This episode happens at the beginning of the series, shortly after the plane has crashed and before Jack has found the caves.*

Ethan shows up in Jack's tent with a suitcase full of pharmaceuticals that he suggests belonged to a hypochondriac. He thanks Jack for being rational about the situation and thinking long-term, rather than believing, like everyone else, that they'll be rescued soon. He says he knows Jack is thinking of Claire, and assures him he is not alone. Jack says if she does go into labor he's glad he'll have an assistant. Ethan's face shadows over and Jack apologizes. Ethan tells Jack that his wife died in childbirth and the baby didn't make it. He hopes they're wrong and the rescue boats are on the way.

It's likely Ethan is making up his story to ingratiate himself to Jack, but what if he's telling the truth and his wife died in her second trimester on the island? Could this be why he's so serious about his job, and so obsessed with the health of Claire's baby? This episode explains why Jack has such a huge stash of medication.

Episode 11: Jin Has a Temper-Tantrum
on the Golf Course (January 14, 2008)

Written by: Drew Goddard

Context: *This episode would fall in the first half of season 1, when Jin is still seen as a harsh character, he's still wearing the handcuff, and Michael isn't spending all his time building the raft.*

This episode is exactly what the title says it is. Hurley, Michael and Jin are on Hurley's golf course, and Jin has to sink the putt to win. He misses, Hurley congratulates Michael, and Jin has a hissy fit, screaming at them in Korean. Hurley looks at Michael at one point and mutters, "I think I heard our names in there somewhere." He screams at the sky that he hates the island, hates the game of golf, wanted one moment of happiness and is frustrated no one understands him. Hurley prevents Michael from comforting Jin, saying he should probably get this out of his system. Hurley suggests they take a break from golf for a while, and Jin sits on the ground crying and saying he's so alone.

This one is my favorite of the mobisodes. It's hysterically funny, and Daniel Dae Kim is brilliant. It doesn't really add anything to the series, yet feels like one scene that would have been great to have had in an episode.

Episode 12: The Envelope (January 21, 2008)

Teleplay by J.J. Abrams and Damon Lindelof, Story by Damon Lindelof

Context: *This scene takes place during the opening flashback of "A Tale of Two Cities."*

Using stock footage from the season 3 premiere, this mobisode opens with Juliet pulling her muffins out of the oven, burning her hand, and opening the door for Amelia, the older woman who lives in New Otherton and attends Juliet's book club meeting. Amelia asks Juliet if Ben has made his feelings for her clear, and Juliet avoids the question. She finally tells Amelia that she thinks they're all in trouble, and asks Amelia if she'll swear secrecy if Juliet shows her something. Amelia nods, and Juliet begins to pull a large envelope out of her utensils drawer. Just as she's about to remove Ben's X-ray, the doorbell rings.

This mobisode is actually a deleted scene from "A Tale of Two Cities," which would have introduced Ben's X-ray earlier, and also would have suggested Ben has feelings for Juliet before we find out he does explicitly in "The Other Woman." It's not clear why Juliet still has the X-rays (she took them over to Ben's house the previous day, so one would think he would have kept them), but it shows Juliet's possible recklessness with telling secrets. Considering her house is probably bugged by Ben, he was probably watching this scene play out and knew she was going to reveal his secret to someone else. Amelia, by the way, shares a name with Amelia Earhart, whom some fans have speculated could be the female body lying in the caves.

Episode 13: So It Begins (January 28, 2008)

Written by: Drew Goddard

Context: *This episode happens moments before the opening minute of the pilot episode, and actually segues into that scene.*

The episode opens with a dog's-eye-view of the island, with Vincent sniffing at some open luggage. There's a whistle, and Vincent follows it . . . to Christian Shephard, in a suit and white tennis shoes. Christian tells Vincent he needs him to find his son, and he points to a spot in the jungle. Vincent heads off, and Christian stands up and says, "He has work to do." The piece cuts to the opening of the pilot episode, with Jack waking up in the jungle and Vincent running up to him.

This could be the most important of the mobisodes, and definitely has an impact on season 4. Christian Shephard plays a bigger role in season 4 than ever before (see "Cabin Fever"), but this missing piece does raise questions about what form Christian has taken. Is he corporeal? How can he touch Vincent? Is he still dead or not? It also suggests that if Christian does have strong ties to the island, and says Jack has work to do, that the island has a role for Jack to play, much in the same way it did for Michael.

4.11   Cabin Fever

Original air date: May 8, 2008
Written by: Elizabeth Sarnoff, Kyle Pennington
Directed by: Paul Edwards
Guest cast: Nestor Carbonell (Richard Alpert), Doug Hutchison (Horace Goodspeed), Phil Abrams (Gellert), Amanda Carlin (ER Nurse), Sarah Duval (Melissa), Matthew Pederson (Physical Therapist), Holland Roden (Teenage Emily), Caleb Steinmeyer (John Locke Age 16), Rebecca Tilney (Emily's Mother), Patrick Torres (ER Doctor), Mandy June Turpin (Florence), Charles Henry Wyson (John Locke Age 5)

Flash: Locke

As Keamy and his merry band of mercenaries prepare to torch the island, Locke and his merry band of Jacobites try to find the cabin. We discover that the island had chosen Locke long before 815 crashed there.

"Destiny, John, is a fickle bitch." When it comes to Ben, Locke, and this island, were truer words ever spoken? In the last two seasons, John Locke has become a problematic character for some fans. In season 1, he was the true believer on the island, the character whom many thought may be the key to why that particular plane crashed on this particular island. In season 2, his beliefs were shaken by Jack, who challenged him constantly and made Locke appear like the sort of kid who was once stuffed into lockers. In season 3, Locke's actions became even more confusing, as he sank the sub, blew up the Flame station, and seemed to thwart every chance of getting off the island. By this season, Locke has headed up a mutiny against Jack, splitting the survivors into two camps.

But there always seems to be a method to his madness. Locke, at his core, believes he is acting in the best interests of everyone. If he can keep everyone on the island, he can eventually show them why the island is the place to be. He knows in his heart that the island is special, and that everyone on it is blessed to be walking on these hallowed grounds, but he needs to take drastic measures so everyone can appreciate it the way he does. Locke's actions mirror his faith. In season 1, his ability to walk was restored and he had complete faith in the island. The smoke monster showed itself to him and he believed it was a powerful sign: "I've looked into the eye of this island, and what I saw . . . was beautiful." When he found the hatch but was unable to open it, his faith was shaken. Then he met the smoke monster again, and the eye of the island had lost its sparkle and turned against him. His faith continued a downward slope in season 2 as Jack challenged him, and when he realized he'd made a mistake in not pushing the button, Locke began looking for signs from the island that might tell him what to do in season 3. He listened to the island, and the island gave him his father, whom he got Sawyer to kill; and he also saw Jacob. But then he was shot and left for dead, and decided suicide was the only way out. But the island sent him a message again, told him what to do, and he's had faith ever since.

Throughout Locke's life he has trusted the wrong person, and second-guessed himself. He trusted his father over and over again, only to be disappointed and abused at every turn. His instincts told him to walk away, and he didn't trust them. He trusted Eddie, the kid who turned out to be a cop, in "Further Instructions," and was turned away by the people who had embraced him. He believed the button should be pushed every 108 minutes, but when Jack battered him long enough, he questioned his convictions, and decided not to push the button, with catastrophic results. Since that moment, John has changed. He does what comes to him, despite the fact everyone else looks at him like he's crazy. He blew up the Flame station and sank the sub because doing those things felt right. As the leader of New Otherton, he is stern with Kate and Claire and anyone else who questions him because he's made his decision and is going to stick with it, even if deep down he has insecurities about leading — insecurities Ben senses and stirs up.

In "Cabin Fever," we get another flashback of Locke. So far this season we are getting flashforwards of the Oceanic 6 only, and the other survivors are getting flashbacks (since their future is still a mystery the writers don't want to reveal). For the most part, it told us what we already knew about Locke — he was in a foster home, his birth mother had the maternal instinct of a popsicle stick, he was a loser, he loved backgammon, and he had given up on ever walking again. But throw in a little Richard Alpert, Matthew Abaddon, and a walkabout, and you have the makings of a brilliant

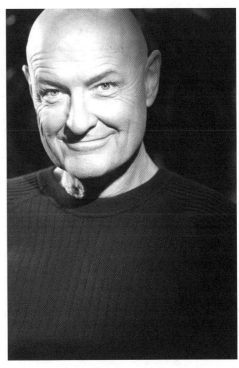

The brilliant Terry O'Quinn won an Emmy for his portrayal of John Locke, who becomes the Chosen One in "Cabin Fever." (AP PHOTO/RICHARD DREW)

flashback. What we see in the two flashbacks of Locke as a child and a teenager are the beginnings of him second-guessing himself and going against his true instincts. As a teenager, his guidance counsellor urges him to attend a science camp because he's gifted, but John, despite knowing he loves science, wants to be one of the cool kids. He longs to play sports — because that's what teenage boys are supposed to want — even though that's not where his strengths are. The repetition of Locke's mantra, "Don't tell me what I can't do," seems to be nothing more than a link to the post-crash John, but it's more important than that. It shows that even at a young age, John did things he thought he ought to do, not what he was best at. If someone told him he wouldn't be prom king, he would put all his efforts into doing just that simply because he wanted to prove them wrong. In the end, he wouldn't be prom king, the other person would be proven right, and John would have wasted his time.

In the earlier flashback, when Richard Alpert visits him, he lays six objects on the table: three are boring (a vial of sand, a compass, and the Book of Laws), and three would be exciting to a child (a baseball mitt, a knife, and a comic book). John grabs the vial of sand and the compass, and Richard looks like he's going to burst from the excitement he's trying to contain, and John's eyes move to the Book of Laws . . . but he goes against his instinct and grabs the knife. Viewers may have thought that was the correct choice, because Locke is always identified with his knives, but perhaps the fact that was the "wrong" choice means he was never meant to focus so much on knives and he's spent his life following the incorrect path. Alpert abandons him, and he's once again left alone. In the final flashback, he meets Matthew Abaddon, who tells him about the walkabout, ensuring Locke will get on the plane. For some reason Locke trusts this man, and for better or for worse, ends up on the island. Did he trust the right person in this case, or was it once again a bad decision?

So why is Richard Alpert featuring so heavily in John's flashbacks, again not having aged a day? If we link his presence to season 4's overriding theme of time travel, it would suggest Alpert is traveling back to recruit John after knowing he would one day come to the island. He is aware of John's existence soon after he is born. Is Alpert in touch with the island? Can it tell him things? If so, maybe Locke was chosen by the island at birth, and it kept him alive much the same way it kept Michael alive — because it needed him. The nurse comments that pree-mie John suffered through infections and pneumonia, but always got rid of them. He wasn't supposed to survive, but in a colossal "don't tell me what I can't do" move, John fought all infections off and proved everyone wrong. If the island has somehow chosen John from the beginning, it would explain how he has survived all of the things he has — being grossly premature, his kidney transplant, being thrown out of an eight-storey window. Or perhaps Alpert's visit is similar to Desmond going back in time to see Daniel. Daniel from 2004 needs 1996 Desmond to give him the coordinates that would allow him to harness time travel. Similarly, future-Alpert realizes Locke will be important to the island and he goes back to 1961 to recruit a five-year-old Locke.

As for Alpert's presence, again if you read *Slaughterhouse-Five* (see page 69), it gives the best explanation for these anomalies. In that book, the aliens believe that all time is happening at once. You may think you are 30 years old, but somewhere along the time spectrum you are still 8, 15, and 16 years old. Every moment in our lives is happening simultaneously at different points on the time spectrum, and if someone could figure out a way to move along those points, he or she could visit anyone else at any point in their lives (see page 117). If this theory is to be believed, it would explain why Alpert says the objects already belong to John, and not that they will belong to him in the future. If one actually has glimpses of one's life because of this simultaneous timeline, then it could explain how five-year-old John had drawn a picture of the smoke monster dragging him, which happens in "Exodus, Part 2." It would also explain how Alpert could be present at any point in Locke's life and how he already knows that Locke is special.

The "test" that Locke undergoes with Alpert is also similar to the ritual used to find the Dalai Lama. When a Dalai Lama dies, the High Lamas search for the reincarnated Dalai Lama, which can take up to a few years. Once the boy has been located, the High Lamas visit his home and lay several artefacts before him, some of which belonged to the previous Dalai Lama (and therefore, if the boy really is the reincarnated one, already belong to him). If the boy chooses the correct items, the High Lamas take that as a sign, and they confirm the boy's authenticity with the Living Buddhas and the Government of Tibet. Richard, acting as a sort of High Lama, comes to Locke's house thinking he's found the Chosen One, and is clearly disappointed to discover he was wrong, though deep down he knows Locke is still special.

As we are reminded several times in this episode, Locke wasn't the only one who was special. Ben was originally brought to the island and visited by Richard in the jungle. The island seemed to have big plans for him and give him subconscious messages — "I used to have dreams," he tells Locke sadly — but then it decided he was no longer special. Locke was recruited at an early age, but it took the island 40 years to actually get him there. Walt is the other child who has been called special, but the island let him go. Apparently his specialness was a little too violent for the island's tastes (see page 136). Aaron is a child who may be deemed special in the future — neither Ben nor Locke were raised by their mothers, whereas the psychic Richard Malkin had insisted that Claire raise Aaron herself. Ben and Locke have many similarities (see page 150) and one could make a very strong argument that they actually represent the same person living parallel lives. Locke represents the man who made choices against his better instincts and lived away from the island, and Ben was the man who followed his instincts and lived on the island. They both managed to end up at the same place, and the question will be which one will prevail.

Of course, if Keamy gets his way, no one will prevail. As he moves on to the Secondary Protocol, we see just how serious Widmore is about finding that island

and being the only one alive who knows it exists. The obvious question this scene begs, however, is why Widmore didn't give Keamy this information in the first place? Why not point out that Ben would head to the Orchid so he only has to make one trip to the island, finish his business, and get out of there? Clearly the place Ben is going is so top secret that there's a good chance Widmore will make sure that, if Keamy completes his mission, it will be his last. The island can protect itself, as it has shown time and again, but it has its limitations, and that's why it needs to be saved by Locke.

While Locke was the focal point of this episode, Ben featured prominently as well. He seems to have finally accepted that he is no longer Jacob's man on the island, and that John is the real apostle. When Locke suddenly appeared at the end of "Through the Looking Glass," Ben had a shocked look on his face like he already knew Locke had unseated him. In this episode, Ben sits back and reacts rather than acts. He says he was following Hurley, who is confused since Ben always leads and forces others to follow him. Michael Emerson fills simple lines of dialogue with so much emotion we know that Ben is hurting deeply at having been usurped. He tries to praise John for being like him when John tricks Hurley into believing he chose to stay with them, but Locke's dismissive, "I'm not like you" deflates any pride Ben had in that moment. He tells Locke, "You'll understand soon enough that there are consequences to being chosen," and there is a lot of backstory hanging in that sentence. He says in this episode that losing Alex was his destiny, even though when it happened, he certainly didn't act like it. But in this episode he clearly steps back to let Locke take the spotlight. Is it because he's really accepted Locke as the go-to guy, or does he suspect something dangerous is about to happen and he'd rather Locke be standing front and center? Or, has Alex's death temporarily taken the fight out of him? When Ben watches longingly as John walks up to the cabin, I actually felt sorry for the guy.

Every time the cabin appears we see another feature of it. In "The Man Behind the Curtain," Ben can see and talk to Jacob, and does so in a condescending tone like he's scolding a child. Locke believes Ben is either crazy or playing a huge prank, and threatens to leave until Jacob suddenly shows himself to Locke, and utters the words, "Help me" in a way that only Locke can hear. In "The Beginning of the End," when Hurley looked in the window we could see Christian Shephard sitting in the shadows. There was a second eye at the window (perhaps Jacob's). In this episode, Christian finally moves into the light and talks calmly with Locke. He is enigmatic, asking questions and getting Locke to answer them, rather than coming out and telling him what he needs him to do. It's as if the island needs to make sure they've picked the correct Chosen One this time. Instead of Jacob, Claire sits nearby, casually slumped in a chair, smiling serenely as if the scene playing out is completely normal. What is going on with her has become one of the biggest questions of the season (see **Interesting Facts** below).

Despite the mysteriousness of Christian's questioning, Locke seems to give him the correct answers, and when Locke finally gets his instructions, they are as baffling to us as they are to him. With the words, "He wants us to move the island," this episode hurtles the rest of the season headlong toward what promises to be a mindblowing finale.

If it hadn't been for the Writers' Strike, Nestor Carbonell (Richard Alpert) probably wouldn't have appeared in season 4. (AP PHOTO/SETH WENIG)

Highlight: Ben, Locke, and Hurley as the three stooges was absolutely hilarious, and lightened this otherwise serious episode. From Ben and Hurley arguing over who was supposed to be the leader to Hurley saying, "Guys? Cabin," to Hurley telling Locke he was happy with Locke going in alone, the laughs just kept coming. But the single funniest moment for me was Hurley sharing his chocolate bar with Ben. After everything we know Ben is capable of doing, seeing him sit there and simply enjoy a chocolate bar was a riot.

Timeline: Ben, Hurley, and Locke make camp on the evening of December 28, 2004, and they go to the Dharma Initiative mass grave on December 29, 2004, discovering Jacob's cabin later that evening.

Did You Notice?:
- There was no "previously on *Lost*" for this episode.
- When the episode opens and the mother refers to her daughter as "Emily," it could be either a Locke or Ben flashback at that point, since they both had redheaded mothers named Emily (see page 150).

- Emily was hit by a car running from her mother, just as Locke was bumped by a car running after Emily many years later.
- Emily doesn't ask the nurse to call him John, but instead insists, "His name is John," as if it already was John, and always has been.
- We finally discover the year of the Purge. Horace says he's been dead for 12 years, which puts the Purge on December 19, 1992 (December 19 is Ben's birthday, which is the day he killed his father).
- At the end of the dream sequence, Horace says, "Godspeed." His surname is Goodspeed.
- The casting people actually put a real newborn baby in that incubator. On most other shows, they'd stick a 17-pound six-month-old in there and call it a newborn. The fact that the baby is staring at Emily right before she runs out of the room makes her abandonment of him even sadder.
- In the scene in the hospital, behind Richard, there is a poster with the word CHOICE on it.
- When Hurley says he believes they can see the cabin because they're the crazy ones, John stops and stares at him, as if seriously considering it. In "Something Nice Back Home," Jack's life seemed to be going well until Hurley suggested they're all dead, and then Jack began unravelling. There's something oddly powerful about Hurley's words, even when he means them as throwaway lines.
- Richard says he runs a school for kids who are extremely special, which makes him sound like Xavier in *The X-Men*.
- In the season 1 episode, "Outlaws," Locke tells a story about his foster sister, Jeannie, who fell off the monkey bars and died when he was a boy. He says his mother blamed herself and stopped functioning. A golden retriever showed up at their house and stayed with his mother for the next five years, until she died. However, in this episode his sister's name is Melissa. If there is continuity between these episodes, it would suggest that shortly after Alpert's visit, his foster mother got rid of him and he bounced into another foster environment with Jeannie. Or, Jeannie could be Melissa's sister and we just don't see her in this scene.
- After Richard Alpert leaves young John, his foster mother says accusingly, "What did you *do*?" in the same way Jack said it to Locke when everyone believed he had killed Boone, and after Locke knifed Naomi in the back.

- Ben tells Hurley he should have known better than to shoot Locke and leave him for dead, as if he knows the island won't let John die.
- The folder that contains the Secondary Protocol has the symbol for the Orchid station on it.
- When John steps out of the locker he's been stuffed in, there's a Geronimo Jackson poster on the inside of the door. Geronimo Jackson is a fictional band that has been alluded to several times in the series.
- John's guidance counsellor tells him he's destined to be a scientist, yet John has spent his time on the island arguing for faith over science.
- Caleb Steinmeyer, the actor playing the teenage John Locke, bears a strong resemblance to a young Kevin Tighe, the actor who plays Locke's father.
- Desmond has barely had a line since "The Constant." He simply appears running around behind Sayid and making facial expressions.
- The word "Kahana" is properly painted on the side of the freighter again.
- When Abaddon puts Locke at the top of the stairs, we get a reverse scene from the season 3 episode "Further Instructions." In that episode, where Locke hallucinates that Boone is walking him through an airport, we see a flash where Locke sits in his wheelchair at the base of an escalator while Boone stands at the top. The scene looks like Jacob's ladder from the Book of Genesis, with Locke lying at the bottom of a set of stairs. In this case, Locke is at the top of the stairs, not the bottom. That puts Locke in the position of God.
- One of the pervading theories among *Lost* fans, especially after this episode aired, is that Abaddon is actually Walt as an adult (when we see him as Abaddon, that is Walt time traveling back). Notice when Abaddon visits Locke in the hospital, he refers to him as "Mr. Locke," which is exactly what Walt always called him. He tells Locke that he had a miracle happen to him (he could be referring to his ability to astrally project himself, or simply to his survival of a plane crash) and says he was once convinced he was one thing, but turned out to be another.
- Frank is no doubt a hero, but he'd have been an even bigger one if he'd just crashed the helicopter directly into the ocean on the way back to the island.
- Christian isn't wearing the suit he was buried in.

Interesting Facts: Charles Henry Wyson, the actor who plays John Locke at the age of five, played Dan Vasser's son Zack on the brilliant but tragically short-lived series *Journeyman*.

John Locke and Ben Linus: Cain and Abel?

It's clear that Locke and Ben are the two characters who are linked most closely to the mystical aspects of the island. But the similarities between the two men don't stop there:

- Both have redheaded mothers named Emily.
- Both boys were born prematurely.
- As newborn John is being wheeled away from his mother, she yells for them to call him John; as Ben's mother dies, her last words are to call him Ben. (Interesting that both mothers are insistent on naming their boys something specific, like it was predestined.)
- Neither one is cuddled by his mother after he was born.
- Neither one is raised by his mother.
- There is an island link to both their births: Horace Goodspeed shows up moments after Ben is born; Richard Alpert comes to see John a couple of weeks after he is born.
- Ben is raised by a nasty father; Locke by a nasty foster parent.
- Both are visited by Richard Alpert early in their lives.
- Ben comes to the island because of his father who is given the job of "Work Man" (it's obvious Horace just wanted Ben there and Roger was the conduit to that goal). Locke comes to the island through a plane crash, but only after earlier attempts to get him there via a less bumpy route fall through.
- Horace is a huge influence on Ben; John is visited by Horace who directs him to Jacob's cabin.
- Ben follows an image of his mother into the jungle and meets Richard Alpert; Locke chases his mother through a parking lot, which leads him to Cooper, and ultimately the island.
- Each man blames his father for destroying his life.
- Both men kill their fathers.
- Both believe the island has spoken to them and that the island is something bigger than just a physical place.
- Both have uttered the phrase, "Don't tell me what I can't do!"
- Both have been in wheelchairs.
- Both survived a spinal problem that could have killed them.
- Both have heard Jacob's voice and seen him.
- Both have been "chosen" by the island and believe that it holds special power.

Is it possible John and Ben are linked? Could they be brothers? Or could they be two examples of the same person, showing us the two life paths that were possible, one man living out his life on the island, the other living away from the island. Looks like no matter which way the life was lived, it wasn't good.

There was a lot of fan speculation that Claire actually died in the house explosion in "The Shape of Things to Come," and because someone doesn't necessarily become ethereal on the island, she could be a Dead Woman Walking from that point on. While I'm not quite won over to the argument yet, there are some moments that add credence to it. First, in that episode, when Sawyer grabs her, she says, "Charlie?" as if she's actually seeing Charlie's ghost. More importantly, note Miles's comment when Claire emerges from the bedroom after having a rest. Sawyer asks her if she's all right, and she says, "I'm a bit wobbly but I'll live." Miles, the man who detects ghosts, replies, "I wouldn't be too sure about that." In "Something Nice Back Home," Miles takes an unusual interest in Claire, staring at her constantly, which forces Sawyer to give him a restraining order. (In this episode, we see her about to breastfeed Aaron, and I wrote on my blog that it would be a little difficult for a ghost to do that. One reader commented, "I believe ghost milk is referred to as 'lactoplasm'.") But it's this episode that lends the most credence to the idea. Claire is completely calm and laid-back in this scene, with one leg slung over the arm of the chair and smiling knowingly at her father. She is unconcerned with Aaron's whereabouts, and accepts Christian's statement that Aaron is where he's supposed to be. Perhaps Christian or the island has taken Claire ahead in the future to show her Aaron being happy and well, and that has caused her serenity in this scene. Adding further fuel to the argument, when Frank throws the sat phone package out of the helicopter at the end of "Cabin Fever," it lands on and crushes Claire's tent (you can see Aaron's crib beside it) as if to say she won't be needing it anymore.

When asked if Claire was dead, Carlton Cuse responded, "I think we want the fans to ask, 'What's happened to Claire?' I don't think it's 'Is she dead?' I think it's like, 'Where is she?' and, 'What's going on with her?'" Damon Lindelof added, "What's fascinating with *Lost* is there's a scene where Claire is in the cabin, and she is sitting next to a guy who *is* dead, and nobody is saying 'What's up with that?' They're all asking 'Is *she* dead?' I think the more operative question is 'What is dead?' That's a good question to ask, and one you will certainly be asking over the long hiatus." Opponents of the "Claire is Dead" theory took these statements as a declaration that Claire was alive, but Darlton never actually say anywhere that she's alive, they simply steer questions in a different direction.

Nitpicks: I'm starting to think none of the writers on the show have ever been through a pregnancy or even seen a pregnant woman before. I'll accept that Sun isn't showing at all, even though she's pencil-thin, and that her morning sickness is gone, even though it usually doesn't disappear until the beginning of the second trimester. But Emily is six months pregnant and isn't showing in the least. I don't buy that for an instant. Not even with those generous poodle skirts. You might be able to cover up a pregnancy at six months if you looked like Hurley, but not someone her size.

Oops: In "Further Instructions" we see Locke's driver's license and it says he was born in 1956. Emily is listening to Buddy Holly's "Everyday" right before she gives birth, but Buddy Holly and the Crickets didn't record that song until 1957. Also, when Locke approaches the Dharma Initiative grave, he is holding a machete in his right hand and is using it to hack the occasional branch in his way. Suddenly he stops to turn around, and the camera switches to a different angle where he drops the backpack, and the machete is stuck in the back of it. Finally, when Jack pulls the things out of the backpack that Frank tossed onto the island, he pulls the sat phone out of the bag, but it's not wrapped tightly in the yellow wrapper we saw Frank roll it up in.

4 8 15 16 23 42: Emily says she's almost six months pregnant, so there's a good chance she gives birth at **23** weeks. Horace has been dead for 12 years (**8 + 4**).

It's Just a Flesh Wound: Keamy slams Gault against the wall.

Any Questions?:

- In "Through the Looking Glass," Ben tells Jack that if he makes that phone call, "every living person on this island will die." Are there people on the island who are *not* living? Was he referring to Christian? Jacob?
- Does Sayid feel at all responsible for the pain that is inflicted upon Michael? When Gault tells Keamy he's not the one who gave them up to Ben, Sayid closes his eyes like he realizes he may have been a little hasty in turning him in.
- Did Emily's mother know Richard Alpert? She certainly sputters like she knows who he is. Is it possible that he's Locke's father? Emily's mother said he was twice Emily's age.
- Was Locke's foster mother hoping Richard Alpert would take John away?
- What is the significance of the six objects Richard puts in front of young John? What *does* he mean when he says they belong to John already?
- What is the Book of Laws? Is it an ancient book of the Others?
- Ben tells Hurley he wasn't always the Others' leader. Who was?
- If Locke is fated to be on that island, then Abaddon knows he will make it to Sydney, be turned away at the Walkabout office, and have to return home. Why does Abaddon put Locke on the plane? He seemed to be working for Widmore at the beginning of the season, but now he seems to

Abaddon: The Destroyer?

In the Book of Revelation, John describes the seven angels blowing their trumpets in sequence. When the fifth angel blows his, a star (or angel) falls to earth and opens Hell. Smoke pours out of the abyss, and scorpion-like locusts appear out of the smoke to devour those who are not among God's people. After a graphic description of the locusts, John says, "They have a king ruling over them, who is the angel in charge of the abyss. His name in Hebrew is Abaddon; in Greek the name is Apollyon (meaning 'The Destroyer')." In other Biblical references, Abaddon is the term used for the abyss itself, but it is always used synonymously with Hell or destruction.

The more oft-used name, Apollyon, was used by early Christians as an alternative name for the Devil. The most well-known use of Apollyon is in John Bunyan's Christian allegory, *The Pilgrim's Progress*. Published in 1678, the book is a story recounted by a narrator who falls asleep and dreams of a man, Christian, who leaves "the city of destruction" and heads for the Celestial City. Along the way he meets with allegorical characters like Hopeful, Talkative, Giant Despair, and Hypocrisy (no one ever accused allegories of being subtle). But one of the most memorable characters in Bunyan's book is Apollyon, the ruler of the land of destruction, who meets with Christian after he leaves the Palace Beautiful. Apollyon comes loping across the plain toward Christian, and as the narrator describes him, "Now the monster was hideous to behold: he was clothed with scales like a fish, and they are his pride; he had wings like a dragon, and feet like a bear, and out of his belly came fire and smoke; and his mouth was as the mouth of a lion." Apollyon asks Christian where he is going, and Christian tells him he is heading to Zion and away from the city of Destruction. Apollyon says if he is traveling through this land, then he is one of his subjects, for Apollyon is the ruler of the land. Christian declares his allegiance to his new prince, Christ, and Apollyon becomes angry. The two begin to fight, and Apollyon wounds him in his head, his hand, and his foot. The two wrestle for half a day until Apollyon grabs him around the middle and begins squeezing the life out of him. With his last ounce of strength, Christian grabs his sword and stabs Apollyon, causing the monster to retreat.

At this point in *Lost*, one can only speculate why the writers have named a character after the monster who battles Christian. Perhaps they just cruise around Wikipedia to come up with names — "Hey, I've got one, let's call the shopkeeper B.L. Zebub!" "Ha ha, Damon, that's a good one!" On the other hand, there's a hint that Matthew Abaddon is the enemy of Jacob and the island. If Christian Shephard is Jacob's mouthpiece, then he is aligned with Jacob (who has chosen both Ben and Locke) and by implication, Abaddon is with Widmore. The lines between the two sides are becoming clearer. Notice in "Cabin Fever," when Locke asks Christian what his name is, he simply says, "Christian" as if he has no last name, just like the character in *Pilgrim's Progress*.

be aligned with the Others. Notice he doesn't age, in much the same way that Richard remains ageless. If the Others are somehow traveling back and forth through time and therefore know what is going to happen, Abaddon seems to be a man who puts things in place to make sure they happen accordingly. Why? Is he working against Widmore, but the people he recruited think they're working *for* Widmore?

- What happens with the doctor? If he is killed a day after he is found dead on the beach, does that mean the island is in the future? So if he dies on the freighter and floats through the bubble that protects the island, he time travels to the future where they find him, call the freighter, but they're still stuck in the past where the doctor hasn't yet died? (Did anyone else's brain just explode?)
- Does Ben really believe that the island wants him to die and wants to save Locke, or does he just want to avoid going into the cabin? He seems to have given up completely, because he believes the island proved he was no longer the chosen one by given him a tumor on his spine. But by that same logic, didn't the island bring a spinal surgeon to him?
- *Move the island?!*

Ashes to Ashes: Mayhew was one of Keamy's mercenaries, and was attacked brutally by the smoke monster when he tried to run out of the jungle in "The Shape of Things to Come." Despite shooting his machine gun directly at the monster, it dragged him back into the jungle and probably pulled an Eko on him. Where the monster mercifully killed Eko on the spot, Mayhew didn't die immediately.

Doctor Ray, a dead ringer for Mark Messier, worked as a snarly doctor on the freighter and had the bedside manner of a poisonous toad. He had the rare experience of hearing people joke about how he was going to die as if it had already happened, moments before it actually did.

Captain Gault was a no-nonsense leader who led with pragmatism, not emotion. If a crewmember threatened to desert he would beat some common sense into them. He was sent on a mission to do whatever it was necessary to extract Benjamin Linus, but when he realized what was necessary, he stopped being a willing follower. He was killed by Keamy.

Music/Bands: At the beginning of the episode, Emily is listening to "Everyday" by Buddy Holly and the Crickets. The lyrics practically explain how season 4 feels, saying that every day is getting closer, going faster than a rollercoaster.

✍ *Mystery Tales #40* (April 1956)

When John Locke receives a visit from Richard Alpert when he is only five, Alpert lays six objects on the table and tells John to choose the objects "that already belong to you." One of those objects is a comic book. The comic book is *Mystery Tales*, issue 40, which was released in April 1956 (one month before John Locke was born). The cover features a man with a shocked look on his face, staring out an airplane window at a city sitting in the clouds. A few eagle-eye fans noticed the skyline of the buildings was almost exactly the same as the one that was being used on the series logo to promote season 4 (take a look at the reflection in the water of the palm trees — rather than trees, it's a city skyline). Underneath the cloud city is a second one, as if one city is hidden above another, concealed from the world. The words emblazoned on the cover shouted, "What was the secret of the mysterious HIDDEN LAND?" and "Does it pay to ignore the VOICE OF WARNING?"

One could draw numerous parallels between *Lost* and the cover of the comic book. First, the man is looking out an airplane window. Second, the island appears to be a land that's hidden from the rest of the world, as if it's veiled by something. But fans wondered if the similarities went beyond the cover. Who would be the first to get their hands on a copy?

Surprisingly, there was already one for sale on eBay. Imagine the fortunate person who posted this comic book a couple of days before the episode aired, probably expecting $30 or $40 for his vintage comic book, only to watch the bidding suddenly soar into the hundreds following the episode's broadcast on May 8. Luckily for *Lost* fans, the winning bidders (who paid a whopping $417 for the comic!) were a group of guys from Spain who were massive *Lost* fans . . . and who had every intention of scanning the comic for the rest of us to read.

You can go and check out the comic's *Twilight Zone*–esque sensibilities at www.mysterytales40.com. Here are summaries of the stories. The links to *Lost* (time travel, rich and powerful men, destinies and secrets) are pretty obvious.

The Hidden Land!
Fred Phipps is an accountant who works for Mr. Castin, a rich and powerful man who rose to power very quickly, to everyone's wonderment. Rumor has it that he was a photographer on a museum expedition in Tibet. He got lost, but when he

returned home, he became very wealthy very fast. Castin has become increasingly ill, and is popping pills constantly. One day Phipps finds a ring under Castin's desk. He puts it on and suddenly he is overwhelmed with ideas of how to make money and raise his place in society. He runs outside, where he sees outlines of people staring at him. He floats into the air and finds himself in a temple in Tibet, where a group of monks explain that the ring belongs to them and Castin had stolen it years earlier. They ask him to return it to them, saying one day they will give it to humanity to bring peace to the world. They insist that the ring can't be in the hands of one person or it will destroy him. Phipps gives back the ring, and he is returned to his home. As he walks up the street to his house, he is reminded that he has three children, a wife, and a home, and he's a rich man already.

A Warning Voice!
Sergeant Jim Harmon is returning from a two-year tour of duty in Germany. On a freighter, he hears a voice warning, "Watch out! Watch out!" He tells the captain of the ship, and moments later the ship almost hits an iceberg. He gets off the boat and onto a plane, and in the air hears the voice again. Sure enough, the plane is about to hit a mountain peak, but thanks to Harmon's efforts, averts it. Again, as they're about to land, he hears the voice, and tells the pilot, and they narrowly avoid hitting a car crossing the runway. Finally, on the cab ride home, he hears it again — "Watch out! Watch out!" — and the cabbie just misses dropping the car into a gully. Jim finally arrives at home and as he's hugging his wife, he hears the voice again. His wife says that's not a voice, it's a record his son was playing where the chorus is "Watch out! Watch out!" She explains that the record always gets stuck in that spot. The son had been playing it, hoping it would get his father home faster.

Crossroads of Destiny!
Ernest Falter is a scientist working on a time machine that not only travels to the past or the future, but to the "time-that-might-have-been." When his girlfriend, Martha, begs him to marry her and offers to support him so he can devote more time to the machine, he angrily sends her away. He finishes the machine and travels through time to see Julius Caesar at a "crossroads of his destiny." Caesar is wondering whether he should join the army or become a philosopher; he decides on the latter. Expecting a disastrous outcome, Falter travels slightly ahead to see the aftermath, and to his surprise, discovers the ancient Roman society living in

peace because of Caesar's philosophy. Falter then travels to Genoa to see a young Christopher Columbus decide to be a merchant rather than an explorer. Again, he travels ahead in time to see the Native Americans living peacefully; much later, Europeans happen upon America and decide to adopt the natives' peaceful way of living. Shocked, Falter begins to wonder if he, too, had made the wrong decision, and he zips ahead to see what would have happened had he stayed with Martha. He discovers a happy man who finished the machine sooner and had Martha at his side to support him. He returns to his own time and destroys the machine, worried that if people found out all the wrong decisions that had been made in history, they might focus on the past rather than bettering themselves in the present. He asks Martha's forgiveness, and she agrees to marry him.

Sammy's Secret!

Sammy has a secret: he can fly. He sneaks out his window at night, flying through the night sky. But he must always be careful to not let others see him, and this cautiousness restricts his freedom. One night he decides he's going to fly away and never come back, because he'll never be able to trust anyone with his secret. He flies higher and higher until he leaves the Earth's atmosphere. Suddenly he can't breathe. A spaceship pulls him in, and the people aboard refer to him as Porok. They tell him he was lost years ago on Earth and he was probably raised as an Earthling orphan, but he's actually Porok, from the planet Venus. They take him there and sure enough, the Venusians all fly up to greet him. He joins everyone and finally realizes true happiness.

The Silent Stranger

The town of Bradford Valley has fallen on bad times, and the mayor decides to take down the statue of the town founder, John Denton. His descendent, Abigail Denton, argues that they should keep it up for inspiration, because Denton built the entire town and started its factory. The mayor refuses to listen. A few days later, a man appears in town and refuses to say a word to anyone. Instead he goes to an old, abandoned house and begins taking it apart plank by plank. The townspeople begin to help him, drawn by an irresistible urge to do so. He silently finishes the job and walks the planks over to the town factory, where they begin rebuilding the factory using the parts from the old home and repairing the machinery. After the task is finished, they're all compelled to fix up their own shops and repaint the exteriors, making the main street of town look new. Then they go to work at the factory, completely exhausted but feeling a compulsion no one can explain. Soon after that, some businessmen are driving through the town and think it's lovely. They stop at the factory, which is making pre-fab homes, and put in large orders. The town is prosperous again, and to celebrate, they re-erect the statue of John Denton. When they clean up the statue's face, they realize that he was actually the silent stranger.

March Has 32 Days

Many *Lost* fans point to this instalment as being the one most important to the show, mainly because during the alternate reality game that ran post–season 4, the first email that went out to players had the title of this chapter hidden in its HTML coding. In this story, John Billings wakes up on March 31, tears off the March 30 page of his calendar, and goes to work. He is supposed to inspect a bridge that will be having a grand opening that day, but when his wife calls and asks him to take her to the airport, he obliges. At the grand opening, the bridge collapses, and though no one is hurt, Billings is wracked with guilt. He wishes he could live the day over again, and suddenly hears a voice in his head tell him that even if he did, he would still go to the airport. He wakes up the next morning and lo and behold, the March 30 page is still on the calendar, à la *Groundhog Day*. Realizing he's been given a second chance, Billings races to work and when his wife calls, he tells her he cannot take her to the airport. His co-workers tell him he's being silly, and one colleague says he checked the bridge personally the day before and everything was fine. Reluctantly, Billings gets into his car and is heading home when he realizes he's doing exactly what the voice said he'd do. He races to the bridge, inspects it, and finds a structural flaw, which is quickly fixed, and the opening goes well. He was able to change his destiny. The comic then cuts to a room of astronomers scratching their heads and wondering why there were 32 days in March that year, and they conclude they'll simply never know.

The Travelers

Presented as text only, with just a single illustration, "The Travelers" is a story of the Jesters, a new couple who moves into a "house of the future" full of futuristic gadgets. When the new neighbors come over to welcome them, they're surprised to see the couple completely settled in; the night before, the house had been empty. Ajax Jester says they liked it right away, and that they have moved around a lot because they aren't tied down by time and obligations, at which point his wife gives him a sharp look. One night, the Jesters hold a television party to show off their new television set, but they seem so enthralled by every program they barely pay attention to their guests. One guest, Tom Jackson, accidentally spills an ashtray on the ground, and Ajax absentmindedly sweeps his hand in the air and the garbage disappears. His wife tries to pretend it was a magic trick, but everyone stares in astonishment. When a history show on Ancient Rome comes on, Ajax says it would be nice to travel back to that time and wander around. The next day the house is completely empty, save for some maps that date as far back as antiquity and as far forward as 2500 A.D. The neighbors are confused. But when they find a toga and gold sandals in a closet, Tom admits he had a dream in which he was traveling through space and time. He was heading for Ancient Rome when he suddenly decided he didn't want to go, and so he headed back. He heard a voice telling him to go to Rome or he'd miss everything, but he left. No one ever finds out what happened to the Jesters.

4.12   There's No Place Like Home, Part 1

Original air date: May 15, 2008
Written by: Damon Lindelof, Carlton Cuse
Directed by: Stephen Williams
Guest cast: Nestor Carbonell (Richard Alpert), Byron Chung (Mr. Paik), Michelle Forbes (Karen Decker), Andrea Gabriel (Nadia), Veronica Hamel (Margo Shephard), Lillian Hurst (Carmen Reyes), June Kyoko Lu (Mrs. Paik), Cheech Marin (David Reyes), Esmond Chung (Underling), Noah Craft (Hendricks), Susan Duerden (Carole), Garrett Hughes (Reporter #1), David Michael (Pilot), Souhil Nimeh (Arabic Reporter), Eul Noh (Korean Reporter), Alicia Rae (Blonde Reporter), Joe Sikora (Co-Pilot)

Flash: Oceanic 6

It's a race to see who can get to the Orchid station first, while Dan tries to get as many people off the island as he can. Meanwhile, we see the future of the Oceanic 6 will include tearful reunions, press conferences, birthday parties, and hostile takeovers.

One always expects the end of a castaway story to be about either death or a rescue. Four years ago, when *Lost* was just starting out, some fans must have

"You all look so happy to be rescued!" The Oceanic 6 hold a bittersweet press conference to announce their return. (MARIO PEREZ/© ABC/COURTESY: EVERETT COLLECTION)

imagined that when the series finale came, it would involve some characters being rescued and reunited with their families. Who could have guessed that scene would happen in the *middle* of the series?

"There's No Place Like Home, Part 1" is mostly setting things up for the two-hour finale that happens next. There are many questions raised, with the majority of the answers waiting for us in the next episode. What intrigued fans more than the island action, though, is what happens in the future. This episode opens the same way the first *Lost* flashback did — looking out an airplane window at a blue sky with fluffy white clouds. Rather than beginning in the body of the plane, we open in the cockpit, with two pilots talking about their "cargo." It quickly becomes clear their cargo is the Oceanic 6.

At the press conference, we see the beginning of the lie that Jack perpetuates on the witness stand in "Eggtown" and it's as mysterious in this episode as it was in that one. Even now, off the island, Jack takes charge and orders everyone to "stick to the story" that they've presumably constructed in the time between being rescued and being put on the chartered plane. Finally, in answer to what fans had been nitpicking since "Eggtown," the writers did the math, altered Jack's story, and have put things right. Where before Jack said eight people survived and two died, now he says three people died and then Aaron was born, which makes sense. Until this point, fans assumed that the story would necessarily involve Claire as one of the survivors, since she had to give birth to Aaron after the crash. But now we realize the lie is deeper than originally thought, and they're suggesting Kate is Aaron's birth mother.

The press conference scene is interesting, because Decker first confirms that their plane had gone down near the Sunda Trench, which is not true, but it solidifies the fake plane-crash story. Is Oceanic in cahoots with Widmore? Wouldn't the press question why there were 324 bodies on that plane, but these six people are clearly not dead? Secondly, when the Korean reporter asks Sun if Jin had died on the island, Jack looks at Sun anxiously. Why is it so important that she say no? Do they have a story involving three other people who died, and it's important that Jin can't be one of those people? Clearly the reporters smell something fishy with the Oceanic 6's story, especially considering their pointed questions to Kate regarding her being pregnant with Aaron.

After the group is done with the media, Hurley seems to go back to his old life, Sayid finds happiness with Nadia, Kate and Aaron are doing well, Jack has learned to say goodbye to his father and move on, and Sun has developed the nerve to stand up to her domineering father. However, we know from other flashforwards that Hurley will go mad, Sayid will lose Nadia, Kate will find stability with Jack but will lose it, Jack will degenerate into an emotional carcass, and Sun will mourn the loss of her husband while raising their daughter alone.

Meanwhile, back on the island, Ben's resignation in the previous episode seems all but gone, as he once again takes charge. Now that Locke's new mission necessarily involves Ben — he is the only one who knows what Jacob means by "move the island" — he can once again boss everyone around and make condescending remarks about how slow everyone else is. Hurley is probably rethinking his decision to stay, Locke is starting to lose control, and no one but Ben knows exactly what is about to happen. As they walk directly into the lion's den to meet Keamy and company, Ben seems confident he has things under control. But he thought that about the Alex situation, and look how *that* turned out.

What is so fascinating about this episode is that we know what's going to happen to these people in the next eight days, but the end of this episode still leaves us in suspense. We know who is going to get away safely, but at this point it's the *how* that keeps us glued to our seats. It's one of the few episodes that features almost every cast member, yet it feels completely fleshed-out and never rushed. The Oceanic 6 will be rescued in only a day or two, but by the end of this episode a montage (set to Michael Giacchino's gorgeous score) makes us realize exactly how scattered everyone is. Ben is turning himself over to the baddies. Locke is about to enter a chamber that will allow him to move the island. Hurley is lying in wait. Sawyer and Jack are crossing the jungle in pursuit of Keamy and his fellow psychos, as Jack oozes blood from his appendectomy stitches. Kate and Sayid have been captured by Richard Alpert and the heavily armed Others and are being led somewhere. Dan is ferrying people from the island to the freighter. Michael, Desmond, and Jin are in the belly of the freighter, where they've just discovered a wall of C-4 explosives. Sun and Aaron are standing on the deck of the freighter, with nowhere to escape should the bomb go off.

In other words, just another day on the *Lost* island.

Highlight: The way Sayid blinks when he is reunited with Nadia, as if trying to convince himself he's not dreaming. It's a beautiful moment, rendered heartbreaking because we know how it will end.

Timeline: The events of this episode take place on Day 100 (December 30, 2004).

Did You Notice?:

- The copilot is rubbing a lucky rabbit's foot in the cockpit, and later when Hurley's father gives him the keys to the Camaro, he gives him the rabbit's foot keychain we first saw in "Tricia Tanaka Is Dead."
- When the Oceanic 6 are being brought back to the U.S., it's the first time we've seen baby Aaron wearing clothes.
- The plane lands in Honolulu, so, for the first time, Hawaii gets to play itself on this show.
- Not one of the Oceanic 6 has a sibling who shows up to see them, highlighting just how many characters are only children — Sun, Kate, and Jack (as far as he knows) have no siblings. Hurley has a brother Diego, but either the writers forgot about him or Diego wasn't able to come for some reason. Sawyer, Jin, Claire, Locke, Ben, and Walt are all only children; Boone and

Shannon are only step-siblings. We are never told if Ana Lucia, Michael, Sayid, or Desmond have any brothers or sisters. In fact, Eko, Charlie, and Juliet are the only characters whose siblings seem to play a major role in their lives.

This mansion on Farmers Road in Kahala, Oahu, serves as the exterior of Hurley's lavish house. (RYAN OZAWA)

- When the Oceanic 6 are greeting their relatives, Sun goes straight to her mother and won't even look at her father, and Paik clearly notices.
- The Orchid must be a need-to-know station, because Juliet had no idea what it is or does.
- In "Confirmed Dead," Dan seemed to know less about the island than anyone, and now he seems to know more than anyone.
- When Sawyer and Miles come stumbling out of the jungle, it is the first time Jack has seen Sawyer and Aaron since Sawyer broke ranks in "The Beginning of the End." And the last time Kate saw Sawyer she had just slapped him and walked out on him.
- Sawyer calls the Others' camp "New Otherton," which is the first time it's called that on the show (it's what the crew has been calling it on set).
- When Sawyer decides to follow Jack, he mutters, "Hold up, you don't get to die alone," a great mockery of Jack's famous line.
- Decker says they were found on day 108, and by the Lostpedia timeline, we're currently on day 100.
- The story Decker tells is reminiscent of Rousseau's — six people were stranded on the island when a woman gave birth. (If Charlie was still alive at that point — see **Interesting Facts** below — there would have been six people.)
- Kate lies about Aaron's age (the younger they say he is, the less pregnant she would have been before the crash). She says he's five weeks, when in fact he's a little over two months.
- When Sun ascends the staircase, it's the same camera angle as when she ascended to ask her father for money to pay off Jin's mother. But now she's in a completely different power position.

Filming at St. Patrick's Church in Kaimuki, Jorge Garcia and Naveen Andrews wait between takes of the exterior scene of Christian Shephard's memorial service in "There's No Place Like Home, Part 1." This footage was not used in the final cut of the episode that aired. (RYAN OZAWA)

- When Sun enters the room where Paik is having a meeting, it would seem he has just discovered that someone has bought a controlling interest in his company by putting the money through five different banks, as one of his underlings tells him. Little could he know that person was his own daughter.
- Mr. Tranh and Lady Tranh were apparently rehired. (Remember the bundle of money they accepted in "Tricia Tanaka Is Dead" to leave the place?)

- Hurley tells his dad he doesn't want anything to do with the money. This explains why he drives such a run-down old car (that backfires constantly) and why he is in such a low-rent psychiatric hospital.
- In "Something Nice Back Home," Jack visits Hurley at the hospital and Hurley says he was happy until he saw Charlie. But this episode suggests his unhappiness had started long before then.
- When Locke asks Ben when he was ever truthful, Ben doesn't respond.
- When Daniel, driving the motor boat, drops off the first batch of people at the freighter, he and Desmond acknowledge each other but don't say anything. They have a new connection after Desmond's breakdown, but it seems it will remain silent between them.
- Once again, Jack says Sawyer's "Son of a *bitch!*" line when Sawyer tells him Hurley is with Ben.
- Sawyer doesn't mention Locke is also with Ben, as if he's not important.
- Several times throughout this episode, someone looks at Aaron's face and he's a picture of serenity, and they seem to calm down after seeing him.
- When Ben is giving Locke the instructions of how to get into the Orchid station, he tells him to walk down a hall and go to an alcove on the north wall. This reminds us of one of the sayings on Eko's stick — "Lift up your eyes and look north." Locke took that saying to be prophetic, and it still seems to be important.

Interesting Facts: This episode originally aired on May 15, but two weeks later, they repeated it before running the season finale and added some extra footage from the press conference. In the extra footage, Jack says that the three people who survived the plane crash but who died on the island were: Boone, who died immediately following the crash due to his internal injuries (like the marshal); Libby, who didn't make it through the first week; and Charlie, who died a few weeks before they were rescued. It's not clear why he chose those three, and why Jin couldn't have been one of them, but here's hoping it becomes clearer in a later episode. Also, there's a rumor that they had done a reaction shot of Sun's parents looking shocked when she answers a question in English. That might end up on the DVDs, and by the time you read this, it'll already be there.

Nitpicks: Not to sound like a broken record, but if Kate is going to suggest she was seven months pregnant when the marshal apprehended her, then why didn't the police report mention she was pregnant? I don't care who you are, if you are

Sawyer's Nicknames

Because this season was much shorter than any other, Sawyer didn't have as much time to use his fancy nicknames. But when he did, they were classic.

Desmond: Scotty
Hurley: Ese, Montezuma, Chicken Little
Locke: Colonel Kurtz, Johnny
Walt: Taller Ghost Walt
Charlotte: Red
Karl: Kid
Ben: Yoda, Gizmo
Miles: Bruce Lee, Donger, Genghis
Rousseau, Karl, and Alex: Frenchie and the kids
Frank: Shaggy, Kenny Rogers
Jack: Sundance

a size 0, you will be showing at seven months. If Oceanic ends up paying out large sums of money, they'll probably make the survivors undergo a physical, which would instantly determine that Kate has never had a baby. Even if they don't, if Kate had given birth on the island, the only means of feeding it would have been breastfeeding it. Yet the moment they were rescued, one of the first things she probably requested would have been formula. Wouldn't anyone have questioned that? Or wondered why she has washboard abs and no stretch marks? It just doesn't seem to be something she can pass off so easily.

Also, Dan's urgency to get off the island in this episode shows once again how inserted the Tempest storyline still feels (see "The Other Woman," page 74). In that episode, there was a powerful likelihood that every person on the island was going to die, but Dan and Charlotte hung around the island, chatting with other people, doing experiments, and acting like nothing was a rush at all, and then they got over to the station with minutes to spare and worked madly against hope, assuming it would probably blow and they wouldn't be able to stop it. In this episode, the moment Dan discovers they've gone to the Orchid station and there was a possibility that something bad could happen to the people on the island, he begins ferrying them to the freighter as quickly as he can. Why didn't he feel the same sense of urgency when there was a possibility they'd all be killed?

Claire's mom, Carole, tells Jack all about Claire and apologizes for the timing (mid-funeral), but says, "You need to know." Why does he need to know that his father was unfaithful to his mother and he'd had a child with another woman? His father is dead, and as far as Carole knows, his sister is dead, so what can he do with this information? He can't confront his father about it, and he can't start a relationship with a sibling who is deceased. While I loved seeing Jack's face when he discovered the news, divulging this at his father's memorial service seemed in incredibly bad taste.

Finally, why did Sawyer call Frank a yahoo? The last time he saw Frank, he was saving Sawyer's life by distracting Keamy while Sawyer, Claire, Miles, and Aaron hid in the jungle.

Oops: The memorial service for Christian is held 10 months after the plane crash, in July, but Aaron still looks the same way he did when they were rescued in January.

4 8 15 16 23 42: Ms. Decker says the Oceanic 6 were discovered on Day 108, which is the sum of the numbers. Jack says there were only **8** people left by the time they got to the island. The coast guard plane is number 1717, which adds up to **16**. The crackers Locke hands to Hurley are **15** years old. Hurley sees the numbers on his odometer, showing a whopping **481,516** miles on the car (no wonder they had to change the engine) and **234.2** miles on the tripometer below. The freighter is rigged with C-**4**.

It's Just a Flesh Wound: Ben gets clocked in the head with the butt of Keamy's handgun.

Any Questions?:

- Why are the Oceanic 6 being transported in a cargo plane?
- When Decker first walks back to the Oceanic 6, she nods to a bald man sitting on the right side of the plane. Who is it? Is it just a crew member or someone far more important?
- Daniel flips on the monitor function on the sat phone, and everyone can overhear Keamy's conversation with Frank. Daniel quickly flips it off. Why didn't he keep it running to try to get more information?
- How does Daniel know about the Secondary Protocol? No one else seemed to know what it was without checking the file, not even Keamy. Why did he have a drawing of the Orchid symbol in his notebooks? Has Dan been to the Orchid station before? Did he encounter it with his time travel experiments? Has he been on this island but doesn't remember?

- Also, he'd written earlier that if anything happened to him, Desmond would be his constant. Shouldn't he be staying a little closer to Des?
- What has happened that makes Jack want to lie?
- Are the five survivors the ones who have come up with the lie, or is Oceanic blackmailing them somehow?
- Why did Oceanic (or the 6) come up with the idea of having them land in Sumba? Oceanic Flight 815 would have been traveling eastward to L.A., but Sumba is to the northwest of Australia.
- In "Tricia Tanaka Is Dead," Hurley discovered once and for all that he makes his own luck and that he's not actually cursed. So why is he still so freaked out by the numbers? His upset when all of the numbers are on his odometer is understandable, but why does he tell the reporter that he doesn't want his $150 million? Didn't he decide that money was not cursed after all?
- How could Hurley possibly eat crackers that are 15 years old? Why don't they taste like wood?
- Who was Ben communicating with when he used the flashing mirror? Was it Richard? Richard and company are in the jungle nabbing Kate and Miles — did Ben tell them to do it? Or is he communicating with someone else? Is it possible, as one person suggested on my blog, that he is communicating with a future or past version of himself?
- How much money did Oceanic pay out? If Sun was able to buy a controlling interest in Paik's company, one assumes they received a very large settlement. Then again, if there are several shareholders in the company, and Sun bought a 15 percent stake in the company and the next highest owner has 14, she would have a controlling interest. But even at 15 percent, she would presumably have paid millions of dollars.
- Sun tells her father that he is one of two people responsible for Jin's death. Who is the other?
- Who really put the odometer to those numbers? Something tells me Hurley's being manipulated so he ends up back at the institution. Could Widmore be involved? Did Charlie reset them? Or is it possible Hurley's father is in on everything? Either he had something to do with the odometer numbers, or Cheech Marin is a worse actor than I thought. His "Wow. What a coincidence," is the least amount of surprise he could have possibly shown, considering what his son has just gone through due to those same numbers.

Mirror, Mirror, On the Wall

In Lewis Carroll's *Through the Looking-Glass, and What Alice Found There*, Alice steps through the mirror above her mantle and ends up in the "looking-glass world," where all of the characters are red or white chess pieces, moving around a large board playing an elaborate game. In the world, everything is backwards, just like it would be in a mirror. The season 3 finale of *Lost*, "Through the Looking Glass," was the series game-changer, where suddenly the flashbacks became flashforwards, and similarly, we saw things in opposition to what we were used to. Just as everything in the looking-glass world was backwards, everything in the flashforward shows us the future, rather than the past. In previous seasons, we've seen characters looking into mirrors, but they usually seem to be soul-searching. Desmond stares into a mirror at the beginning of season 2, and he's built a hall of mirrors to allow him to see up the hatch in case of intruders. Juliet looks into a mirror at herself before breaking down in tears. But in season 4, mirrors tend to be destroyed or to represent a negative action that's being played out, and they usually appear in pivotal scenes.

"The Beginning of the End": Hurley smashes his car into a special mirror sale, destroying dozens of them (and goodness knows how many years of bad luck he'll incur by doing that). As he later sits in the police interrogation room, staring into a one-way mirror, he suddenly sees an image of Charlie swimming toward him, before Charlie reaches out and smashes the mirror. It was only a hallucination, however.

"The Economist": Elsa is looking into a mirror as Sayid tells her the truth about who he is, and soon after she shoots him. Sayid then smashes a mirror to get her attention, and shoots and kills her when she enters the room.

"The Constant": Desmond sees himself in the mirror in the freighter's "sick bay" and realizes how old and haggard he looks compared to his 1996 self. He then looks at himself in another mirror in 1996, and mentally compares the two images.

"Ji Yeon": Sun is looking into a mirror and putting on lipstick when she gets her first contractions and goes into labor. Later, she's doing the same thing when Hurley knocks on the door. This is most likely her first interaction with one of the Oceanic 6 since the rescue.

"The Shape of Things to Come": When Ben is in Tunisia, he watches Ishmael in a mirror so he can follow him. This happens moments before Sayid shoots and kills Ishmael, effectively becoming Ben's hit man.

"Something Nice Back Home": Jack looks into a mirror at the beginning of the episode, immediately before we realize Kate is the woman he will be with in the future. On the island, Kate holds up a mirror so Jack can watch his gruesome surgery, until Juliet realizes how ridiculous he's being and orders Bernard to knock him out.

"There's No Place Like Home, Part 1": Ben communicates with someone in the hills by using a mirror and flashing some sort of message at them. He does this right before entering the Orchid station, where everything changes.

- When Desmond tells Hendricks the engine room is fixed, Hendricks tells him he's getting interference and can't see the reef, and unless he gets it working again he can't come closer than five miles from the island. Isn't that a heck of a lot closer than the current 40 miles?
- Who rigged the ship with the C-4 explosives? Is the trigger that thing that Keamy's wearing on his arm? If it was Keamy, where had he been keeping all of the C-4 all this time? It's not exactly something you can hide in a suitcase.
- At Christian's memorial service, Jack said he wrote out some things 10 months ago in a Sydney airport. If Jack was rescued in early January, why did he wait until July to actually hold the memorial service for Christian?
- When Jin and Sun run into the room and see the explosives, Jin tells Sun in Korean that she needs to leave, but there are no subtitles. Why?
- What is Ben's plan?

4.13, 4.14   There's No Place Like Home, Parts 2 & 3

Original air date: May 29, 2008
Written by: Damon Lindelof, Carlton Cuse
Directed by: Jack Bender
Guest cast: Starletta DuPois (Michael's mother), Malcolm David Kelley (Walt), Sonya Walger (Penelope Widmore), William Blanchette (Aaron), Achilles Gacis (Guy in car), Damon Juan (Indonesian boy), Alex Petrovitch (Henrik)

Flash: Oceanic 6

Ben prepares to move the island and Locke finds his new life path. Michael, Jin, and Desmond attempt to disable the freighter bomb and the Oceanic 6 become . . . the Oceanic 6.

The writers on *Lost* all share an inside joke that's been going on since the first season: they use code names to describe the big twist in each season finale. In season 1, they referred to Walt's abduction as "The Bagel." Why? No one knows. Someone said it, they thought it was funny, and it stuck. Similarly, the two men in the blizzard at the end of season 2 were referred to as "The Challah." Last season, when asked for the code word for the twist, Damon Lindelof referred to it as "The Snake in the Mailbox." After the episode aired, the code name actually made sense. Like finding a snake in your mailbox, a flashforward is the last thing one would expect. But this season, when Damon Lindelof referred to the twist in this year's finale as "The Frozen Donkey Wheel," most reporters rolled their eyes and gave up. And then the twist was . . . *exactly that*. Who'd have thunk it?

You have to hand it to Darlton, these guys know how to pull off a finale. This one didn't pack quite the wallop of the season 3 finale, but it certainly brought the season to a close by taking a bunch of story lines and pulling them together, and did so in a beautiful way that left fans itching for the next season, which was eight months away.

Season 4 has been the season of rifts and separations. In the first episode, the survivors divide themselves into two camps, and for the most part, the camps don't see each other again. The four freighter folk come to the island and are immediately separated from each other. On the freighter, people are committing suicide or killing each other. They are split between those who are onside and want to capture Ben and those who don't trust the man who hired them. Even the flashes are divided between flashforwards and flashbacks (notably, only the people who get off the island get flashforwards, and everyone else appears in flashback). As with previous finales, this one split the characters up into various locations, forcing us to wonder how they'll ever come back together again. Never before have they been *this* far apart. A full character reunion is something even Jacob wouldn't be able to muster without help from Smokey, various island spirits, and a couple of polar bears. So where have we left everyone?

The newbies this season were the freighter folk. The four people who drop to the island after Naomi's death each have their own issues. Daniel suffers from severe memory loss and has come to the island to experiment with its unique properties. Miles can see dead people and has presumably come to have long conversations with them. Frank should have been the pilot of 815 and he believes the plane discovered in the Sunda Trench is a hoax. Charlotte is an anthropologist who seemed to be the least interesting of the group . . . until this episode. When Miles asks Charlotte why she would leave when she's spent her whole life looking for this place, it suddenly makes us all look at her a little more closely. Has she been to the island before? When her parachute landed in the tree and she dropped herself into the water in "Confirmed Dead," the first thing she did was smile and splash about in the water, like she was in a familiar place. After that the island doesn't seem to interest her much, but maybe she was hiding her glee from everyone else. Before even coming to the island, when she found the Dharma collar from the polar bear in the desert, she looked pleased, as if she recognized the symbol. She also knew that Ben had used gas to annihilate the Dharma Initiative. Could she have been a child born of the Dharma Initiative? Has she traveled through time somehow (whether or not she knows it) and is actually much older than we think, and previously lived on the island decades or centuries ago? Could she be related to the mystical Adam and Eve we saw in the caves in season 1? Could she *be* Eve? Could she be Annie, the girl Ben was fond of, whom we saw briefly in "The Man Behind the Curtain"? Is it possible that Charlotte was the last person to turn the donkey wheel and was ejected from the island, and has spent years trying to find her way back? Or, as some fans have speculated, is there a chance Annie got pregnant by Ben, left the island to avoid dying, and Charlotte is their child?

Miles has also chosen to stay on the island, probably because the stories the island's dead are telling him have been keeping him entertained and wanting to know more. We've been led to believe that Miles can detect ghosts, yet he seems to know a lot about the living, too. He knows something about Charlotte's past, and he's the one who declared that Michael's name wasn't Kevin Johnson. He knows about Ben, enough that he says he knows how to lie to Widmore and report that Ben is dead. His choice of $3.2 million is a curious number, so there's definitely something afoot, or else why is he bribing Ben for that particular amount? How does Miles know so much about living people? Are the whispers talking to him more clearly than to everyone else and through them he's finding out information about everyone? Or is there a lot more to Miles than we've been led to believe? Either way, I'm definitely looking forward to his unique brand of snark next season.

Frank is the most heroic of the bunch. He saved the lives of Sawyer, Claire, Aaron, and Miles when Keamy thought he heard Aaron make a noise in the jungle. Then he flew the Oceanic 6 (plus Desmond) to safety. While Frank knows that the fake Flight 815 is, indeed, a fake, he doesn't seem to know much else. When he arrives, it seems he's been kept in the dark about what Keamy's people are really there to do; he doesn't understand what Dan's experiments mean; and he knows little about Miles and Charlotte. He's been hired because he is a pilot, but why Abaddon chose him is still a mystery. He's the one person alive who knows with absolute certainty that the Sunda Trench plane was a hoax. Perhaps, if Widmore is sending a team of mercenaries to the island to kill everyone on it who could prove his fake plane to be, indeed, fake, he could also be planning on killing Frank. However, at the end of the season, Frank is on a boat with Desmond, away from the island. He knows about the island, knows that it disappeared, knows what Keamy and his men were doing there, and he is probably a hunted man now. But if he's with Desmond — who is also, most likely, avoiding his future father-in-law — he might stay safe. I don't think we've seen the last of Frank Lapidus. (Jeff Fahey, incidentally, is the only one of the freighter folk who was never made a cast member in season 4.)

Daniel has been a fan favorite from the beginning. Jeremy Davies plays Daniel's jittery, nervous self with aplomb. Daniel has an affinity to Charlotte (some fans have speculated that in the future he and Charlotte are a couple, and he shows such tenderness to her because he's seen the future). He also has a knowledge of the island — for some reason, he knows what the Orchid station is and what it is capable of. Could he have already time traveled to the island in the past? In the future? Is it possible he is Adam? The fact that Dan has lost his memory makes him a tragic figure: if he's been to the future, he can't reliably tell you about it. Therefore, his past and future are as much a mystery to him as they are to us. We leave Dan at the end of this episode floating in the water between the boat and the freighter. The big question is: when the island was moved, did it take Dan with it? Or is he now floating in oblivion? Considering that the people on the boat with him were a bunch of background characters, there's a good chance they will all become major characters. And yet, if we remember the disaster that was Nikki and Paulo, the writers might want to avoid that route. Perhaps we'll get a storyline reminiscent of Hitchcock's *Lifeboat*; or Daniel will get sucked away with the island to be a member of the doomed islanders.

Yes, in one of the more jaw-dropping moments of the season, Ben has managed to move the island. And that puts a bunch of our beloved Lostaways in a new place where no one can find them. Considering it took Penny three years of waiting to discover a blip on the radar when Desmond blew up the Swan station, it makes sense that it will take at least that long for anyone to find these folks again. We have two seasons left, and the flashforwards are showing the action three years in the future, but we have to cover three years of island time in only 34 more television hours, while it's taken 85 hours to cover three months. Perhaps all those scenes where we saw time moving differently on the freighter than it did on the island were a hint at what's to come. Maybe in the island's new location, three years in the outside world can pass in a matter of weeks of island time. That way we could still follow the islanders on a daily basis, while time on the outside will jump around.

Left on the island is Sawyer, who is sitting with Juliet on the shore. Sawyer has turned into a superhero this season. Whether it's running through a hail of bullets to save Claire's life or finally taking a leadership role and marching Claire, Aaron, and Miles across the island, or following Jack back to the mercenaries so he doesn't bleed out on the way, or (gah!) jumping from the helicopter and sacrificing his only chance at rescue so the rest of them could actually make it back, Sawyer has become the character who has evolved the most. No longer is he that self-centered jerk who pretended he had Shannon's asthma medication just so he could get a kiss from Kate or the guy who took all the camp supplies and declared himself sheriff. We know that Sawyer has spent his life hunting down the real Sawyer, who destroyed his life, and when he finally finds him in "The Brig" and kills him, his lifelong goal has been reached. He no longer has a purpose in life, so he must find a new one. And he's certainly done that. Of course, he still has his moments of jerkdom, like when he told Kate he didn't want her to have his baby, but when he emerged from the jungle holding Aaron in "There's No Place Like Home, Part 1," the look on Kate's face was of pure shock. Season 4 was the only season so far that hasn't had a Sawyer flashback, but his presence on the island has been so strong, fans barely noticed.

Is there a possibility he and Juliet will become an item? (Those shippers have already declared themselves the "Suliets," since the term Jawyer — meaning Jack and Sawyer — was taken long ago.) Juliet was originally married to Edmund Burke, who, it seems, has a proclivity for affairs with his research assistants, and that marriage ended. Since then, she's been the other woman in Goodwin and Harper's marriage, and in Jack and Kate's on-again, off-again relationship. Why not become the other woman in the Sawyer-Kate hookup? We leave Juliet sitting on the beach drinking herself into oblivion as she looks at the freighter with a comical look on her face. It's like she's realized that the idea of rescue is a farce, and she's starting to wonder if she's doomed to wait on the island for all of eternity like a character in a Beckett play.

Claire is also on the island. Now separated from Aaron, she seems to be serene and comfortable with Christian Shephard. It's not clear if she's dead, but she now has a strong connection to Christian, and therefore to Jacob, and therefore to the island. The producers have already said Claire won't be around much in season 5, but her story is not finished yet, and we'll be seeing more of her in the final season.

To film the scene where the gang in the helicopter crashes into the ocean, the *Lost* crew went to Waianae in Oahu, filmed the scene just offshore, and then in post-production made it look like they were miles from civilization in a vast ocean. Top left: Yunjin Kim, Naveen Andrews, and Matthew Fox are in the water as Jorge Garcia pulls Evangeline Lilly into the boat. (Note the children playing on the beach in the background, showing the cast was very close to shore when filming the scene.) Top right: Evangeline Lilly looks off the side of the boat (right) as Jorge Garcia cradles "Aaron" and Naveen Andrews pulls Yunjin Kim aboard. Bottom left: Jorge Garcia, Evangeline Lilly, and Jeff Fahey stand under umbrellas while Matthew Fox stands further up, shielding his eyes from the sun. Bottom right: The cast and crew wait between takes on the public beach. From left: Henry Ian Cusick, Jorge Garcia, Matthew Fox, Evangeline Lilly (wearing sunglasses and sitting in a chair), Yunjin Kim (facing away from us), Jeff Fahey, and Naveen Andrews. (RYAN OZAWA)

Neither Rose nor Bernard made it onto the Zodiac raft, so they are somewhere on that beach as well. Bernard has referred to Locke as a murderer, and Rose feels the same. But considering Rose believes the island has healed her in the same way it healed Locke, and Locke has now been proven right (in that Keamy came to kill everyone on the island) could Rose and Bernard end up joining the Others? Or will they stay with Sawyer, Juliet, and the remaining background characters to become an opposing force? Either way, this probably means a bigger role for Bernard and Rose on the show.

Most of the background survivors have been disposed of now. We started off with 33 of them, and one by one they've been offed in one scene or another, including three killed in "The Shape of Things to Come" during Sawyer's shootout (more may have been killed offscreen by Keamy's men or upon the entrance of the smoke monster) and three more were presumably blown up on the freighter in this episode. Since Juliet and Sawyer are alone, Locke joined the Others on his own, and Claire is with Christian, it would seem the only background survivors left are currently floating in Dan's Zodiac raft or they're fending for themselves in the jungle.

After being used as a pawn by the island and the Others, the much-abused Michael is finally dead. Christian tells Michael his work is finally over, and he's free to "go." So what exactly was his ultimate role, what did the island need him for? The information he provided to Ben didn't seem to protect Ben at all; it simply allowed Ben to catch other people off guard as he recited their biographies to them. He destroyed the engine, but he also got it working again. It seems his role was to keep the battery cold long enough for Sun to get away on the plane. Either way, he's now gone; but we know from Hurley's flashforward that Walt seems to know his father returned to the island after being in New York, because he comments to Hurley that his father was one of the ones who needs to be protected. Michael's story is over, but Walt's may still continue. From everything we already know about Walt, it would seem strange to leave his story unfinished.

Jin, too, appears to die in the freighter explosion, but it's not clear. His death didn't seem as legitimate as Michael's — Michael had to keep spraying the battery with liquid nitrogen, so he couldn't leave, but there was no reason Jin should have stayed behind . . . or even have been there in the first place. Desmond leaves the hold because there's no way he's going to get this close to Penny and not see her, and Jin stays. But is he dead? On a common sense level, the obvious answer is yes. But this show has never been about common sense. Could Jin have a purpose, too?

If he does, the island would keep him safe by telling him to jump in the water before the explosion. Or maybe the freighter was close enough to the bubble surrounding the island that he suddenly teleported off the freighter (yes, I'm being a little too hopeful now). A screen capture taken from the nanosecond before the freighter blows up shows no one standing on the deck, but then again, the production team probably used an empty freighter to add the CGI effects of an explosion. Could Jin still be alive? It would be a great story line if Sun believed that her husband was dead, only to one day return to the island and find him alive.

Desmond has spent more time on the island than any of the survivors, and he's finally departed after three very long years. The reunion between Desmond and Penny is the stuff of old-fashioned romance films, and it was filled with all the violin-swelling emotion one would expect. Like the reunion between Sayid and Nadia in the previous episode, this is a beautiful moment that the story line has been building toward since we first met Penny and Desmond, and the audience believes 100 percent that they are soul mates. The wild-eyed shock in Desmond's eyes is matched only by Penny's speechlessness as she looks down from the top of the boat. Widmore told Desmond he would never be good enough for Penny: notice in this scene how Desmond comes up to her level and she comes down to his so they meet in the middle, which is symbolic of how they have sloughed off the class distinctions that could hold them apart. Desmond has held onto his love of Penny for three years, and she's proven herself to be just as devoted by searching the world for him — and actually finding him, which is more than her father has been able to do. Desmond represents the notion that love is the key to survival. Because his story comes full circle in this episode, my initial instinct was that his story might be over, and this is the last we'll see of him. However, his connection to Widmore — and the fact that Ben will be on the hunt for Penelope a year later — means Desmond is not yet free of the island.

The Oceanic 6 have finally made it to the mainland, but the joy we would expect at their rescue is overshadowed by our knowledge of their futures, which is what makes this show so fascinating. So many questions we've had the rest of the season were answered, while other questions are raised (would it be *Lost* if that weren't the case?).

Both of the presumed deceased characters on the freighter are connected to Sun in some way. If Michael's purpose had been to ensure Sun's rescue, then it would suggest the island has big plans for her — and Ji Yeon. Some have speculated that Aaron and Ji Yeon could be the island's Adam and Eve. Considering that time doesn't seem to be important around these parts, it's possible they could go back in time to be the island's first inhabitants. Sun will return to Korea and continue to stick to the lie that everyone died in the plane crash (or shortly after) except for the Oceanic 6. Jack says they need to lie to keep the others safe, but since Jin is dead, does Sun really care as much about the others? By saying he died she is denying those months on the island where Jin and Sun fell in love all over again, more deeply than they had before. She's denying Ji Yeon's conception and the heroic thing Jin did to ensure she and the baby would be safe. Of everyone who is perpetuating the lie, this situation will be hardest on Sun. (Yunjin Kim, by the way, gives a stunning performance in this three-hour finale, from her hysteria at leaving Jin behind to the deadness in her eyes on the cargo plane to the vengeful confidence she shows her father.) She returns to Korea a hardened woman. She buys a controlling interest in her father's company and approaches Widmore independently, telling him they have common interests. When Sun tells Hurley in "Ji Yeon" that the others aren't coming, it seems as if she has broken ties with them. In the previous episode, she tells her father that he is one of the two people responsible for Jin's death, but it's not clear who she believes is the other one. Is it Widmore for sending the freighter folk? Could it be Keamy for blowing up the freighter? Or Ben for killing Keamy and setting the bomb off? Or Frank for leaving the boat so quickly and not waiting a few extra seconds for Jin? Or does she blame herself for putting Jin in a position where he boarded Oceanic Flight 815 in the first place? Jack believes she blames him; but then again, Jack always thinks people are talking about him.

Jack will return to the world, do all the talking for everyone, and settle back into life at the hospital. He'll lay his father to rest (which is a huge element in Jack's ability to move forward, considering how his daddy issues have held him back so often in the past). He'll experience the happiness with Kate that eluded him on the island, but the spectre of Sawyer will once again come between them. Jack, the one who had the most responsibility heaped upon him while on the island, will be the one who is the most badly broken in the end.

But he wasn't the only hero on the island. In "Something Nice Back Home," Jack gets upset with Kate when he realizes she is doing a favor for Sawyer, and he shouts at her, "I *saved* you!" How did he do that? In the final moments, it was Sawyer who made the sacrifice and jumped out of the helicopter. Kate and Sayid bartered their way off the island by working with the Others, and if they hadn't done that, they wouldn't have made it to the helicopter, Jack or no Jack. Is it because he stops her from going after Jin on the boat? Also, in that episode Jack says Sawyer made his choice and left them, where Jack stayed with her to prove his love. That's an interesting way of looking at it, since if Sawyer hadn't jumped from the helicopter, perhaps none of them would have made it. Despite Sawyer being on an island that has moved (and for all Jack knows, he is floating in the water, dead), Jack is *still* feeling threatened by him.

Kate will tell the world she is Aaron's mother and spend the first few months deflecting questions about the specifics of it and why she doesn't appear to have ever given birth. Her biggest fear on the island was the trial that inevitably awaited her at home, but she manages to get through it *and* put her mother issues behind her at the same time. Perhaps when she's searching for Clementine (for that was Sawyer's final message to her: see **Any Questions?** below) she will discover who Clementine's mother is. Will she renew her friendship with Cassidy that started in "Left Behind"? Of the Oceanic 6, she may be the one who most resists a return to the island. She will continue to be a fierce and protective mother to Aaron, but will be haunted by dreams telling her she needs to return to the island. Many fans suggested Aaron was hugely important to the island, and we might soon find out if that's true, if he and Kate return.

Hurley will be haunted by more than just dreams. When the Oceanic 6 first return, Hurley has a joyful reunion with his parents at the airport. He seems to settle into his life pretty quickly, but despite discovering on the island that he can make his own luck, Hurley falls apart the moment he sees the numbers again. Between Jack's pressure on him to keep quiet and the numbers showing up in the Camaro, Hurley will probably break ties with all of the Oceanic 6 except Sun, who invites him alone to come to see Ji Yeon. Perhaps next season we'll see more of what happened to Hurley between coming home and going into Santa Rosa, because a lot of his backstory was kept from us. He still seems to be the one person everyone trusts — and the only one Walt decides to visit. Will he willingly return to the island?

If all these stories don't seem sad enough, along comes Sayid to make a person want to give up on the notion of lifelong happiness. After the Oceanic 6 press conference, Sayid is reunited with Nadia, whom he immediately marries (he's wearing a wedding band at Hurley's birthday party), but she is dead within a year. Blinded by vengeance for Nadia's death, Sayid is recruited by a now-off-the-island Ben to become a hit man, and he stops communicating with the other Oceanic survivors. Despite his resolution on the island to leave the torturer in him behind,

The Hoffs-Drawlar funeral home is a dressed-up building on Liliha Street in Kahana, Oahu. Hoffs-Drawlar is an anagram for "fastforward." (RYAN OZAWA)

he is now an executioner, doling out "justice" in the name of Ben and the island, and presumably against Widmore. He returns to Hurley only after he finds one of Widmore's men (probably one of the people on Ben's list) watching Hurley. Here's hoping we see a few happy Sayid flashforwards when he's still with Nadia, despite the fact they'll be tinged with the sorrow of what is to come.

All of the characters say they have been visited by Jeremy Bentham, the man in the coffin, who turns out to be . . . John Locke. Many fans picked Locke as the guy in the coffin, because he's the sort of guy who would make Kate turn her nose up at going to his funeral, and the one who would fill Jack with such deep ambivalence. However, because the writers worked so hard to make us think it was Michael — going so far as to create a phony obit that said he lived in New York, had a teenage son, and had committed suicide — my money had been on him. Neither Jack nor Kate would be happy about attending his funeral because he'd betrayed them to get off the island with Walt, but Jack would still feel guilty because, well, Jack feels guilty about everything.

Several questions arose after we saw Locke in that coffin. First, how did he get off the island and why? Jack says that "some very bad things happened" after everyone left. What were they? Why would those things be Jack's fault? Why does Locke believe he needs the Oceanic 6 back in order to put things right again? How did Locke die? And why do they have to take him back with them? Could the island actually restore life? It's one thing to make a paralyzed man walk again, but quite another to bring a man back to life (especially considering, by the looks of his corpse, he's been embalmed). But then again, if the island could resurrect Christian, it could probably bring its savior back to life. Clearly Locke's referring to himself as Jeremy Bentham to throw other people (namely Widmore) off his scent, especially if Widmore somehow knows John Locke was alive and well on the island. Tom was sent off the island to bring Michael back because the island needed him, and now Locke is visiting everyone (including Walt, for some reason) to make them come back. Does Walt need to return, too? Why else would he have visited him?

In the present, Locke has ascended to the leader of the Others. He has been chosen by the island, and Ben has been ousted (quite literally). Locke is being thrown into a role of leadership, but he doesn't quite know what he's getting himself into. He'll have Richard Alpert as his second-in-command, just as Ben did; but we've seen in the past that Richard can affect change and get rid of any messiah who doesn't seem to live up to his expectations. In season 3, he handed Locke the file on Sawyer to help him carry out his task of killing his father, and he seems bent on getting rid of Ben. Richard is always at the beck and call of the island (in this episode he steps up to save Ben's life so Ben can fulfill his duty of moving the island) and Locke will rely on him to advise him what to do. But just like with anything Locke does, things promise to get out of hand, and surely he'll be out of his league soon. He is handed a group of people who will follow him without question, but he doesn't know what to do with them. Will he be able to lead them for a while before outside forces work against him, or will he fall apart immediately? Even though Locke lacks confidence in many ways, he still has an intuition that one hopes he'll use to his advantage.

Making Locke the leader of a ragtag group of hopeful people who will look to him for guidance puts him in the same position as Jack immediately following the crash. Jack seemed like an effective leader in the beginning, but many of his actions were self-centered. He tried to help people because of his single-minded compulsion to fix situations, and when someone died, he was angrier at himself for not having fixed them than he was sad to lose them. As Jack has said on many occasions, he never asked to become leader, instead leadership was thrust upon him. The pressures put on him were immense, and in the end, he did manage to keep a lot of people safe, even if he lost control on many occasions. Now Locke is in charge, and there must be some part of him subconsciously comparing himself to Jack, who had become his arch-nemesis by the end. Whenever Locke and Jack have disagreed on fundamental issues, Locke has been right. Locke said the freighter folk were not going to rescue them, and Jack said they would. Locke said they had to push a button every 108 minutes or something bad would happen, and Jack disagreed. Locke told Jack that if he left the island, one day he'd find he'd need to return. Jack thought Locke was insane, but Locke was right. Jack's steadfast refusal to believe anything that comes from Locke even extends to him refusing to accept what he sees before his own eyes, such as when the island disappears as they're all looking at it. When Hurley says with astonishment that he can't believe Locke has finally moved the island, Jack responds with a snide remark, "No he didn't." Jack doesn't believe in miracles; even when one happens right in front of him, he remains agnostic.

Ben, on the other hand, is like Locke in that he will do anything to protect the island. In "Through the Looking Glass," when Mikhail questions why Ben kept the Looking Glass station running and jammed all signals, Ben responds, "You have to understand. Everything I did, I did for the island." He has lived most of his life on the island, he was one of the original converts, he helped wipe out the Dharma Initiative when he thought they were a threat to the island, and he has been the leader of the Others for years. As Jacob's mouthpiece, Ben believed in the powers and magic of the island long before Locke crashed to its surface. Which is why Ben's final task on the island is such a difficult one. As he enters the underground chamber and hacks away at the ice, declaring, "I hope you're happy now, Jacob," there is anger and immense sadness in him. Emerson has been incredible this season, but his performance as he turns the frozen donkey wheel deserves awards.

This scene also makes the opening scene of "The Shape of Things to Come" a lot less confusing. Now we understand that Ben enters the chamber, ripping the arm of his parka on the way down the broken ladder. He turns the wheel, moves the island, and as the island moves, a flash of light comes out of the center of the wheel he is turning. Ben is ejected from the island and sent through space and time to the Saharan desert in October 2005. He awakes in the desert, breathes out some cold air (we see the vapor come out of his mouth when he opens his eyes), vomits because of the physical disorientation of time travel, sees the rip in his jacket, and tries to get his bearings. Suddenly two Bedouin appear, and Ben, true to form, adapts to the situation instantly. He gets to the hotel, realizes he's been sent 10 months into the future, and happens to see a news flash on the television about how Sayid's wife has died and has been brought to Tikrit for burial. Ben's daughter had just been killed three days earlier (from Ben's perspective) and he knows Widmore was the man who orchestrated the circumstances that led to her murder. He immediately puts together a plan where he'll meet Sayid and recruit him using a photo of Ishmael Bakir, and that way he'll be able to make his way to Widmore, one person at a time. When Elsa is shot (from "The Economist") after contacting her boss about Sayid, Sayid tells Ben they'll know he's coming, and Ben responds, "Good." Now that Widmore knows someone is executing his people, Ben appears to him and threatens Penny. That scene (which I analyzed in detail on page 110) ends with Ben telling Widmore he's going to kill Penny, and Widmore saying you'll never find her. Is it possible Penny and Desmond somehow made their way to the island, the place Widmore believes Ben cannot return to, and that's where she's hiding out? It's unlikely Desmond would return, but it's even less likely he'd leave Penny's side.

The final flashforward we get chronologically has Ben and Jack talking about returning to the island. Locke has visited each of the Oceanic 6 (plus Walt) and has told them they need to return to the island together. Sayid is with Hurley, and because Sayid is working for Ben, he'll probably return to the island because he believes to do so would hurt Widmore. In "The Beginning of the End," when Jack and Hurley play basketball, Hurley says he thinks the island needs him to go back, so he probably won't object to returning. Jack obviously will take no convincing. When Kate rushes into Aaron's room after having the nightmare about Claire sitting there, she breaks down beside his bed and tells him she's sorry over and over. What is she sorry for? That she's lied to him about being his mother? That she left his real mother behind? That he had such a rough beginning to his life? Or that she knows they need to go back, and she must take him with her? Kate will take the most convincing.

And then there's Sun. Her little meeting with Widmore casts her as the wild card in this scenario. What could she be up to? If Ben is the other person she blames for Jin's death, she could align herself with Ben's mortal (or immortal) enemy out of revenge. She's broken ties with everyone but Hurley, and that's because Hurley has mostly been a neutral party in all of this. In each flashforward where we've see Sun — going into labor, visiting Jin's grave, confronting her father, and meeting Widmore — she is always wearing black and white, as if it's unclear if she's a good guy or a bad guy. If Sun becomes an enemy to the other five survivors, it would make things very interesting. (Also, if she has to return to the island, does Ji Yeon have to return as well? Technically, she was on the island, too.)

The next season is shaping up to feature flashforwards of the Oceanic 6 trying to get back to the island; Charlotte learning more about the island and getting closer to the truth she is seeking; Abaddon featuring more heavily in the fates of the people on the island; Desmond, Penny, and Frank attempting to get far away from the action but inevitably being pulled back in; Sawyer, Juliet, Bernard, Rose, and a few remaining survivors figuring out how to live without Jack leading them; Locke having more visits with Christian and/or Jacob and learning about the leadership on the island through Richard, for better or for worse; and flashforwards of "Jeremy Bentham" meeting with the Oceanic 6.

But, as I said in the guide to "The Shape of Things to Come," the ultimate theme of the series is the race for control of the island, which is a game being played between Charles Widmore and Benjamin Linus. Like an elaborate game of chess, these men are moving their pieces around for control of the board, and one of them will become the ruler, effectively checkmating and destroying his opponent. Both of them want to get back to the island, but Ben has been ousted by the island, and Widmore can't find it (one wonders if perhaps at some point in the past *he* moved the island and that's why he can't find it). They both know the island will bring back the Oceanic 6 if it needs them, and so these two are piggybacking on the ride. If Widmore can follow Sun, and Ben follows the others, and they bring Locke's body back, then everyone makes it back to the island, and the chess game will continue there, where it was meant to be played.

And that is when we will discover who, if anyone, becomes king.

Highlight: Ben's response to Locke after Locke watches the Orchid orientation video and asks if he just saw what he thinks he just saw: "If you mean time traveling bunnies, then yes."

Timeline: Most of the on-island events happen on Day 100, December 30,

2004. Penny's boat discovers the Oceanic 6 and Desmond in the early hours of December 31, 2004. One week later, on January 7, 2005 (Day 108), the Oceanic 6 pull their raft up on the shore of an Indonesian fishing village.

Did You Notice?:

- The beginning of this episode picked up exactly where the season 3 finale ended. While the crew had to recreate the scene to make sure they matched — including getting the puddles just right, straightening Kate's hair, and imperfecting Jack's bad beard — part of the scene was actually filmed in 2007 with the material for "Through the Looking Glass."
- Kate says she's spent three years trying to forget what happened, which puts this scene at the end of 2007. Considering Jack seemed to be fine in August 2007 (the date of the newspaper he reads the morning he wakes up and steps on Aaron's toy), his deterioration was pretty fast.
- If things seemed a little awkward between Jack and Hurley when they first meet up, it's because he hasn't seen him since Hurley urged so many people to join Locke and abandon Jack.
- After Alpert momentarily stops Keamy by shooting him in the back, Kate helps Sayid up and smiles at him, but Sayid doesn't return the smile. He's probably feeling guilty that all their efforts went toward letting Ben go free.
- After Locke and Jack have their verbal smackdown in the greenhouse at the Orchid station, it's the last time they'll look at each other on the island.
- Apparently Dan's Zodiac raft is running on solar power, since it's making it to and from the boat repeatedly without refuelling.
- Rose seems to have picked up Sawyer's affinity for nicknames in his absence. In "Something Nice Back Home" she refers to Charlotte as "Red," and in this episode she calls Miles "Shorty."
- The Orchid station is very deep, like they're descending into hell. *The Third Policeman* — the book Desmond was reading in season 2 — features a scene where the characters descend into eternity via an elevator that seems to go on forever. Once they reach the bottom, there is a series of halls and the two men accompanying the narrator tell him he can try any of them. Every hall he goes down has the two men standing at the end of it, proving the place really is eternity, with the narrator doomed to repeat the same actions forever (see page 200 of *Finding Lost* for a complete analysis of the book).
- There is a great moment when Locke asks Ben if the chamber in the Orchid

station is the magic box, and Ben stares at him for a brief moment in bafflement before responding in complete exasperation, "No, it's not." The comic timing between the two is impeccable, and this moment must have really bugged Ben. He was speaking in metaphor in "The Man from Tallahassee," and Locke is such a literalist he took the magic box as an actual physical thing on the island. "And *this* is the guy you're replacing me with!" Ben must be thinking to himself.

- The Orchid orientation film that fans were able to watch ahead of time was different than the one shown in the episode.
- The actor in the orientation videos goes by a different name in each instance, but his name always has a reference to candles in it. In the Swan orientation film, he was Marvin Candle. In the Pearl video, he was Mark Wickmund. And in the Orchid video, he is Edgar Halliwax.
- When the Orchid video begins rewinding, Locke looks sped up as he tries to make it stop, as if time is moving differently for him, too. (Or it could have just been a production glitch on the episode.)
- When Sayid sees Hurley, he smiles and hugs him, yet the last time he saw him Hurley was walking him into a trap set by Locke. Sayid clearly forgives him because he knows how badly Hurley felt about doing that.
- Ben tells Michael that when he's at war, he'll do what he has to do but he won't kill innocent people. Apparently if you kill his daughter, he changes his own rules.
- Despite Ben often oozing pure evil, there's something about him that makes me think there's a heart in there. Even if it's a tiny piece of charcoal, there's a heart. Locke jumps on Keamy after Ben stabs him, and tells Ben that he's just killed everyone on the boat, to which Ben replies, "So?" His coldness comes across as just that, but I think he's been broken by Alex's death.
- Jack takes over even on the helicopter.
- Watch poor Hurley's face when Frank says he'd feel better if they could lose a few hundred pounds.
- Jack reassures Kate they'll go back for Sawyer, after telling Hurley they'd go back for Claire. He's still making empty promises. It must be said, however, that no one else is expected to answer such questions. If Hurley had asked Kate if they'd go back to save Claire, would she have answered differently?
- When Christian appears to Michael, he says, "You can go now," which is the same thing Miles said to the ghost in his flashback in "Confirmed Dead."

Checkmate

Lost might end up being the story of two men playing an elaborate chess game with each other, using all the characters we've come to know and love as pawns. Chess has become an ongoing motif in the series, the most obvious being the constant references to Lewis Carroll's *Through the Looking-Glass, and What Alice Found There*, which is a book based on an actual chess game, with the characters making the correct moves to get themselves across the board. Damon Lindelof has even used chess as a metaphor for what it was like during the season 2/3 era when fans were starting to lose faith in the series. "I feel like we're playing a chess game," he said, "and in the first six moves, we've lost our queen and two bishops, and the audience is saying 'They are the worst chess players in the world!' What they don't realize is that we're nine moves away from checkmating you. If we lose, we lose. But that's the play, and we're standing by it." Here are the other chess occurrences in the series:

- When the island is briefly seen on Penelope's radar, the two men sitting in the hut in the blizzard are playing chess ("Live Together, Die Alone")
- Locke plays a chess game against the computer at the Flame station, despite Mikhail's warning that the computer never loses ("Enter 77")
- Two of the Others are playing chess in their makeshift camp when Ben tells them to go to the beach and bring back the pregnant women ("Greatest Hits")
- Mikhail is playing chess with Richard Alpert when Ben tells him to go to the Looking Glass station and stop Charlie ("Through the Looking Glass")
- When Abaddon comes to see Hurley at Santa Rosa in the future, he sits down at a card table with a chess board on it ("The Beginning of the End")
- When Keamy is holding a gun to Alex's head, Ben tells him she was nothing but a pawn to him ("The Shape of Things to Come")
- Hurley is playing a game of chess with an invisible Mr. Eko when Sayid comes to break him out of the hospital ("There's No Place Like Home, Part 3")
- In the mobisode, "King of the Castle," Ben is playing chess with Jack as they talk about Jack leaving the island

- Many of the people who make it off the island are motivated from that point on because they lost their loved ones due to Widmore's design: Ben lost Alex; Sun lost Jin; Hurley lost Charlie; Sayid lost Nadia.
- On Sun's business card, the P in Paik looks like a tidal wave.
- Ben says to Locke, "Sometimes good command decisions get compromised by bad emotional responses. I'm sure you'll do a much better job of separating the two than I ever did." His comment is a sarcastic one, since Ben knows better than anyone that Locke falls prey to bad emotional responses all the time, especially when it's Ben pushing his buttons.

- Richard says, "Welcome home," as if John is returning to a life he once had.
- When Ben was in the snow cave, there were hieroglyphics all over the rocks.
- When Ben moved the turnstile, it made the same noise as when the Swan hatch imploded/exploded. The sky turned purple again and that deafening sound caused everyone to cover their ears again.
- Maybe the island healed Jack's stitches quicker than they would heal in another place, but it's pretty amazing they didn't break open during the chopper crash.
- After the helicopter crash, we see Jack floating in the water and waking up face down, whereas after the initial plane crash, we first see Jack waking up face up.
- John Tenniel's drawing of the White Rabbit from the *Alice* books is on Aaron's bedroom door.
- Jack bristles when Kate says that Aaron surviving that fall is a miracle. There's something more to that statement than simply making Jack feel all superior and agnostic . . . Aaron has survived a *lot* of stuff so far and seems completely fine.
- The rescue boat suddenly appearing is like the end of season 1, complete with the little search light.
- When Ben talks to Sayid at the end of "The Economist," he tells him he's killing the people on Ben's list to "keep your friends safe." In this episode we discover that's actually true. By killing Widmore's people, he prevents them from getting to the island.
- When everyone comes onto the rescue boat and Desmond introduces them to Penny, Jack is the only one who speaks. It's like everyone has decided to already let Jack do all the talking for them.
- If Locke hadn't moved the island, Penny could have saved whoever wanted saving, since her boat was in the vicinity of the island.
- We get a time indicator at one point that says, "One week later." This is the first time the present day events have jumped forward in time.
- It must have been difficult for Sun to dock in that fishing village, considering where Jin came from and always seeing him with his poles and nets on the island.
- Locke has become Ben, not only taking over the Others, but traveling off the island under pseudonyms.
- Ben says to Jack, "*We're* gonna have to bring him, too," as if Ben will be accompanying them.

Interesting Facts: When Hurley is trying to unwrap the Fruit Roll-Up in the hospital, where the flavor should be listed it instead says, "Molly Fisher." The Molly Fisher Rock is a boulder in Kent, Connecticut, named for a woman named Molly Fisher, born in 1750, who was a healer in the area and who would visit the rock often and claimed it had healing properties. The stone has an inscription etched into the side of it, and to this day no one has been able to decipher the meaning of the symbols.

In the Orchid orientation video, Dr. Halliwax says, "The unique properties of this island have created a kind of Casimir effect, allowing the Dharma Initiative to conduct experiments in space and time." A Casimir effect is caused when two uncharged metallic objects create a force between them, measured through quantum electrodynamics, even though on a purely classical electromagnetic level, there doesn't appear to be any force between the two of them.

Last season, someone by the name of lostfan108 revealed the entirety of the final episode a week before the episode aired. The person remains anonymous, as no one has been able to trace who he or she is. This season, to try to contain the huge reveal at the end of the episode, the *Lost* team filmed two alternate endings to try to trick any crew member who might try to give it away. The morning after the finale aired, *Good Morning America* aired the two alternate endings, and they featured first Sawyer, then Desmond, in the coffin at the end of the episode. (If you want to watch it, go to YouTube and type in "Lost season 4 alternate endings.") Their ploy failed, by the way — lostfan108 revealed the plot of "There's No Place Like Home" (including Locke being the man in the coffin) a week in advance of its broadcast.

Harold Perrineau was contacted before the finale script went out to the actors and told that Michael would die in the finale episode, and that his story was finished. He was not happy with the way his character left the show, as he told TVGuide.com: "I'm disappointed, mostly because I wanted Michael and Walt to have a happy ending. I was hoping Michael would get it together and actually want to be a father to his kid and try to figure out a way to get back [home]." He believes fans hate Michael for what he did on the island, and he felt like Michael being first beaten by Keamy and then killed "was sort of pandering to some fans who wanted to see Michael punished because he betrayed people." In his most contentious comment, he accused the show of racism: "Listen, if I'm being really candid, there are all these questions about how they respond to black people on the show. Sayid gets to meet Nadia again, and Desmond and Penny hook up again, but a little black boy and his father hooking up, that wasn't interesting? Instead, Walt just winds up being another fatherless child. It plays into a really big, weird stereotype and, being a black person myself, that wasn't so interesting."

After this section of the interview was quoted in countless newspapers, Perrineau qualified his statement in *Entertainment Weekly*, and said his opinion was his opinion only, and he would never deign to suggest he could write the scripts better than Darlton. He added, "I should probably think more before I say things. I should especially think before I say anything racial, because I recognize that when you make a racial comment it polarizes people." Even though many fans saw Michael's final act as one of redemption, Perrineau didn't think Michael was redeemed, simply because no one he betrayed actually saw him trying to help them. "I didn't think he got to redeem himself especially to the people who I feel like he wronged. I wanted Michael to go back and do something for them so that they felt like he really put out and that he did something to satisfy his own guilt and their anger. . . . I think he was probably going to be a good father. I wish Michael would have gotten to be the father that he had always wanted to be, because he's a good dude."

Many fans point to Darlton's comments in their podcasts as being canon, but one of the biggest claims Damon Lindelof made during the show's first season has already proved to be untrue. In an interview with *SciFi Wire*, Lindelof stated, "I don't think we've shown anything on the show yet . . . that has no rational explanation in the real world that we all function within. We certainly hint at psychic phenomena, happenstance and . . . things being in a place where they probably shouldn't be. But nothing is flat-out impossible. There are no spaceships. There isn't any time travel." Oops. It's safe to assume any claims Darlton make from season 4 on should be considered canon, however, because in season 1 they hadn't fully mapped out how the series was going to end, and now they claim to know exactly how it will end.

Nitpicks: Walt asks Hurley why none of the Oceanic 6 came to visit him. But in "Meet Kevin Johnson," Michael's mother says that he and Walt changed their names and are in hiding, so how would the Oceanic 6 have been able to *find* Walt? Speaking of which, how did Locke manage to find him?

Oops: Following the helicopter crash, when Jack comes up from under the water we see Hurley leaning over the raft wearing an orange lifevest. When the camera switches to a close-up, Hurley's suddenly not wearing it as he pulls Aaron into the raft. Also, when the Oceanic 6 get off the raft, there's no one there holding a camera, despite Decker saying a fisherman took a picture of the 6 touching land for the first time. Finally, when Ben was turning the wheel, he still had bruising around one eye, but in "The Shape of Things to Come," when he wakes up in the desert, there's no bruise on him. Considering his arm still has the fresh gash on it from the cave where he turned the wheel, it can't be explained away by saying the time travel healed it.

4 8 15 16 23 42: The first number in Kate's license plate is **4**. Alpert shoots Keamy in the back **4** times. The rabbit has a **15** on it. Michael says at one point that he has a 1/4 tank of nitrogen left. When Frank notices the fuel is dropping, it's at **4**. When the helicopter crashes into the ocean, there are **8** people on it. When Sayid asks the man in the car what time it is, he says **8:15** just before Sayid shoots him.

It's Just a Flesh Wound: One of the mercenaries has his neck broken, another is tripped and killed, another gets an electric dart in his neck that kills him, Omar is killed by a grenade. Sayid and Keamy fight each other, with Sayid getting punched and kicked and Keamy getting stabbed and beaten with a stick. Alpert shoots Keamy four times in the back. Ben stabs Keamy repeatedly in the neck. The people on the helicopter suffer cuts and bruises from the impact of the chopper hitting the water.

Lost in Translation: There is some debate about what Sawyer says to Kate, but the gist is the same. Most fans agree he says, "I have a daughter in Albuquerque, you need to find her. Tell her I'm sorry." Some fans can hear him say Alabama rather than Albuquerque (that's actually what I hear, too), but because we learn in an earlier episode that his daughter Clementine lives in Albuquerque, they're going with that as the translation. In Kate's dream, the audio we hear of the person on the other end of the phone is played backwards. Played forward, it's a man's voice saying, "You have to go back. The island needs you before it's too late." When the raft pulls up to Penny's boat, the men in the boat are shouting in Portuguese. First they yell to point the light over to the survivors, then one shouts, "A raft filled with people. There are eight of them" (it's interesting that at that distance they could see Aaron). A few of them begin yelling, "Where did they come from?" As the raft gets closer, one yells, "Get some blankets. And the first-aid kit. Bring them here now!" And finally, one yells, "A raft with people, Ms. Widmore! Ms. Widmore, come to the front of the boat!" Sadly, I haven't been able to find any whisper transcripts for this episode.

Any Questions?:

- Kate asks Jack a valid question in the opening: why does Jack believe Locke of all people? He never believed anything Locke said no matter how much evidence Locke could show him — he didn't even believe Locke had moved the island, despite the fact it disappeared right in front of him. Why does he believe him now?

- When Walt's grandmother visits Hurley at the hospital, she wants to know if he's dangerous. Her question seems to be significant: could Hurley be a danger to Walt? Could his knowledge potentially hurt him?

- What are those crackers made of? They're 15 years old, yet Hurley and Sawyer both think they're pretty good. I have opened packages of crackers in my cupboards that taste like cardboard after having been open for only a month. Because these crackers seem to be receiving an inordinate amount of screen time, one can assume there's something more there than we might think. Could time be moving at such a strange pace that even if they were left in that spot 15 years ago, the crackers are only a few days old? Stranger things have happened.

- When Sun tells Michael that she's pregnant, he looks at her very strangely. It's probable that the discomfort in his face is because he knows that if the bomb goes off, it's even worse than he'd originally thought. But could there be something more? Was there a tryst between Sun and Michael? In one of the mobisodes, "Buried Secrets," Sun and Michael almost share a kiss before they are interrupted. The writers must have included that particular missing piece for a reason.

- Why does the orientation video begin to rewind? Is the actual video going back in time?

- Why can't Frank find the freighter when he still has Sawyer in the helicopter? The boat had moved closer so it's now only five miles off the south coast of the island. The flight should have taken only a few minutes. Had the boat moved so far off Dan's bearing that Frank was too far away from it?

- Now that we know what Kate was doing for Sawyer, why didn't she just come out and tell Jack in "Something Nice Back Home"? "Sawyer had a daughter and asked me to track her down. Turns out I actually know the girl's mother, so we've been reconnecting." Is she such a compulsive liar that she has to lie about everything, even when she doesn't need to?

- Why does Sayid remove Hurley from the mental hospital? Is it time to return to the island? Or does he really sense a close threat from Widmore and needs to keep Hurley safe?

- In "Through the Looking Glass," the flight attendant hands a newspaper to Jack, with the page folded back so the obituary is facing him, as if she was handing it to him on purpose. Later in that episode, Jack seems surprised when the funeral director tells him no one showed up to the funeral. In this episode, Sayid knows about Bentham's death. Did he see the obituary? Had the obituary been placed for the Oceanic 6 to see it? Did Locke warn them ahead of time to keep their eyes on the death pages of the paper?

- "Checkmate, Mr. Eko." Are the "dead" people really dead or not? Is it possible we'll see Eko again? That said, Sayid not seeing Eko sitting there would point to him not actually being there. Unless Hurley is the key to the whole thing . . . Is there a significance to the fact Hurley sees Charlie and Eko? Is it because they are two people who have seen the smoke monster?

- What interests does Sun have in common with Widmore? Finding the island? Bringing down Ben? Is it possible Sun might believe Jin is still alive?

- What does Sun mean when she says "we're not the only ones who left the island"? Is she referring to Ben? Locke? Or Frank and Desmond? Is it a veiled threat, considering one of those people is with Penelope?

- Is Sun looking to join forces with Widmore? After all, the only reason the 6 are telling the lie is to protect the island and its inhabitants from Widmore, and now she admits to Widmore they've been telling a lie.

- Ben says to Locke, "I'm sorry I made your life so miserable." What does he mean? Notice he doesn't say he's sorry he's made the last three months of his life miserable, but his *life*. Has he been watching John Locke for as long as Richard has? Could he have been the one who sent Richard to spy on John? Has he somehow orchestrated the lifelong misery that has befallen John?

- Why are the Others such willing followers who will do whatever John (or Ben, or whoever is the leader that week) tells them to do?

- What exactly is that room underneath the Orchid? Jacob's Fortress of Solitude? When had it been used before? Why is it so cold? What was the blinding white light that shot out when Ben turned the wheel? How did Ben know about this protocol?

- What is the link between Jacob and the kerosene lamp? Ben and Locke light the lamp before entering the cabin, and now we see Ben lighting it when he gets to the cave with the frozen donkey wheel.

- What did Ben do? Did he move the island in space *and* time?
- How can Desmond be Daniel's constant if they can't contact each other?
- Kate's not kidding when she says it's a miracle Aaron survived the helicopter crash. How did she possibly hold onto him as the helicopter hit the water?
- In "Cabin Fever," Locke has a dream of Horace Goodspeed giving him information that was true, and Ben mentions that he used to have dreams, too. Now Kate has a dream where Claire urges her not to bring him back. Was that dream sent by the island? Is it an indication that Claire is dead? Who is Claire referring to when she tells Kate not to bring "him" back? Aaron? Locke? Ben?
- How will Desmond stay away from Widmore?
- What sort of conversations happened during the week between Penny rescuing everyone and the Oceanic 6 heading to that fishing village? Did Sayid tell everyone what Gault told him about the fake plane crash? Since Sayid and Desmond knew that the freighter belonged to Widmore, and Hurley saw firsthand what Widmore's people were capable of, did they tell Penny what her father had done and how dangerous he was? If Jack was one of the few people who didn't know about Charles Widmore and any background on him, the others are going to have to do some talking, regardless of Jack's plan to let him take care of it.
- Jack throws Desmond's line back at him as a wink, saying, "See you in another life, brother." Will he? Jack also says, "Don't let him find you," which would indicate that they all know Widmore is dangerous.
- Why do the Oceanic 6 have to return to the island? Is it to bring Aaron? Locke? Why did Locke tell Jack that it was his fault things are going haywire on the island? Did he think the only way to bring Jack back was to stroke his ego? Why do they *all* have to return?
- Will returning to the island bring Locke back to life? Or could it have the same effect on him as it had on Christian Shephard, who is dead in the outside world, but appears to be alive on the island? Would it at least allow Locke to be a spirit guide like Christian so he could continue to lead people?

Ashes to Ashes: Michael Dawson was one of the survivors of Oceanic Flight 815. A devoted father, he was never given much of a chance to prove his love to his son. After killing two other survivors and reluctantly making a deal with the devil to recover his son, Michael was the first survivor to make it back to the mainland, but he returned after only a few weeks. He redeemed himself by saving Sun, her unborn baby, and Desmond, and offering Ben information that ironically kept the survivors safe.

Martin Keamy was a brutal former U.S. marine who has more recently worked with several mercenary groups. He was hired by Widmore to head up a mission to extract Ben Linus and dispose of everyone else on the island. He is *not* someone you want to mess with. He was killed by Ben.

Kocol, Lacour, Redfern, and Omar were mercenaries working with Keamy. The first three were killed by the Others in the battle to retrieve Ben, and Omar was killed by Keamy when Keamy kicked a grenade in his direction to deflect it away from himself.

Music/Bands: When Jack is driving to the funeral home he's listening to "Gouge Away" by The Pixies, from their 1989 album, *Doolittle*. This song is apparently about the Old Testament (specifically Samson and Delilah, because Black Francis mentions cutting one's locks and pulling down the pillars). There's a line in the song, "sleeping on your belly" which indicates a snake, which from Jack's perspective, could mean Locke.

Jeremy Bentham (1748–1832)

The Enlightenment philosopher John Locke believed that in a state of nature, man was essentially born good and over time was written upon by experience. He believed citizens needed a government that would protect them, but that they should rebel against what they believed to be tyranny. Jeremy Bentham, on the other hand, believed the idea of a state of nature was "nonsense upon stilts," and that government was necessary to protect the happiness of the people.

Looks like our bald-headed buddy has switched his ideas over the years.

Jeremy Bentham was born in 1748, and was a child prodigy. His father dreamed of him becoming Lord Chancellor, and enrolled him at Oxford University when he was 12. By the time he was 15 he had his Bachelor degree, and his Master's was earned three years later. While he never practiced as a lawyer, most of his writing pertained to the law, whether he thought it was essentially unfair or whether he was writing about how to reform it.

Bentham is widely considered the father of utilitarianism. While he didn't coin the phrase "greatest happiness for the greatest number," despite what many think (that phrase was written by Joseph Priestley, a philosopher and political theorist who discovered the element of oxygen), it was that phrase that appealed to Bentham, and he began basing all of his philosophies on that very simple idea. Human beings were, quite simply, motivated by pleasure or pain, and spent their lives chasing that which would cause the most pleasure and the least pain.

Bentham first came to prominence with his scathing critique of the philosophies of Sir William Blackstone, who was a proponent of John Locke, in his anonymously published *Fragment on Government* (1776). Bentham attacked Blackstone and others who appealed for a social contract and based their philosophies on the idea of a state of nature. If people have always been part of societies, then there is no state of nature, he said. If liberty corresponded with pleasure and the law sought to restrict that, creating pain, then the law was evil. However, as long as law is protecting the interests of the many and creating the greatest happiness for the greatest number, then it was effective.

Bentham's philosophy has been criticized widely for not having a practical application. For example, if one must govern oneself to maximize one's pleasure and minimize one's pain, but society must also make sure that the happiness for the greatest number comes before individual happiness, then what about a person who is publically tortured? If seeing that person hurt brings pleasure to those people but immense pain to the one being tortured, does that actually work?

To try to work out these kinks in the theory, Bentham developed what is known as the hedonistic calculus, where he said that in order to figure out what action to take, one had to first calculate if it was a benefit or a detriment. The calculator worked thusly, according to the *Penguin Dictionary of Philosophy*:

When determining what action is right in a given situation, we should consider the pleasures and pains resulting from it, in respect of their *intensity, duration, certainty, propinquity, fecundity* (the chance that a pleasure is followed by other ones, a pain by further pains), *purity* (the chance that pleasure is followed by pains and vice versa), and *extent* (the number of persons affected). We should next consider the alternative courses of action: ideally, this method will determine which act has the best tendency, and therefore is right. Bentham envisaged the calculus could be used for criminal law reform: given a crime of a certain kind it would be possible to work out the minimum penalty necessary for its prevention.

Many of Bentham's ideas were quite modern for his time (and therefore were largely ignored in his lifetime). He argued for animal rights, women's rights, the right to divorce, and homosexual rights (he wrote a paper explaining that consensual homosexual sex was pleasurable to those involved, and therefore should be supported and not punished). He argued for slavery to be abolished, and for people to have freedom of speech, and he was a critic of the death penalty.

Despite later criticizing them, Bentham was actually heavily influenced by the political theories of John Locke and David Hume. Locke had written in his *Essay Concerning Human Understanding*, "Reason must be our last judge and guide in everything." Bentham admired his emphasis on the importance of reason over tradition, and upheld that value in much of his writing.

One of the reasons Bentham's utilitarian philosophy was so overlooked was its negativity toward sovereignty. As writer Robert Clark states, "He did not realise in 1776 the degree to which the self-interest of those in power would resist such a principle." He argued for the separation of the church and state, for example, acknowledging that the two usually went hand in hand, creating rules in each other's best interests, essentially preventing the society from actually being a democracy.

Aside from utilitarianism, Bentham is often remembered as the originator of the panopticon, which was a prison system where inmates were constantly watched by unseen guards, and would never know when they were being watched. The prison cells would be on the inside wall of the tall, tube-like structure, with the guards in a tower at the center (think of the structure of the prison on HBO's *Oz*, and imagine the guards in the center were hidden, and you'll get a sense of Bentham's idea). Bentham invested years of his life in trying to get one made, but it never happened (interesting, in the context of *Lost*, that when the final plan for a building fell through, Bentham was monetarily compensated with £23,000). He spent so much time working on the panopticon that his political theories fell by the wayside, and he wasted much of his potential.

English scholars often compare Bentham to Mr. Gradgrind of Charles Dickens' *Hard Times* (Desmond is a big Dickens fan) who boils everything down to facts and takes the fun out of all learning. His name is also conjured in Dickens studies because his panopticon was eventually adopted, in a way, when it became the basis for several workhouses for the poor. Using his utilitarian principles, Bentham suggested it was in the interests of the greater good to put everyone to work. As Clark writes, "Whilst evidently to a degree sympathetic to the plight of the poor, these papers were hard-headed in their application of utilitarian principles, analysing the poor into a hierarchical tree of categories by cause of poverty and willingness to work, and seeking to motivate the workless by placing them in coercive environments."

It's examples like this that show some of the shortcomings of Bentham's philosophies: on the one hand he puts the onus on the individual to make the best decision for his/herself by choosing what will bring the most pleasure; on the other hand, he puts that decision in the hands of the state. Most of Bentham's writings weren't published in his lifetime, but were published long after by scholars who had been immensely influenced by him, and that could also be the root of some of the problems in his argument.

Regardless, Bentham's ideas were groundbreaking at the time, and were hugely influential on later philosophers like John Stuart Mill and Adam Smith. When Bentham died, he willed his estate to University College in London, and is considered the godfather of the college, since he made sure it would be built and would provide education for those who might not otherwise afford it. He also asked that his body be preserved and embalmed and placed in a wooden box, known as the "Auto-Icon," and be put on display at University College, sitting in his favorite chair. To this day Bentham's body is on display — minus the head, which was damaged during preservation and suffered through several student pranks, destroying it further; it's currently locked away in another room. His head, instead, is a wax likeness. According to the UCL Bentham Project website, "One of the most commonly recounted [anecdotes] is that the Auto-Icon regularly attends meetings of the College Council, and that it is solemnly wheeled into the Council Room to take its place among the present-day members. Its presence, it is claimed, is always recorded in the minutes with the words *Jeremy Bentham — present but not voting*. Another version of the story asserts that the Auto-Icon does vote, but only on occasions when the votes of the other Council members are equally split. In these cases the Auto-Icon invariably votes for the motion." It's not clear why Bentham had his body preserved in such a way, though some have speculated that it may be "regarded as an attempt to question religious sensibilities about life and death."

So why is John Locke on *Lost* now calling himself Jeremy Bentham? At this point, we can only speculate, since his name change has happened during a period in which we haven't seen him. In season 3, he ran New Otherton like a dictatorship (while insisting it was not one), which goes against Bentham's ideas of every man deciding for himself what would be his best path. Locke keeps insisting that everything he was doing was in service to the island and to everyone's greater good. Perhaps somewhere along the way he realized the philosopher John Locke believed a tyrannical leader needed to be overthrown, and he needed to change his way of thinking. It's interesting that the body of Jeremy Bentham sits amongst the University College students still, just as John Locke's body will be transported back to the island with the Oceanic 6. Bentham has been brought back to life, in a sense, just as Locke might have life restored to him should he return to the island. Has Locke tried to form a utilitarian society on the island? Has he moved to a panopticon way of thinking, and is watching everyone in a Big Brother kind of way, without them knowing?

Or did the writers just think "Jeremy Bentham" would be a funny inside joke to all of us who had already spent so long rereading our old philosophy books on John Locke?

Flashforward Timeline

Since realizing the flashback in "Through the Looking Glass" was actually a flash-forward, fans have been on a journey into the future, seeing what will unfold for Jack, Kate, Sayid, Sun, Hurley, and Aaron. Only a couple of the flashforwards have mentioned solid dates, but that's enough to help us sort out their order (to bridge the gaps in some of the times, I'm speculating on what could have happened and when).

The Oceanic 6 are discovered on a raft on January 7, 2005. A press conference is held only a few days later. Kate is probably charged with the crimes she was facing prior to the crash, but because of the widespread publicity focused on the Oceanic 6, the courts delay the trial until a later date to give the trial its best chance at an impartial jury. Sayid is reunited with Nadia, and they waste no time in getting married. In the spring, Sun buys a controlling interest in her father's company, and travels to his office to confront him about it, telling him they'll work out the details after she's given birth. Hurley's parents throw a birthday party for him, which is attended by Sayid and Nadia, and Kate and Aaron (Jack is on his way but says he'll be late). In July, 10 months after the crash, Jack holds a memorial service for his father, which is attended by Sayid and Nadia, Kate and Aaron, and Hurley. At this point it seems all of the Oceanic 6 are keeping in touch with one another, with the exception of Sun, either for reasons of distance or because she partly blames the other survivors for the death of her husband. At that service, Jack finds out that Claire is his sister and Aaron his nephew. He begins to distance himself from Kate because he can't bear to look at Aaron without remembering that he left Claire behind, and that the island took his sister from him.

In Korea, Sun goes into early labor. (She seems surprised by the onset of contractions, and is preparing her bag for the hospital, something that is usually done weeks in advance.) This is probably in June, since Ji Yeon was actually due in July. When Hurley comes to visit Sun, she has lost all the baby weight, but Ji Yeon doesn't look more than a month old (or two months for a premature baby), so his visit probably falls in August. (Then again, Claire lost all baby weight the moment she gave birth, so it could have been a week later.) Now that Jack has distanced himself from Kate and by extension, the rest of the 6, and Hurley has started seeing the numbers again, Hurley is happy that the rest of the Oceanic 6 won't be attending.

In October 2005, Nadia is murdered in Los Angeles, and a grief-stricken Sayid accompanies her body to Tikrit to bury her with her family. He runs into a time-traveling Ben probably on October 25 or 26 (on October 24, Ben sees a news piece of Sayid returning to Tikrit to bury the body), who convinces him Nadia was killed by one of Widmore's men. Sayid kills the man, and becomes Ben's assassin.

Ben travels to England at some point afterward to tell Widmore that he's going to kill Penelope, and that he's moved the island so Widmore will never find it. He might visit him after recruiting Sayid, or he might do it a year later, after the Elsa chapter in Sayid's life, when Sayid tells Ben that the others will know he's after them now, and Ben replies, "Good."

Within the next few months (it's not clear when, but it's before Kate's trial because Jack is living in an apartment), Hurley goes into a convenience store and sees Charlie standing there. He leads police on a chase throughout L.A., and is caught and admitted to the Santa Rosa Mental Health Institute, where "Charlie" begins to visit him on a regular basis. While he's in there, Matthew Abaddon comes to visit him and asks if "they" are still alive. Jack visits Hurley in the institution and they play basketball, but mainly Jack wants to make sure Hurley's going to stick to their story.

Shortly after Hurley's institutionalization, Kate's trial begins. Jack appears as a character witness after having lost contact with Kate months earlier. After the trial is over, Kate asks Jack if he might want to reconsider coming to see Aaron, and Jack says no. He soon changes his mind, and comes to see him, and realizes having a relationship with him won't be as difficult as he thought. He moves in with Kate, and they begin to raise Aaron together. Kate begins searching for Sawyer's daughter.

Meanwhile, Sayid has become a full-blown assassin for Ben, killing people whose names are on a list and who work for Widmore. He's gone beyond just walking up and shooting people on golf courses, but instead does it through a long con, like Sawyer would have done. He goes to Germany in the winter of 2006–2007, meets a woman named Elsa, develops feelings for her, and is shot by her, but he manages to kill her before she can finish the job.

As things move along well with Jack and Kate, things with Hurley aren't going so well. He's being visited by other island spirits, and he stops taking his medication and believes his doctor doesn't exist. By August 2007, things have gotten so bad with him the doctor calls Jack in. Jack visits him and Hurley tells him that Charlie said Jack wasn't supposed to "raise him." Hurley wonders if the note means Aaron. Soon after, Jack begins having visions of Christian Shephard in the hospital. He rushes home and proposes to Kate, hoping that will fix things, but it doesn't. Within a week of visiting Hurley, Jack has begun taking clonazepam, has become distrustful of Kate, and reminds her that she's not related to Aaron. He finds out she's been doing a favor for Sawyer, and becomes angry. She kicks him out of the house; he begins a long downward spiral during which he believes his father is alive again (he refers to him as being upstairs in the hospital and drunk) and increases his dosage of clonazepam considerably.

Sometime in the fall of 2007, John Locke gets off the island, adopts the pseudonym of Jeremy Bentham, and begins visiting the survivors. He goes to see Kate, Jack, Hurley, Sayid, Ben, and even Walt. He tells everyone they need to come back to the island (whether he's including Walt in that is not clear) and he tells Jack specifically that things have gone very badly since they all left, and it's Jack's fault for taking them all away. On one of his good days, Hurley is visited by Walt in the hospital, who asks him about meeting Jeremy Bentham and asks him why they're lying. Jack becomes increasingly obsessed with returning to the island while Kate tries to ignore the pull the island has over her.

Meanwhile, Sun travels to London, England, to confront Widmore. She tells him they have similar interests and that they're all lying about where they've been. She reminds him that the 6 aren't the only ones who left the island, most likely referring to Ben, but also possibly meaning Locke. It's unclear what her intentions are, or if Bentham has visited her. If he needs them all to return, it would make sense that he would visit her, but there's no mention of it by the end of season 4.

At the end of 2007, three years after leaving the island, Jack spots an obituary for Jeremy Bentham that seems to have been placed in the paper as a code to the Oceanic 6 and he contacts Kate, telling her they have to go back to the island. She meets him and tells him angrily that she is not going back and she can't believe he is listening to Bentham. After Kate drives away, Jack gets back in his car and drives straight to the funeral home, where he opens the casket and stares at the face of John Locke. Ben appears in the doorway and tells him he has some ideas about how Jack might convince the others to return. While Ben is visiting Jack, Sayid kills one of Widmore's men who is camping outside the institution and breaks Hurley out. Hurley's immediate reaction is, "We're not going back, are we?"

That night, or soon after, Kate has a dream of going into Aaron's room where Claire is sitting by his bed saying, "Don't you dare bring him back." She wakes up and runs to Aaron's room, apologizing to him. It seems even she has realized they all need to return.

Sources

"About Type A and Type B Personalities." Discovery Health. Online. Accessed October 14, 2008.

Adalian, Joseph. "'Lost' set for three more years." Variety.com. Online. May 6, 2007.

Adelstein, Richard. "The Origins of Property and the Powers of Government." *The Fundamental Interrelationship between Government and Property.* Ed. Nicholas Mercuro and Warren J. Samuels. Routledge: New York, 2003.

Ausiello, Michael. "Exclusive: Sopranos Scene-stealer Gets Lost!" TVGuide.com. Online. August 19, 2007.

——. "*Lost* Introduces the *Other* Others?!" TVGuide.com. Online. August 1, 2007.

"The Auto-Icon." UCL Bentham Project. <www.ucl.ac.uk/Bentham_Project> Online. Accessed October 28, 2008.

Bianco, Robert. "'Lost' Rescues a TV Season That's Adrift." *USA Today.* January 31, 2008.

Bim, Cathy S. "Jeff Fahey Biography." Thespian.net. Online. Accessed September 6, 2008.

Cain, George and Dana Longo. "Philip K. Dick: Confessions of a SF Artist." *Denver Clarion.* October 23, 1980.

Carroll, Lewis. *The Annotated Alice.* Ed. Martin Gardner. New York: Penguin, 1960. 1970.

Casares, Adolfo Bioy. *The Invention of Morel.* Trans. Ruth L.C. Simms. New York Review of Books: New York, 1940. 2003.

Clark, Robert. "Jeremy Bentham." *The Literary Encyclopedia.* <www.litencyc. com> Online. September 15, 2002.

Dahl, Oscar. "Comicon 2007: Lost Season 4 Panel, with Carlton Cuse, Damon Lindelof and Harold Perrineau." BuddyTV.com. Online. July 26, 2007.

Dick, Philip K. *VALIS*. New York: Vintage Books, 1981. 1991.

Dos Santos, Kristin. "Is Claire Dead? Are they Really Time Traveling? *Lost's* Bosses Speak!" E! Online. May 9, 2008.

Fienberg, Daniel. "'Lost Comic-Con Panel: Everything that's fit to blog." Zap2it.com. Online. July 26, 2007.

"The Gnostic World View: A Brief Summary of Gnosticism." *The Gnosis Archive.* Online. www.gnosis.org. Accessed September 15, 2008.

"Harold Perrineau Dishes on his Lost Exit (Again)." TVGuide.com. Online. Accessed May 30, 2008.

Hunter, Jason. Email interview with author. October 22, 2008.

——. "Lost: A Theory on Time Travel." www.timelooptheory.com. Online. Accessed July 25–November 4, 2008.

Internet Movie Database. <www.imdb.com> Online.

Jensen, Jeff. "'Lost': Five Fresh Faces." EW.com. Online. August 29, 2007.

——. "'Lost': Mind-Blowing Scoop from its Producers." EW.com. Online. February 20, 2008.

——. "Lost Scoop: Jeff Fahey Joins Cast." EW.com. Online. August 27, 2007.

——. "Lost: Unhappy Jack." EW.com. Online. May 2, 2008.

Jensen, Jeff, and Dan Snierson. "'Lost' and Found." *Entertainment Weekly.* Issue 921. February 16, 2007.

Kim, Jina. "Ask the Expert: Korean Naming Practices." *My Asian Heritage.* Online blog. Accessed October 8, 2008.

Kowalczyk, Jameson. "Interview: Jeremy Davies." IONCinema.com. Online. July 2, 2007.

Lachonis, Jon "DocArzt" and Amy "hijinx" Johnston. *Lost Ate My Life: The Inside Story of a Fandom Like No Other.* ECW Press: Toronto, 2008.

Lindelof, Damon. "Mourning TV." *The New York Times.* November 11, 2007.

——. "Why We Write." Nikki Finke's Deadline Hollywood Daily. Online. January 9, 2008.

Lost. TV Series. Exec. Prod. Carlton Cuse, Damon Lindelof. ABC. 2004–.

"Lost Answers Are Out There." *SciFiWire.* January 24, 2005.

Lostpedia. <http://www.lostpedia.com> Online.

"The Lostpedia Interview: Thomas Hannsz." Lostpedia.com. Online. Accessed July 19, 2008.

"Lost TV Season 4 Secret Clues." Yahoo Australia. Online. Accessed October 13, 2008.

Mautner, Thomas. *The Penguin Dictionary of Philosophy*. New York: Penguin, 2005.

Murphy, Joel. "One on One with . . . Lance Reddick." Hobo Trashcan. Online. October 2005. Accessed October 29, 2008.

"NBC's Ben Silverman Blames 'Mean, Ugly' WGA Nerds for Ruining His Golden Globes Prom." Defamer.com. Online. January 8, 2008.

Nik at Nite. <nikkistafford.blogspot.com> Online.

Santa. "Lost's Writing on the Wall?" Lostpedia Blog. Online. October 21, 2007.

Schneller, Joanna. "Awards season: when words matter." *The Globe and Mail.* January 18, 2008.

Shakespeare, William. "The Tempest." In *The Late Romances*. Ed. David Bevington. New York: Bantam. 1988.

Shostak, E.M. "Lance Reddick Biography." Brief Biographies. Online. Accessed October 29, 2008.

Snierson, Dan. "Exclusive: Harold Perrineau clarifies the record on his departure from Lost: 'I was disappointed . . . I wouldn't say I'm bitter.'" EW.com. Online. June 2, 2008.

Spooner, Clifford C. "The Story of Molly Fisher and the Molly Fisher Rock." Online. <http://members.skyweb.net/~channy/SpoonerMF.html> Accessed October 17, 2008.

Sweet, William. "Jeremy Bentham." Internet Encyclopedia of Philosophy. Online. Accessed October 26–30, 2008.

Vonnegut, Kurt. *Slaughterhouse-Five*. New York: Delta Fiction, 1969. 1999.

WGA America. "Why We Fight." November 5, 2007. Online video clip. YouTube. Accessed October 23, 2008. <http://www.youtube.com/watch?v=oJ55Ir2jCxk>

Wikipedia. <http://www.wikipedia.org> Online.

"'Wire' Star Gets 'Lost'." Zap2it.com. Online. August 22, 2007.

Yuan, Jada. "Jeremy Davies Gives the Skinny on 'Rescue Dawn'." *New York Magazine*. July 11, 2007.

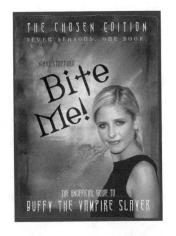

Bite Me!: The Unofficial Guide to Buffy the Vampire Slayer

The Chosen Edition / Nikki Stafford
$17.95 U.S., $19.95 Cdn

Revised and updated, the 10th Buffyversary edition of *Bite Me!* contains exhaustive episode guides to every episode of all seven seasons of this groundbreaking series, chronicles what happened to all of its stars, gives the background story to why the series ended and what legacy it has had, and contains information about the new *Buffy* "season eight" comic book series from Dark Horse. *Bite Me!* is the definitive guide for all *Buffy* fans.

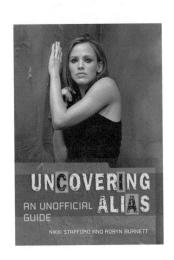

Once Bitten: The Unofficial Guide to Angel

Nikki Stafford / $17.95 U.S., $19.95 Cdn

"Nikki has been an intricate part of the Joss-verse being, not only, an early admirer of both the *Buffy* and *Angel* series but by attending many of the industry events that have given her an uncommon perspective on what made both these shows cult hits with critics, their viewers and within academic institutions all over the world. Her skills as a writer and humorist take front page. . . ."
— Cityofangel.com

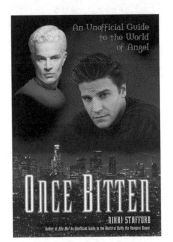

Uncovering Alias: The Unofficial Guide

Nikki Stafford and Robyn Burnett / $17.95 U.S., $19.95 Cdn

Double agents, international terrorist rings, family relationships, and forbidden love are among the themes discussed in this companion guide to *Alias*, ABC's fast-paced drama series about the life of CIA operative Sydney Bristow. An extensive episode guide and explanation of the complex storylines offers a comprehensive perspective on the series' first three seasons. A map of Rambaldi artifacts uncovered, locations that Sydney visited, profiles of the James Bond–like gadgets used, and a discussion of continuity errors make this roll call of favorite and unknown facts about *Alias* essential for devotees and new fans of the drama.

"*Uncovering Alias* is the perfect guide for any *Alias* fan."
— *The Midwest Book Review*

Feed Your TV Addiction

Lost Ate My Life: The Inside Story of a Fandom Like No Other

Jon "DocArzt" Lachonis & Amy "hijinx" Johnston / $19.95 U.S., $19.95 Cdn

Filled with behind-the-scenes anecdotes and expert analysis, *Lost Ate My Life* is an exploration of fan involvement in the metamorphosis of *Lost* from high-concept "cash-in" to high art. Key media spokesfan "DocArtz" and insider "hijinx" detail how the breakdown of barriers between the show and the viewers created a series — and a fandom — like no other.

Saving the World: A Guide to Heroes

Lynnette Porter and David Lavery and Hillary Robson / $14.95 U.S., $16.95 Cdn

Saving the World: A Guide to Heroes features essay analyses of the hit show's driving forces, which keep *Heroes'* audience tuning in each week: the history of comic books making their way to the screen, and how this show has been affected by the decades of superheroes that precede it; the series' archetypal characters; the fandom surrounding the show; its link to other current series such as *Lost*; and the driving force behind the show, creator Tim Kring.

Frak You!: The Ultimate Unauthorized Guide to Battlestar Galactica

Jo Storm / $17.95 U.S., $19.95 Cdn

Examining the universe of *BSG*, *Frak You!* looks at the ways apocalyptic events are depicted in science fiction; how the show blends political commentary into a sci-fi setting, dealing with subjects like treatment of war prisoners, armistice breaking, and the rules of engagement; and how the current show compares to the original 1970s series. It also features an interview with the show's executive producer, Ron Moore, and bios of the seven principal cast members.

with a Little Help from ECW Press

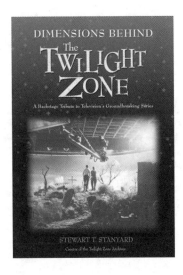

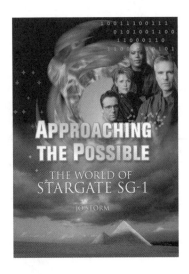

The House That Hugh Laurie Built: An Unauthorized Biography and Episode Guide
Paul Challen / $17.95 U.S., $19.95 Cdn

Who is the man behind the cane and acerbic wit? A musician, a motorcyclist, a comedian? Hugh Laurie is all these things and more. This biography sheds light on his childhood struggles; his prestigious education; his comedic career; his own personal struggle with depression; and how he came to be the best-loved curmudgeon on TV. *The House That Hugh Laurie Built* also serves as a magnifying glass on the show, providing episode analysis, cast biographies, and production bloopers and medical mistakes that only a sleuth like Dr. House could expose.

Dimensions Behind the Twilight Zone: A Backstage Tribute to Television's Groundbreaking Series
Stewart Stanyard / $21.95 U.S., $24.95 Cdn

"Stanyard's book is an amazing, insightful journey into the creation of what is perhaps the best show ever on television. Brimming with behind-the-scenes anecdotes and rare photos, *Dimensions Behind the Twilight Zone* is an absolute must-have for any fan of Serling's. I loved it!"
— J.J. Abrams, creator of *Lost*, *Alias*, and *Fringe*

Approaching the Possible: The World of Stargate SG-1
Jo Storm / $19.95 U.S., $22.95 Cdn

"A comprehensive episodic exploration, which will be appreciated by new viewers and old fans alike, covering everything from the background details of myth and science presented in the shows to interviews with cast, crew members and all involved."
— *Midwest Book Review*

The essential companions to the first three seasons of **LOST**

Finding Lost:
The Unofficial Guide
$17.95 U.S., $19.95 Cdn

Finding Lost, Season
Three: The Unofficial Guide
$14.95 U.S., $16.95 Cdn

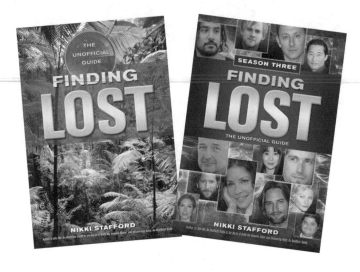

"Stafford has a gift for writing about television and this book is an interesting read and definitely a must for any *Lost* fan."
— The Medium Online

"Nikki Stafford [is] . . . one of the show's leading scholars."
— *Newsday*

"Stafford brings the symbolism, themes, and mythology to the forefront, so that casual viewers and devoted fans have a better understanding of what is happening in each episode."
— About.com

Each instalment of the *Finding Lost* series includes:

- a comprehensive episode guide and bios of all of the major actors on the show
- chapters examining major references on the show, such as the real John Locke and Jean-Jacques Rousseau (and how they compare to the fictional ones), the blast door map, the Dharma symbol, Stephen Hawking's theories, and much more
- sidebars chronicling trivia such as Sawyer's nicknames for people; what Hurley's numbers could represent; comparing the Others to the Losties; what Kate's aliases really mean, and more
- summaries of the show's literary references, including *Watership Down, The Third Policeman, Our Mutual Friend, Of Mice and Men, Through the Looking Glass* and many more
- exclusive behind-the-scenes photos of filming in Hawaii